The Great Fiscal Experiment

RUDOLPH G. PENNER, Editor

The Great Fiscal Experiment

HJ
2051
.G74
1990

[TH]E URBAN INSTITUTE PRESS
[Wa]shington, D.C.

Library of Congress Cataloging in Publication Data

The Great Fiscal Experiment/Rudolph G. Penner, Editor

1. Budget deficits—United States. 2. Balance of trade—United States. 3. Fiscal policy—United States. 4. United States—economic conditions—1945–
I. Penner, Rudolph Gerhard, 1936–

HJ2051.G74   1990   336.73—dc20   90-43204
                                                            CIP

ISBN 0-87766-485-4 (alk. paper)
ISBN 0-87766-484-6 (alk. paper; casebound)

Urban Institute books are printed on acid-free paper whenever possible.

Printed in the United States of America.

9 8 7 6 5 4 3 2 1

Distributed by:
            University Press of America
4720 Boston Way   3 Henrietta Street
Lanham, MD 20706   London WC2E 8LU ENGLAND

THE URBAN INSTITUTE is a nonprofit policy research and educational organization established in Washington, D.C., in 1968. Its staff investigates the social and economic problems confronting the nation and government policies and programs designed to alleviate such problems. The Institute disseminates significant findings of its research through the publications program of its Press. The Institute has two goals for work in each of its research areas: to help shape thinking about societal problems and efforts to solve them, and to improve government decisions and performance by providing better information and analytic tools.

Through work that ranges from broad conceptual studies to administrative and technical assistance, Institute researchers contribute to the stock of knowledge available to public officials and private individuals and groups concerned with formulating and implementing more efficient and effective government policy.

Conclusions or opinions expressed in Institute publications are those of the authors and do not necessarily reflect the views of other staff members, officers or trustees of the Institute, advisory groups, or any organizations that provide financial support to the Institute.

ACKNOWLEDGMENTS

I would like to thank the Andrew W. Mellon Foundation for the financial support that made the conference on which this book is based possible. Numerous individuals, inside and outside The Urban Institute, also contributed to its success. Clementine Taylor provided invaluable organizational and secretarial support and Kyna Rubin expertly edited the volume. The participants in the conference provided valuable comments on my introductory chapter and I would especially like to thank Vito Tanzi and David Mathiasen for their detailed reviews. They should take no blame for any deficiencies, however, since I did not accept all their criticisms.

CONTENTS

Tables

Figures

FOREWORD

The 1980s witnessed large swings in macro fiscal and monetary policies and significant changes in national priorities. This book focuses on the macro fiscal policy changes and asks what we have learned from this turbulent decade about the effects of fiscal policy on the economy. The analysis examines both the international and domestic impacts of changing budget deficits, and a concluding chapter asks about the effect on government itself. Do significant tax cuts curb the overall level of government spending?

It is somewhat unusual for The Urban Institute to study macro-economic issues. Our work typically involves policy analysis at the micro level. However, the papers in this book clearly show that it is harder and harder to draw a distinct line between micro and macro analysis. The economics profession has, in recent years, made great progress in attempting to develop a micro foundation for macro phenomena. Much of this work involves studies of private behavior, but there are obviously strong linkages between macroeconomic events and micro policies. Macroeconomic changes affect the design and impacts of micro policies, and the incentives created by policies at the micro level have important effects on the overall economic health of the nation.

Such considerations are especially important with regard to programs for the poor and disadvantaged, which are the focus of much of the analytic work of The Urban Institute. Thus, it is appropriate that from time to time The Urban Institute, known for its micro-level research on such programs and policies, be a forum for discussions of the larger issues such as fiscal policy.

This book is the result of such a forum. Through the generous support of The Andrew W. Mellon Foundation, on October 23, 1989

The Urban Institute held a conference that gathered together leading experts on U.S. fiscal policy to discuss the economic policies of the 1980s. This volume resulted from that conference.

William Gorham
President

THE GREAT FISCAL EXPERIMENT
OF THE 1980s

THE GREAT FISCAL EXPERIMENT
OF THE 1980s

Rudolph G. Penner

For most of its history, the United States has been highly conservative in its fiscal policy. Before World War II the notion that budgets should be balanced had a strong moral impact and deficits were small except during times of war and recession.

The nation began to fall from grace after World War II.[1] But although during the 30 years following the war deficits tended to be higher than in past history, they were not high enough to cause the national debt to grow faster than the GNP. Indeed, the ratio of the debt in the hands of the public to the GNP fell fairly steadily from over 100 percent at the end of the war to a low of 24 percent at the end of fiscal year 1974. The fall partly reflected the erosion in the debt's real value that resulted from unanticipated inflation. The ratio remained fairly flat through the end of the Carter administration before beginning a rapid rise during the 1980s.

Fiscal responsibility may be good for a nation, but it makes life difficult for research economists. It is difficult to assess the impact of large swings in the deficit, if the deficit remains fairly stable except during wars and recessions, for in such times available statistical techniques are not very good at separating the impact of a rising deficit from the impact of the traumatic event that caused the deficit to rise.

INTRODUCTION

During the 1980s the nation experienced a new phenomenon. The federal deficit rose as would be expected in the recessions of 1980 and 1982, but was not substantially reduced by the subsequent healthy economic recovery. The deficit started the decade in fiscal year 1980 at 2.8 percent of GNP, reached a recession-induced peak of 6.3 percent of GNP in fiscal year 1983, but was still at 5.3 percent of GNP in fiscal year 1986. The implied fiscal policy may have been deplorable, but it provided valuable new data points for economists. The episode did not, however, provide a pure laboratory experiment, for it was contaminated by a series of contemporaneous events, which will be described later.

After 1986 the deficit improved considerably, falling to close to 3 percent of the GNP by 1989—still an enormous deficit by historical standards given that the nation was enjoying peace and prosperity. Before entering into a discussion of the macroeconomic effects of these massive swings in fiscal policy, it is useful to explore briefly the sequence of micro and macro policy changes in the 1980s that led to the macro fiscal mess. Although brevity comes at the cost of some oversimplification, enough will be revealed to indicate that it was a complex decade in which there were more profound changes in national priorities than is usual in American history. It is not surprising that there is still enormous controversy over which policy changes should get the credit or blame for the good and bad economic developments that followed.

The late 1970s was not a happy time for the American economy or U.S. foreign policy. The inflation rate rose every year between 1976 and 1979, and although the unemployment rate fell steadily over this period, it abruptly jumped upward in 1980, while inflation remained at double-digit levels. Simultaneously, the nation appeared impotent in the face of the Iranian hostage crisis and the Soviet invasion of Afghanistan. Tax burdens rose rapidly at the federal, state, and local levels, and tax revolts spread throughout the land as the public lost confidence in government's ability to do anything right. The economics profession also lost public confidence because of its failure to forecast the economic problems of the 1970s and because of its lack of cures for the stagflation gripping the country.[2]

The voters reacted to what President Carter had dubbed "a national malaise" by giving Ronald Reagan a smashing electoral victory in 1980. More surprisingly, they also gave Republicans control of the Senate.

The new administration, brimming with confidence and seduced by a new breed of supply-side economists who had jumped into the void left by traditional economics, sought to cure all of the nation's problems simultaneously. The military buildup, earlier launched by President Carter, was accelerated, and the growth of civilian spending was to be reined in. Massive tax cuts were expected to increase work effort and private saving, thereby unleashing the rapid economic growth necessary to balance the budget. Meanwhile, the growth of the money supply was to be lowered to cure rampaging inflation. The program did not compute arithmetically. Rapid growth in nominal GNP was necessary to bring about the balanced budget promised for 1984, but the promised restraint on the money supply meant that that growth could not be financed unless the ratio of the GNP to the money supply, i.e., the velocity of money, grew at unprecedented rates. It was then reasonable to assume that the deficit would soar to a range of $75 to $100 billion. Such deficits seemed a horror at the time. President Carter had been forced by an adverse market reaction to withdraw his 1980 budget (covering FY 1981) because it only held the forecast deficit to $15.8 billion.

But there was a suspension of disbelief in the Congress. Traditional economists were in such disrepute that even their ability at arithmetic was doubted. Republican House members formed an effective coalition with Southern Democrats to push through the main elements of the Reagan program, and Senate Republicans, who enjoyed a majority for the first time since 1954, could hardly be expected to thwart a newly elected Republican president. In Senator Baker's famous phrase, they were forced to engage in a "riverboat gamble."

As things turned out, some parts of the gamble succeeded and other parts failed miserably. Monetary policy turned out to be more restrictive than in the Reagan plan, and the velocity of money fell rather than rising at a rapid rate. The economy fell into the deepest recession since the Great Depression, but as a result the Reagan administration and the Federal Reserve triumphed over inflation, which fell at a far more rapid rate than deemed possible by most economists.

But the deficit soared to levels that made the interest bill on the national debt a major problem. The deficit began to feed upon itself as the interest bill rose over 88 percent or by over 17 percent per year between 1981 and 1985. The administration and the Congress had some success in restraining the growth of nondefense, noninterest spending, which fell from 15.2 to 14.3 percent of GNP between 1980 and 1985 (quite an accomplishment given the inexorable growth of previous decades), but defense spending plus interest rose from 7.0 to 9.7 percent of GNP over the same period. Thus, total spending rose from 22.2 to 24.0 percent of GNP.

The fiscal history of the period since 1981 has consisted of a series of steps, often modest and sometimes confused, to correct the error of 1981. Over time, a large portion of the initial tax cut was taken back. Particularly large tax increases were enacted in 1982, 1983, and 1984. All together, tax revenues, not including automatic payroll tax base increases, were raised over $100 billion on a static basis in the period 1982–1989, or by more than 2 percent of the GNP above where they would have been had the 1981 cuts remained in place. But the total tax burden still fell from a recent high of 20.1 percent of GNP in 1981 to 19.2 percent in 1989.

Civilian, noninterest spending growth continued to be constrained over the period, and starting in 1986 defense budget authority was reduced by about 2 percent per year in real terms. The tax increases and spending constraint, combined with the longest peacetime recovery in history, began to bring the deficit down relative to GNP in 1987, and by 1989 it equaled about 3 percent of GNP.

Although the rapid rise and subsequent slow decline in the deficit come about as close to a controlled experiment as economists ever witness, this brief history of the experiment makes it clear that it was sullied by rapid changes in national priorities and by an attack (via monetary policy) on the inflation of the early 1980s. The nation may have been at peace while the deficit rose, but the defense buildup bore some similarity to a wartime effort. Although the deficit continued to rise absolutely during a period of recovery, the deep recession of 1982 had a long-lasting impact on the budget through its effect on interest costs and the structure of the economy, since in combination with the rapid rise in the value of the dollar, it devastated the manufacturing sector. In addition, through the 1980s the tax system was massively reformed and marginal tax rates tumbled. This may not have had the miraculous effects promised by supply siders, but it would have been disappointing if it had had no beneficial effects on economic efficiency. It did not, however, seem to have much of an effect on the private savings rate, which fell dramatically in the 1980s. Perhaps the savings rate would have fallen even more had it not been for the decline in marginal tax rates, but clearly, the effects of the marginal rate cuts did not overwhelm whatever else was going on.[3]

Despite the lack of purity in the fiscal experiment, it did teach us a great deal. Before the fact, most economists would have predicted a major upward movement of real interest rates and falling private investment. They would have expected inflows of foreign capital to mute these effects to some degree, but few foresaw the massive capital inflows that actually ensued or the large increase in the current account and trade deficits that had to follow. Few, therefore, foresaw that gross investment could maintain its share of GNP, even though domestic saving fell and real interest rates rose above their level of the 1960s and 1970s. The large current account deficits had a cost, however. By conventional measures, the United States was quickly transformed from the world's largest creditor to its largest debtor. Some say these measures exaggerate the indebtedness of the United States, but it is clear that even if it was not the world's largest debtor by the end of the 1980s, it will be in the early 1990s. This book is the result of a conference held on October 23, 1989 at the Urban Institute to grapple with the fiscal issues of the 1980s. Three papers, each followed by two discussants, provided the framework for the conference discussion, and are published here in edited form. Financial support for the conference was provided by the Andrew W. Mellon Foundation.

THE FISCAL AND EXTERNAL DEFICITS

The first paper in this book, by John Helliwell, asks how much of the growth in the trade deficit in the 1980s can be attributed to changes in the fiscal deficit. Professor Helliwell approaches the problem by bringing together the results of major multicountry, econometric models of economic activity and trade.

As a first step, he simulates the effects of increasing debt-financed, U.S. government spending by an amount equal to 1 percent of real GNP. The increase is sustained for six years. At first, the government's deficit rises less than the rise in spending, because the latter stimulates the economy, increasing income and therefore tax revenues. For the first two years the deficit increase averages about 60 percent of the initial increase in spending, or about 0.6 percent of GNP. But the cumulative interest costs of deficit financing become evident, and the deficit begins to grow, surpassing 1 percent of GNP in the fourth year.

Under Helliwell's simulation, the current account deficit quickly rises to 0.25 percent of GNP. The initial effects reflect the stimulative impact of the deficit on U.S. incomes, but interest rates rise, attracting foreign capital and raising the value of the U.S. dollar. At first, the higher dollar alone counters the stimulative effects of the increased budget deficit on the current account by lowering import prices and raising export prices, but its effects on U.S. competitiveness soon show up and the higher dollar adds to the deterioration of the current account. By the second year of the six-year simulation, the current account deficit has grown sharply to 0.35 percent of GNP. It continues to grow more slowly as the effects of the loss in competitiveness continue to accumulate and the nation has to make growing interest payments on its accumulating foreign debt. Throughout the period, the increase in the current account deficit averages slightly less than the budget deficit, that is, the two deficits tend to grow together, even though they are far from being twins.

The models used by Helliwell indicate that the stimulative effect of the increased budget deficit on the U.S. economy is short-lasting. GNP initially rises by 1.4 times the increase in spending, but the effects decline rapidly and by the sixth year the increase in the GNP equals only 0.5 times the spending increase. The effects on GNP are smaller if so-called rational expectations are assumed. That is to say, if economic decision makers have some understanding of the effects of changes in fiscal policy, they will take actions that tend to speed up the long-run deleterious effects of the policy, so offset some of its initial stimulative impact.

Helliwell goes on to try to simulate the effects of actual fiscal policy in the 1980s. This is difficult because it is hard to know what alternative fiscal policy should serve as a baseline. But making some reasonable assumptions in this regard, he obtains results that are similar to those in the initial simulation. He finds that the fiscal policy of the early 1980s was responsible for about one-half of the rise in the current account deficit.

The results very clearly illustrate the long-run costs of fiscal expansion. Using rational expectations models, the increase in the national debt accumulates to $1,000 billion by the end of the decade, while the foreign debt rises by $500 billion. The servicing of the latter reduces American incomes, as measured by the GNP, by 1 percent relative to American production, as measured by the GDP.

If fiscal policy caused half of the deterioration of the current account in the 1980s, the natural question is, "What caused the rest?" Interestingly, none of the blame is assigned to monetary policy. A monetary expansion has two roughly equal, opposite effects on the current account deficit. It lowers interest rates, thus lowering the value of the dollar and increasing American competitiveness, but it also induces a domestic expansion, thus increasing the demand for imports and leaving less resources for exports.

Some of the leftover deterioration of the current account may have resulted because speculation in foreign exchange markets caused the dollar's value to overshoot its longer term equilibrium level in the mid-1980s. Tax cuts favoring U.S. investment may also have contributed by inducing foreign investment that raised the value of the dollar. It was also a period in which foreign fiscal policies were becoming tighter, and this may have contributed to about one-fifth of the deterioration.

Helliwell concludes by drawing some lessons for the 1990s. Because monetary policy was shown to be ineffective in altering the current account balance, Helliwell suggests that fiscal policy must be the main policy instrument for reducing the current account deficit in the 1990s. But he goes on to say that once a current account deficit is low enough to be sustainable, it should no longer be a concern of policymakers. A current account deficit is sustainable if foreign investors believe that for the foreseeable future, the resulting debt can be serviced without the need for a major fall of the dollar's value in the interim. This can be interpreted to mean that foreign investors are confident that the current account deficit will soon be small enough to imply that the increase in the external debt each year is equal to or less than the growth of GNP. If this condition is not satisfied, the costs of servicing the external debt will continue to grow faster than income, and those costs may eventually become a major part of a growing current account problem. Arithmetically, the deficit can explode to infinity, but the process would be short-circuited by a collapse of the dollar before it proceeded very far.

John Williamson, the first discussant of John Helliwell's paper, begins his comments by stating his general approval of Helliwell's methods and results. He then focuses his critique on Helliwell's statement that a "lower value of the dollar only has a material effect on the external deficit when it is caused by [lower] domestic spending." This seems to leave no role for an explicit exchange rate policy, and to Williamson that seems inconsistent with the finding that a significant part of the current account deterioration was caused by an unexplained increase in the value of the dollar. Williamson prefers to say that "a lower dollar must be accompanied by lower domestic spending if it is to yield a balance of payment improvement rather than simply more inflation." That way of phrasing the same point allows an exchange rate change to be the initiating force in the adjustment process.

Williamson also disagrees with the notion that once the current account deficit becomes sustainable, it should no longer be of interest to policy-makers. While agreeing that there is no need to aim for perpetual balance in the current account, he feels that there is a need for constant monitoring so that moves toward unsustainability can be quickly countered.

In his formal discussion of the same paper, Jacob Frenkel agrees with this point and further suggests that even if a current account deficit cannot be traced to a fiscal deficit, it might still be a symptom of bad policies, since it might have arisen because the incentives affecting the private sector's saving and investment decisions were distorted by an inappropriate structure of taxes and subsidies or by inappropriate monetary policy.

Frenkel praises the breadth of Helliwell's paper, but stresses that more detail is necessary to establish the nature of the links between fiscal policy and the external balance. Knowing the change in the budget deficit is not enough, he believes. It is necessary to ask what type of spending or taxes changed because, for example, it is important to know whether changes in spending affected markets for traded or nontraded goods or whether tax changes affected labor or capital. Because the composition of spending and taxes is so important, it is not surprising that it is so difficult to establish a simple correlation between changes in the overall budget deficit and the current account deficit. Because Helliwell assumes that the increase in the deficit was caused by a change in spending when tax cuts were also important, Frenkel finds his empirical results somewhat suspect, especially given that the models used by Helliwell suggested much less of a dollar appreciation than actually occurred. Clearly, states Frenkel, something else might be going on that is not explained by Helliwell's approach.

Frenkel notes the importance of Helliwell's conclusion that domestic policies alone are incapable of curing the U.S. current account deficit. This suggests that higher growth abroad is also required, which further suggests the need for international coordination. Frenkel states that until recently, G-7 coordination was governed by the "tango principle." The U.S. was to reduce its budget deficit and others were to replace its stimulative effect by engaging in their own stimulative policies, just as one partner's foot precisely replaces the other's in dancing the tango. This was appropriate, says Frenkel, when there was a fear of the world sinking into recession, but with the G-7 partners operating at almost full capacity, accelerating inflation is now the greater danger and the tango principle is no longer appropriate. However, coordination still provides a helpful framework through which governments can take actions that are in their own interests but which they might not do without the cooperation and peer pressure of other governments. Such actions include structural reforms designed to improve productive capacity. In any case, the "tango principle" assumed that fiscal policies were much more flexible than they are in fact. Frenkel believes that it is probably just as well that they are inflexible or else countries would be tempted to use them much more for fine tuning, which frequently turns out badly.

Much of the general discussion of Helliwell's paper at the conference focused on the issue of sustainability and what factors would determine whether a current account deficit at present U.S. levels was, in fact, sustainable. John Williamson pointed out that if the ratio of the current account deficit to GNP remained constant at its level in the late 1980's, the nation's external debt would eventually stabilize at about 30 percent of GNP, roughly Canada's current level. But he noted that the United States might face problems sooner than Canada because the U.S. debt is denominated in its own currency, whereas Canada promises to pay much of its debt in foreign currencies. This makes foreign investors much more sensitive to U.S. policies that might alter the exchange rate. Indeed, if there was a consensus in the discussion, it was that sustainability would be largely determined by foreigners' evaluation of the wisdom of the future policies of the country. They could worry that the United States might try to inflate its way out of the problem (von Furstenberg), resort to protectionism (Frenkel), or not show any concern for its current account deficit at all.

FEDERAL DEFICITS AND THE DOMESTIC ECONOMY

The second paper in this volume, by James R. Barth, George Iden, Frank S. Russek, and Mark Wohar, investigates the effects of changing deficits on the domestic economy. The conventional view is that a higher budget deficit will cause real interest rates to rise, investment to fall, and consumption to rise. This view has been challenged by proponents of the Ricardian theorem put forth most prominently by Robert Barro. The Ricardian theorem argues that consumers are farsighted and altruistic toward future generations. They are smart enough to know that lower taxes now imply higher taxes later, if not on them, then on their descendents, and they raise their savings now to compensate for this future burden. Put another way, increased private saving exactly offsets increased public dissaving and it is irrelevant whether long-term government spending is financed by taxes or by issuing debt. This theory leads to a complicated conclusion. Changes in the deficit caused by anticipated tax changes do not affect interest rates and national saving, but changes in spending and unanticipated tax changes may.

Barth et al. survey numerous empirical studies that are relevant to deciding which view is right, but conclude that no firm conclusion emerges. Perhaps this is not surprising given the complexity of the statistical and conceptual issues that arise in doing empirical work on these issues. Even if the conventional view is right, it is devilishly difficult to document that fact for a number of reasons. First, the United States has been fiscally responsible through most of its history, and deficits have typically emerged only during wars and recessions. The period of the 1980s is highly unusual and does not by itself provide much of a sample period. As stated further above, when deficits arise during wars and recessions, it is hard to disentangle the effects of the deficits from the effects of the traumatic event that caused them. Second, the effect of deficits on interest rates may be positive, but weak enough to be countered by inflows of foreign capital or by a propensity of the Federal Reserve to target interest rates. Third, enormously complicated measurement issues arise in any empirical study. The budget deficit can be measured in a variety of ways. It is necessary to a) choose between the unified or cash budget and the slightly different version of the deficit appearing in the national accounts, b) decide whether the measure should be adjusted for inflation and the state of the business cycle, and c) determine whether to attempt to differentiate between anticipated and unanticipated deficits. Having decided such issues, it is then necessary to determine whether to try to distinguish different impacts from changing taxes and spending, as the Ricardian equivalence theory would suggest, and whether to take explicit account of foreign capital flows and domestic monetary policy.

Having done all of that, it is necessary to measure real interest rates, and that requires an estimate of expected inflation. But what sort of interest rate should be used, a short-term or long-term rate? If the desire is to determine the effect of deficits on private investment and savings, a whole new set of issues emerges as to how those variables should be measured. And if all of that were not complicated enough, it is often assumed that economic impacts operate with a time lag, and frequently the theory being tested provides little guidance as to the form of time lag that should be specified.

Various analysts approach these problems in various ways, and although no firm conclusions emerge, Barth et al. do detect certain patterns in the literature. Studies attempting to show a relationship between budget deficits and long-term interest rates tend to be more successful than those using short-term interest rates. Perhaps this is an indication of the stronger befuddling effects of monetary policy and foreign capital flows on short rates. Studies using annual data tend to be more successful at showing effects than studies using quarterly or monthly data. Generally, studies using a cyclically adjusted deficit work better than those using the actual deficit, as do studies using an expected, rather than actual, deficit. As both conventional and Ricardian theorists would expect, government spending seems to be a more powerful explanatory variable than taxes, and studies using the debt rather than the deficit as an explanatory variable also seem to work better.

These results would seem to offer some comfort to the proponents of the conventional view of deficits, since it is possible to establish statistically significant relationships if variables are chosen appropriately, but Barth et al. quickly raise the discomfort level by showing that none of the conclusions is very statistically robust. Small changes in the time period studied or the way that the statistical tests are specified can change positive results to negative results and vice versa.

To some degree, the literature that attempts to link deficits and interest rates is a residue of a time when it was not too inaccurate to consider the United States to be a closed economy. When international capital markets are brought into the picture, changes in the budget deficit may have no discernible effects on interest rates, but that does not mean that they have no effects on the economy. Even if international capital flows mute the effects on interest rates, there can be important effects on national savings and the composition of domestic output.

Unfortunately, firm conclusions are no less elusive when researchers attempt to investigate the effects of deficits on the composition of output or the level of national saving. There has been some success in showing that larger deficits tend to depress private investment, and this conclusion tends to be substantiated by the large econometric models. But even here it is possible to get contrary results. Studies of the effects of budget deficits on private saving are evenly mixed between those that find a significant result and those that do not.

Although Barth and his colleagues do not reach definite empirical conclusions, they do reach a firm policy conclusion. It may be impossible to determine if deficits are benign or have substantial effects on interest rates and investment, but if they are benign it couldn't hurt to reduce them and if they have harmful effects, it is very important to do so. Moreover, in seeking to identify the impact of deficits, there may be a tendency to impose overly restrictive statistical tests. It is typical to start with the hypothesis that deficits have no effect, then to ask whether this hypothesis can be rejected with a high degree of statistical confidence. For example, a rising deficit may be shown to affect interest rates positively, but the usual statistical test might indicate that such a relationship would show up only 15 percent of the time (because of random factors) even if no true causal relationship exists. Although the 15 percent probability that the result is an accident seems low, statisticians tend to be very demanding and would conclude that the probability of an accident cannot be confidently rejected, even though the probability that it is not an accident may be far greater than 50 percent.

Barth and his co-authors also note that the empirical work they surveyed only investigates the deficit's effects on interest rates and investment. Deficits could do additional harm if they put pressure on the Federal Reserve to create money, thus causing inflation. There is no sign of that happening in the 1980s, but in the extreme the Fed may have little choice if the deficit becomes so large as to explode because of soaring interest costs. If one cannot borrow anymore because of a soaring interest bill and it is politically impossible to raise taxes or cut spending substantially, there is no other choice but to declare bankruptcy or finance government by creating new money.

In his discussion of the Barth et al. paper, John Makin praises the authors for their thorough and evenhanded survey of the literature, but wishes that they would have been more opinionated in identifying what they thought was the best approach to the problem. Makin strongly disagrees with the common view that a rise in the deficit requires a rise in the level of interest rates to clear the market for debt. He believes that the level of interest rates is determined by the stock of debt relative to wealth or its proxy, the GNP, and that the change in the stock of debt or the deficit should be associated with the change in interest rates. Since it is quite possible to have a rise in the deficit-GNP ratio while the debt-GNP ratio continues to fall, it is not surprising that it is difficult to relate the level of interest rates to the deficit.

The issue has been complicated during the 1980s by the relaxation of controls on capital outflows from Japan and by a huge increase in the stock of wealth outside of the United States. During the early 1980s, the acceleration of the growth of the U.S. debt-GNP ratio may have been sufficient to overcome the effects of increased foreign demand for U.S. assets, and the fiscal policy of the time was probably responsible for the increase in U.S. interest rates and the attendant appreciation of the dollar. But since 1985, the growth of public spending has slowed, the deficit has been stabilized, and the growth of the debt-GNP ratio has slowed accordingly. The current account deficit has also fallen relative to GNP since 1987, and in 1989 the foreign demand for U.S. assets was sufficiently robust to force central banks to sell dollars in order to forestall an increase in the exchange rate.

Although the empirical results regarding the domestic effects of the budget deficit may be unclear, the developments of the last few years lead John Makin, the first discussant of the Barth et al. paper, to a clear policy conclusion: a budget deficit remaining constant at about $150 billion is definitely sustainable into the indefinite future, and those who worry that it could cause some sort of foreign exchange crisis are misguided. If one wants to argue that the budget deficit should be reduced, the argument must be based on grounds other than sustainability.

Frank de Leeuw, the second commentator on the Barth et al. paper, also praises the evenhanded nature of the paper, but asks whether it might contain leads that would help to resolve the dispute between the conventional and Ricardian equivalence views of the problem.

First, deLeeuw sees great value in the paper's challenge to certain extreme views. For example, the finding by Paul Evans that there is a strong negative relationship between interest rates and deficits is shown to be transformed if the par value rather than the market value of the debt is used as an explanatory variable. Similarly, Robert Eisner's finding that deficits and investment are positively related evaporates when a few more years of data are added.

Second, the patterns discerned by the authors also contribute to loosening the deadlock between the opposing camps. Their findings that the cyclically adjusted deficit works better than the actual deficit, that debt works better than the deficit, that future deficits seem more important than present deficits, and that long-term interest rates seem more affected than short rates all suggest to de Leeuw that the permanence of the budget deficit has an important bearing on its impacts. DeLeeuw then uses this point to attempt a reconciliation of the conventional and Ricardian approaches. He suggests that consumers may alter their savings plans in response to a temporary change in the deficit. For example, it is clear that the temporary postponement of an earlier announced tax increase will not have a significant effect on private consumption. But an increase in the deficit that is perceived to be long-lasting may not affect private saving, because the day of reckoning is put off so far into the future.

TAXES AND GOVERNMENT SPENDING

While the first two papers discussed above examine the effects of budget deficits on U.S. external accounts and on the domestic economy, the last paper, by George von Furstenberg, examines the effects of the deficit on the government itself by investigating the theoretical and political links between the level of the tax burden and the level of government spending.

Von Furstenberg begins with the arithmetic truth that for the very long run, the present value of taxes must equal the present value of noninterest spending plus the value of the debt. If the present value of taxes falls short of this amount, the debt will expand without limit, and the government will eventually have to default, most probably by printing money to finance government rather than borrowing, thus taxing away the debt through inflation.

It is this arithmetic relationship that leads to the Ricardian equivalence theorem, which states that a far-sighted public that is completely altruistic toward future generations is not impressed by a tax cut given a certain level of noninterest spending. They know that it has to be paid for later, so politicians offering tax cuts without spending cuts cannot gain in popularity.

As von Furstenberg explains, there are at least two problems with this argument. First, the public is not altruistic; second, it is not far-sighted. Using arithmetic examples, von Furstenberg shows that selfish individuals who have little concern for their descendents can gain substantially through deficit financing in their lifetime. Moreover, it may be easy to delude people into thinking that the full cost of government is reflected in their tax bill. Borrowing thus makes government feel cheaper than it really is, and people may demand too much of it.

Yet the arithmetic linkage between long-run spending and taxation does ultimately reassert itself. Von Furstenberg uses the Italian case as an example of how a long period of fiscal profligacy is on the verge of forcing a much larger tax increase than would have been required had more conservative fiscal rules been followed in the past. Because Italy has accumulated a debt equal to 100 percent of

GNP (compared to 42 percent in the U.S.), and because they will soon face an interest cost on the debt greater than their economy's growth rate, the Italian government will have to raise tax rates to a level considerably in excess of noninterest spending in order to stabilize the situation.

Thus, there are two ways that a tax cut can actually raise government spending—first, by making spending look cheap to the current generation, and second, through the effect on the deficit and the interest bill. But Milton Friedman has argued strongly that government will automatically spend what it takes in through the tax system plus whatever else it can get away with. Thus, tax increases will raise spending, and tax cuts should curb it.

However, there has been little evidence of the latter effect from recent U.S. history, and the experience of countries such as West Germany, Singapore and the United Kingdom strongly suggests that it is possible to raise taxes and simultaneously exert enough constraint on spending to bring about budget balance. Von Furstenberg's review of the longer run historical experience of the United States suggests a somewhat more mixed message. There is some suggestion that if the tax increase is sufficient to create a budget surplus, it may result in added spending unless debt reduction becomes popular for its own sake. But debt reduction for its own sake has not been popular since 1870. However, there also seems to be a negative relationship between defense spending and tax burdens, suggesting that if the government feels the need for a peacetime defense buildup, it must provide tax cuts at the same time to obscure its cost. More generally, it is clear that tax burdens and spending tend to vary together, but the line of causality seems to run more from spending to taxes than the other way around.

However, von Furstenberg makes the important point that the timing of tax and spending changes may reveal nothing about the line of causality. For a variety of reasons outlined in von Furstenberg's paper, economists argue that tax burdens should be smoothed over time. A government adopting that goal would raise taxes in advance of an anticipated increase in spending. The tax increase would come first, but it would have been caused by a later spending increase and not vice versa. Although this is a nice theoretical point, von Furstenberg shows that it does not seem to have had much influence on U.S. fiscal history. The need for greater future spending had become apparent well before U.S. entry into World Wars I and II and before the escalation of the Vietnam War, but in each case tax increases lagged behind spending increases.

Having reviewed the theory and the evidence, von Furstenberg ends with the strong conclusion that "The policy of cutting taxes to lower government spending is literally bankrupt." Cutting taxes, he believes, is more likely to increase public spending, even beyond the added cost of interest on the national debt.

William Niskanen begins his discussion of von Furstenberg's paper by wishing that public officials were more cognizant of the long-run linkage between spending and taxes so clearly described by the author. But there is no apparent linkage in the short run that can be obtained from time-series data or cross-country studies. Niskanen thinks that no clear empirical relationships emerge because different countries operate under different fiscal rules defining acceptable behavior, and for each country those rules change over time.

Niskanen earlier studied the link between deficits and spending and believed the data suggesting that deficits increase spending because they appear to make it cheaper. Later data raise some questions about this result, but Niskanen still believes that it was a good description of reality in the United States from 1953 through 1985 and in the United Kingdom throughout the 1980s. But there is also a sense in which the United States operated under the Friedman rule in the 1980s, spending all that it took in plus the proceeds of whatever borrowing was tolerable. Unfortunately, everyone underestimated how much borrowing was tolerable.

Niskanen argues that the passage of Gramm-Rudman-Hollings, despite its many flaws, significantly changed the rules of the game. Given a deficit target, the law requires tax cuts to be matched by spending cuts and spending increases to be matched by tax increases. In other words, the budget must be balanced at the margin, a rule that Niskanen himself proposed as early as 1973. And Niskanen believes that despite its many loopholes, the law has introduced a new sense of discipline. But the law also implies that in the short run, with a given set of deficit targets, any tax increase will quickly be spent. As a result, Niskanen will only accept a tax increase if it can be combined with a reduction in Gramm-Rudman's deficit target.

Edward Gramlich, discussing the same paper, agrees with von Furstenberg's analysis of Ricardian equivalence. The most persuasive evidence against it, he argues, comes from the popularity of politicians promising tax cuts or at least no tax increases.

Gramlich goes on to offer four points regarding von Furstenberg's paper. Although agreeing that discussions of fiscal policy are value-ridden, he points out that the values determining one's attitudes toward the appropriate size of government may have little to do with one's values regarding the appropriate size of the deficit and its effect on national savings. People who favor big government might favor high taxes and low deficits or the reverse. The same is true for those who would keep government small.

Second, Gramlich is disturbed by von Furstenberg's implicit reliance on a stable debt-GNP ratio as an indicator of fiscal prudence. Gramlich argues that it is necessary to ask whether the debt-GNP ratio is being stabilized at a desirable level.

Third, Gramlich notes that the Milton Friedman view that tax increases are always spent is too simple-minded regarding the nature of the budget bargaining that actually occurs every year. To the extent that there is any concern over the deficit at all, this view opens the door to conservatives bargaining for a cut in expenditures in return for acquiescing to a tax increase.

Fourth, Gramlich would have liked to see more of an attempt to use econometric analysis to help resolve the issues raised in the paper.

CONCLUSION

The analysis provided by the papers and the discussion at the conference suggest that as we enter the 1990s there are many important theoretical and empirical issues regarding the impact of 1980s fiscal policy left unresolved. Yet much has been learned over the past ten years and this conference had a very different tone than it would have if the same issues had been discussed in 1979. Certainly, the 1980s taught us the importance of analyzing domestic fiscal policies in an international context. Although we knew that intellectually in 1979, it was not yet ingrained in economic discussions and it often entered as an afterthought.

The growing prominence of the Ricardian equivalence theorem and other theoretical developments in economics have also altered the nature of the discussion regarding the domestic political and economic impacts of fiscal policy. This author, along with many others, is not one to give much credence to the Ricardian theorem, but its proponents have done a great service by forcing more focus on the role of expectations on the effects of fiscal policy. Policies must now be analyzed in a dynamic, long-term context, and economists now tend to assume much more sophisticated responses than they did previously. This makes the analysis of fiscal policy much more difficult theoretically and empirically.

The fiscal policy of the 1980s provides economists with a rich database with which to analyze these difficult issues, and the experience will be debated for many years to come. Let us hope that the 1990s provide somewhat less excitement.

Notes

1. James M. Buchanan and Richard E. Wagner attribute the change to the Keynesian Revolution. See *Democracy in Deficit: The Political Legacy of Lord Keynes*. New York: Academic Press, 1977.

2. John Helliwell believes that these criticisms are unfair in that the economics profession could not possibly have been expected to forecast the rise in oil prices, and that once stagflation hit, some useful analytic work was done. See his "Comparative Macroeconomics of Stagflation," *The Journal of Economic Literature* 26, 1 (March 1988): 1–28. Whether unfair or not, the criticisms certainly reduced the influence of traditional economists in Washington policymaking.

3. Some argue that this is misleading because savings are not measured properly in the national accounts. More specifically, if capital gains are added, the picture is more optimistic, but capital gains do not immediately and directly provide more resources for investment.

THE FISCAL DEFICIT AND THE EXTERNAL DEFICIT: SIBLINGS BUT NOT TWINS

THE FISCAL DEFICIT AND THE EXTERNAL DEFICIT: SIBLINGS BUT NOT TWINS

John F. Helliwell

At the end of the 1970s the U.S. government and external accounts were both in rough balance.[1] Over the course of the 1980s, the federal fiscal deficit and the current account (external) deficit both grew dramatically. The federal fiscal deficit, on a calendar-year national accounts basis, peaked at $206 billion in 1986, while the current account deficit, after initially growing more slowly, reached $139 billion in 1986. Both deficits were approximately $150 billion in 1987.[2]

The purpose of this paper is to describe the linkages between these two deficits. First I will outline some of the simplified approaches that have been used to explain the evolution of the current account, especially the approaches that focus on the possible linkages between the fiscal federal and external deficits. I will then examine more thoroughly some of the available evidence about the extent to which the two deficits were linked during the 1980s. After reviewing the linkages between 1980s fiscal policy and the 1980s current account deficit, I will conclude by assessing the extent to which the current account might respond to possible future changes in fiscal policy. The linkages between fiscal policy and the current account in the 1990s might be expected to be different than they were in the 1980s, since the U.S. external position has changed from large net creditor to net debtor, changing the extent to which interest rates and exchange rates influence the U.S. current account.

APPROACHES TO EXPLAINING THE EXTERNAL DEFICIT

Both partial and macroeconomic approaches have been used to explain the evolution of the current account.

Partial Approaches

The most popular and longstanding partial approach to understanding the current account is to view the evolution of imports and exports separately, with each being determined by relative prices and spending in the United States and in its trading partner countries. Some of these analyses focus on the relative rates of spending growth, and on the income elasticities that measure the extent to which U.S. imports respond to growth in U.S. spending, and the extent to which U.S. exports respond to increases in foreign spending. A separate estimation of U.S. import and export equations frequently shows that import levels respond to increases in U.S. spending more than U.S. export levels respond to increases in foreign spending. This results in concern that there may be a secular decline in the U.S. trade balance unless there are continuing falls in the real value of the U.S. dollar or higher rates of spending growth outside the United States.[3]

Other studies emphasize the role of relative prices in the determination of import and export levels. These studies focus on three key factors: the pass-through of the exchange rate into trade prices, the influence of trade prices on trade flows, and the possibility that initial import price effects are sufficiently larger than volume effects so that a drop in the value of the dollar may initially lead to a worsening of the nominal current account, even though real imports are falling and real exports rising.

With respect to the first question, the influence of exchange rates on trade prices, the traditional assumption has been that primary commodities are sold at prices set in world markets, while most manufactures are sold at prices set separately by each supplier. Under this simple view, a drop in the value of the U.S. dollar would lead to a corresponding increase in the U.S. price of Japanese cars, because the U.S. price would be equal to the fixed Japanese yen price multiplied by the higher number of U.S. dollars required to buy enough yen to pay for the car. However, recent research[4] and even casual observation have revealed that most manufacturers selling into large foreign markets are acutely aware of pressures on their market share, so tend to absorb, at least in the short-run, much of the effect of exchange rate changes. Their doing so insulates U.S. import prices from the initial effects of exchange rate changes. This tends to defer the eventual volume adjustments, but if the initial import volume effects are sufficiently small, the lag in the "pass through" of exchange rate changes to import prices may actually improve rather than worsen the U.S. nominal trade balance, at least in face of a drop in the value of the dollar.

'Elasticity pessimism" is the expression used to desc....
that the volume of trade responds so little to a change in the exchange rate that the nominal U.S. current account might actually worsen in response to a lowering of the value of the dollar. Most empirical evidence suggests that there is a short-term worsening in the current account in response to a lower value of the dollar, but that this effect is reversed by the second year.[5] The initial worsening of the nominal current account, followed by a subsequent improvement, mainly poses problems because of its effect on expectations. If a large drop in the value of the dollar is followed by further worsening of the current account, market participants are likely to become pessimistic about the future prospects for U.S. "competitiveness", which could lead to still larger drops in the value of the currency. The same influence, in reverse, may well have been part of the story of the dramatic rise in the value of the dollar between 1982 and 1985.

Partial approaches to explaining the current account are helpful in understanding some key elements of trade decisions. However, they do not help to unravel the linkages between fiscal policy and the current account, because they stop short at expenditures and relative prices, the proximate determinants of trade flows. To get further, we need to adopt a more macroeconomic approach, in which the levels of aggregate expenditure, prices and exchange rates are themselves determined.

Macroeconomic Approaches

Several simplified macroeconomic approaches have been used to explain the evolution of the current account. In these simple approaches, the determination and role of the exchange rate, and of relative prices more generally, are suppressed, or at least treated in an implicit manner.

The core of these approaches is the national income and expenditure relationship, shown as

$$Y = C + I + G + (X - M)$$

wherein the level of real national output Y is the sum of final domestic expenditure (equal to the sum of consumption, investment and government spending on goods and services, often referred to as domestic absorption) plus net exports $(X - M)$.

THE ABSORPTION APPROACH

The absorption approach makes use of the fact that the current account, or net exports of goods and services in this simple exposition (which excludes foreign transfer payments such as foreign aid and immigrants' remittances, and ignores the special factors determining net investment income), is equal to the excess of output over absorption. Thus anything that increases absorption, such as an increase in government spending, will increase the current account deficit by the same amount, except to the extent that the increase in government spending is offset by reductions in consumption or investment spending, or provided by increases in output. A "supply-side" approach to U.S. fiscal policy in the early 1980s would have argued that the tax cuts could have induced enough output to provide for the extra spending by governments, private consumers, or businesses with higher after-tax incomes, to avoid large buildups in either the fiscal deficit or the current account.

THE KEYNESIAN MULTIPLIER APPROACH

An important variant of the absorption approach is provided by a demand-oriented open-economy Keynesian multiplier approach, in which aggregate income is increased by the increase in government spending, and the current account worsened by the induced change in imports, by an amount roughly equal, under fixed exchange rates, to the marginal propensity to import times the increase in income.

Under flexible exchange rates, the effects of fiscal policy on the external deficit depend on the degree of capital mobility and on the nature of exchange rate expectations. If there is no capital mobility, under fiscal expansion the currency would depreciate by enough to close off the import leakage, thus insulating the current account from the fiscal deficit. Under perfect capital mobility, with static expectations about exchange rates and prices, this model[6] forces the domestic currency to appreciate under fiscal expansion by enough to fully crowd out any increase in income, thus forcing the induced fiscal deficit to be matched by an external deficit of the same size.

THE SAVINGS-INVESTMENT APPROACH

A number of more recent macroeconomic approaches have set up the same national income relationship in a different way, so as to emphasize the identity between domestic investment and total savings. Rewriting the familiar national income identity to show investment on the left-hand side, and adding taxes to allow a distinction between private and public saving, domestic investment can be seen to be equal to the sum of private, government and foreign saving:

$$I = (Y - T - C) + (T - G) + (M - X).$$

Seen this way, net foreign savings, which are net imports of goods and services, and hence are simply the current account deficit, are the amount by which investment spending exceeds net national savings, which in turn is the sum of private and government savings. Thus any increase in the fiscal deficit would lead to a one-for-one increase in the current account deficit (i.e., net foreign savings), unless there were offsetting reductions in domestic investment (for example being crowded out by higher domestic interest rates) or increases in private savings (generated, for example, by higher income levels, or by tax changes influencing saving decisions, as emphasized in some supply-side approaches).

Four particular cases of the savings-investment approach are worthy of special mention.

The "Twin Deficit" View. Known earlier in the United Kingdom as the "New Cambridge" approach, this view maintains there is a one-for-one offset of changes in government savings, i.e., in the fiscal surplus, and foreign savings, as measured by the current account deficit. Thus any increase in the fiscal deficit would be matched by an increase in the external deficit—a reduction in public savings being offset by an increase in foreign savings. The assumption here is that any induced changes in domestic investment are exactly matched by changes in private savings. If the higher fiscal deficit led to a net reduction in private investment spending—with "crowding out" caused by higher interest rates exceeding the "accelerator effects" from the higher levels of output—a reduction in private savings would be required in order for the twin deficits view to hold precisely. If the higher fiscal deficit led to higher incomes and hence higher private savings, then the current account deficit would be smaller than the fiscal deficit, unless induced private investment more than exhausted the induced private savings.

The View That National Savings Determines Domestic Investment. This view stresses the long-established correlation between national savings rates—the sum of private savings and government savings—and domestic investment rates—the amount of capital expenditures in the domestic economy. Feldstein and Horioka (1980) analyzed this evidence in an important paper arguing that measures to increase national savings, whether by governments or the private sector, would be likely to lead to higher investment rates, and hence to greater economic growth in the future. To the extent that the link from national savings to private investment flows through interest rates, according to this view, a greater fiscal deficit might lead to some increase in the current account deficit to the extent that the higher interest rates induce a higher real value of the dollar.

The Intertemporal Approach. Espoused by Frenkel and Razin (1987a), this approach assumes full employment, perfect foresight, and perfect international markets for capital and tradeable goods. It examines how the international implications of government deficits depend on the source and timing of the deficit, the relative saving propensities of the public and private sectors, and the relative extent to which public spending falls on tradeable and non-tradeable goods. As would be expected, a fiscal deficit caused by a temporary increase in spending is more likely to increase the current account deficit if the spending is concentrated on tradeable goods (Frenkel and Razin 1988b, 20-27). The effects of tax changes are especially complex, depending on which type of tax is being changed and on the timing and preference factors coming into play with changes in government spending.[7]

As Dornbusch (1989) and others have pointed out, one implication of the perfect markets and farsighted optimizing behavior assumed in this approach is that there is no policy significance to any current account or fiscal imbalances.

One of the most important benefits of the intertemporal approach has been to focus attention on the likely timing and duration of fiscal actions, and on the nature of private expectations about future government spending and taxes. As we shall see later, temporary and permanent changes in spending can have very different effects on output, interest rates, exchange rates, and the current account.

The Ricardian approach (Barro 1974, 1989) is a special case of the intertemporal optimization approach. It assumes that (infinitely) long-lived consumers foresee the future taxes eventually required to finance deficits created by current tax reductions, and reduce their current consumption correspondingly. Thus, there is no link between fiscal deficits and the current account, at least to the extent that the deficits are caused by changes in tax rates.[8]

The Sustainability Approach. This approach, as espoused, for example, by Krugman (1988), also focuses on savings and investment balances, but differs from the intertemporal optimization approach by raising the possibility that markets are insufficiently forward-looking, or insufficiently consistent in their macroeconomic expectations, to foresee the future consequences of today's external deficits. In particular, the approach calculates whether the market's expected rate of future decline of the dollar in real terms, as measured by current real interest rate differentials, is large enough to eventually stop the growth in the ratio of external debt to GNP. If it is not, then the current level of the exchange rate is described as unsustainable. The application of the approach by Krugman was based only on the impact of the exchange rate on the current account balance, and put aside the other links between final spending and the current account. Other versions of the savings and investment approach emphasize the spending links more directly, with the exchange rate playing a facilitating role by moving far enough to enable continual matching of the current account with desired capital movements.

Further removed from the savings and investment approaches, but sharing with the Krugman approach the view that market participants may value the dollar at unsustainable or undesirable levels, is the Fundamental Equilibrium Exchange Rate (FEER) approach of Williamson (1985) and Williamson and Miller (1987). This approach addresses the sustainability issue in a different way, by starting with an assumption about the desired accumulation of net foreign liabilities, and then calculating the exchange rate path that would be "expected to generate a current account surplus or deficit equal to the underlying capital flow over the cycle, given that the country is pursuing 'internal balance' as best it can and not restricting trade for balance of payments reasons" (Williamson 1985, 113).

The evidence reported in the following sections of this paper does not focus directly on the question of sustainability for either exchange rates or current account balances, except to the extent that these issues arise in particular models. The main focus of attention will be on the empirical linkages between fiscal deficits and external deficits. All of the models used to provide the evidence are both macroeconomic and international, and provide for determination of trade flows, interest rates, and exchange rates for all of the major countries. Some of the models presume fully forward-looking behavior by consumers and investors, and some do not; the differences between these two types of models will be examined after a preliminary review of the evidence from a larger sample of models.

HOW CLOSELY RELATED ARE THE FISCAL
AND EXTERNAL DEFICITS?

It is not very helpful to examine simple correlations between fiscal deficits and external deficits, either over time for a single country or across countries, since both variables represent the results of many forces, some of which make the two deficits move together, and others which make them move apart. For example, a self-inspired investment boom in the United States would tend to raise U.S. GDP, to lower the fiscal deficit and to raise the external deficit. On the other hand, a drop in U.S. exports caused by a fall in foreign demand would tend to lower U.S. GDP, and to raise both the fiscal and external deficits, with the effects on the external deficit being generally greater than those on the fiscal deficit.

As for the impact of government spending on the current account, the size of the effect is much in dispute, although most approaches would show some positive connection. They would show that an increase in the fiscal deficit would also tend to increase the external deficit, to the extent that it also raised real income, domestic prices, interest rates, and the exchange rate. How can the size of the effect best be measured? Since simple theoretical models cannot help to establish the magnitudes, and complex theoretical models soon become ambiguous in their predictions of even the net direction of effects, there is no realistic alternative to the use of empirical models that represent the key elements of macroeconomic structure.

In order to capture the exchange rate and foreign trade effects of fiscal policy, the frameworks or models used must also capture the trading decisions of other countries. To do this in a consistent manner, a number of models have been developed that treat the main industrial countries in a fairly complete and symmetric manner, usually with a more limited treatment of income and trade determination in the rest of the world.

Over the past five years the Brookings Institution, the Federal Reserve Board, the IMF, and the Japanese Economic Planning Agency have sponsored several workshops to compare the major multicountry models of economic activity and trade and to assess their implications for major policy issues of the day.[9] Since one of the key issues has been the explanation of the U.S. external deficit, including the linkage between fiscal policy and the external deficit, the collaborative research resulting from the workshops has focused on the twin deficits question.

What does the evidence show? I will first present some results, then discuss some reasons for caution. The basic results illustrate the consequences of an increase in debt-financed U.S. government spending, sustained over six years, equal to 1 percent of real GNP. Figure 1.1 shows the effects of this increase in debt-financed U.S. government spending on the fiscal deficit and on the external deficit, in both cases measured as a percent of baseline GNP.[10] These results represent an average of the results from ten multicountry models.[11] To give some approximate measure of the spread of the results, a band (plus and minus one standard deviation) is drawn about each of the averages.[12]

In all cases, the initial effect of government spending on the fiscal deficit is less than the initial size of the spending, reflecting the positive effect of the spending on income and tax revenues. As time progresses, however, the size of the induced deficit increases as a share of baseline nominal GNP, mainly because of the interest payments on the increasing public debt, but also partly because of the higher interest rates and price levels. For the first two years, the net effect on the fiscal deficit averages about 0.6 percent of GNP. It increases thereafter, passing through 1 percent in the fourth year.[13]

The current account deficit effect starts at .25 percent of GNP, increasing sharply to .35 percent in the second year, and then growing more gradually thereafter. The second-year growth reflects the working through of the J-curve effects of the higher value of the U.S. dollar, while the continuing increase thereafter reflects both the continuing loss of competitiveness in response to the growing real value of the dollar, and interest payments on the growing external debt.

Figure 1.2 brings together the effects on the fiscal and external deficits to show the extent to which the two deficits move together in response to an increase in government spending. In the first year, the ratio of the induced external deficit to the induced fiscal deficit is just under one-half (.48). It rises in the second year, reflecting the sharp second-year increase in the external deficit effects described above, and then returns to just below one-half, ranging between .45 and .49 for the rest of the six-year period. The fairly narrow bands around the average illustrate that the models, despite their diversity of structure, all show that the two deficits are closely related but far from being twins.

Figure 1.3 shows that the increasing effects of government spending on the two deficits are not due to continuing growth of real spending and output. On the contrary, the average real GNP effects of the fiscal expansion show multipliers of about 1.4 in the first two years, dropping steadily thereafter, to average 0.5 in the sixth year. Figure 1.4 shows that the real GNP effects are smaller in the models with forward-looking

Figure 1.1. AVERAGE CURRENT ACCOUNT DEFICIT AND GOVERNMENT
DEFICIT GNP SHARES

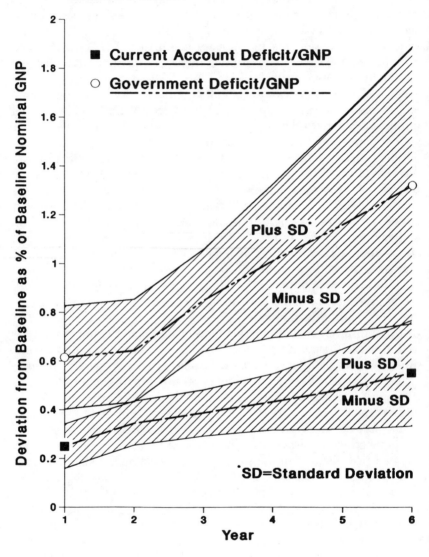

Figure 1.2. AVERAGE RATIO OF CURRENT ACCOUNT DEFICIT TO GOVERNMENT DEFICIT

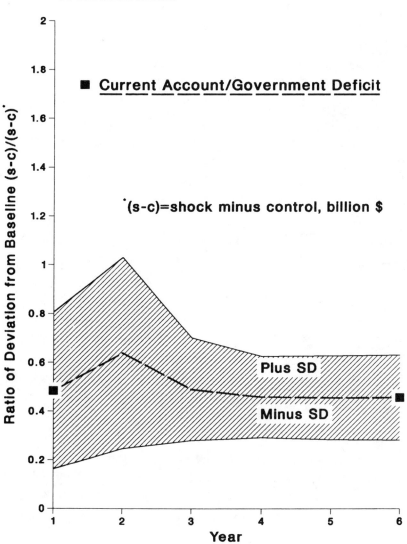

Figure 1.3. AVERAGE U.S. GNP MULTIPLIERS

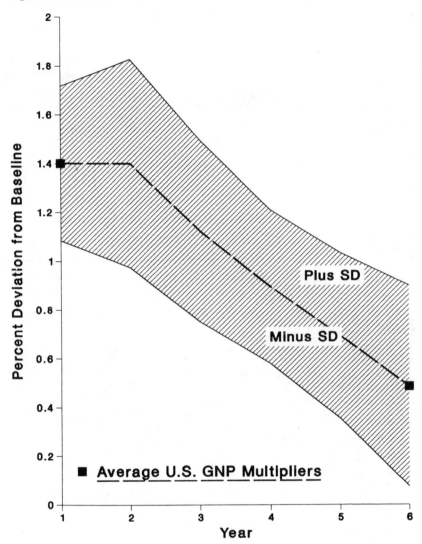

Figure 1.4. AVERAGE U.S. GNP MULTIPLIERS: CONSISTENT AND ADAPTIVE
EXPECTATIONS

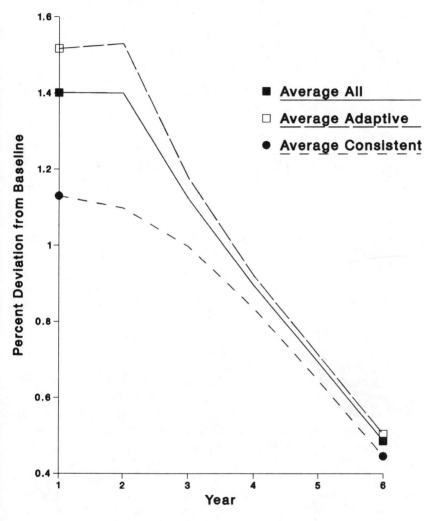

or model-consistent expectations, usually referred to as rational expectations. This happens because in these models the future crowding-out effects are foreseen, especially in financial and foreign exchange markets, so that long-term interest rates and the exchange rate rise more, and much sooner, than in models where expectations adjust adaptively.[14] Although the real exchange rate crowding out occurs faster in the models with consistent expectations, the effects on the nominal current account build up more slowly, as the J-curve effects take a year or more to work themselves out.

WHAT IF FISCAL POLICY HAD BEEN DIFFERENT IN THE 1980s?

To get a rough answer to the question of what would have happened if fiscal policy had been different in the 1980s, simulations based on the INTERMOD multicountry model[15] have been used to estimate how different the U.S. deficit and debt position in the 1980s might have been if U.S. fiscal policy had been less expansionary in the first half of the 1980s. This can only be done in a very approximate manner, since there is no way of knowing what the alternative fiscal policy might have been, and even less way of knowing the extent to which the actual fiscal policy changes were foreseen by financial markets, a factor that has great importance in models with forward-looking expectations. To avoid making any personal guesses on the nature of the alternative policy, I use the Helkie/Hooper (1988, Table 2-15) estimates of the cumulative federal government fiscal expansion between 1980 and 1985, which are approximately equal to the IMF estimates of federal government fiscal expansion, which total some 3.5 percent of GNP. On the presumption that the broad features rather than the year-to-year variations of the fiscal expansion were foreseen by financial markets, the increases are spread evenly over the years 1980 to 1985. The fiscal expansion is then left constant in real terms (about $100 billion 1980 dollars) for the rest of the decade, and then subsequently removed.[16]

Figures 1.5 and 1.6 illustrate the results of this fiscal policy experiment, using both adaptive and consistent expectation versions of INTERMOD. Figure 1.5 shows the effects on the fiscal (government) and external (current account) deficits, and also on the ratio of the external debt to GNP, while figure 1.6 shows the effects on interest rates and the exchange rate, under the assumption that the

Figure 1.5. INTERMOD: CURRENT ACCOUNT DEFICIT, GOVERNMENT DEFICIT
AND NET FOREIGN LIABILITY GNP SHARES

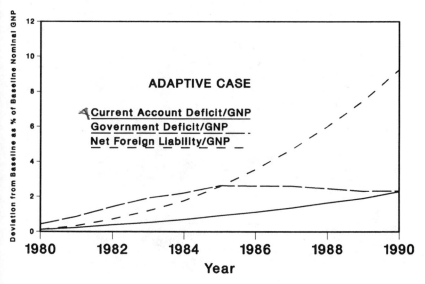

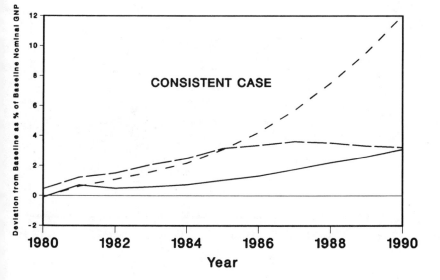

Figure 1.6. INTERMOD: EXCHANGE RATE AND INTEREST RATES

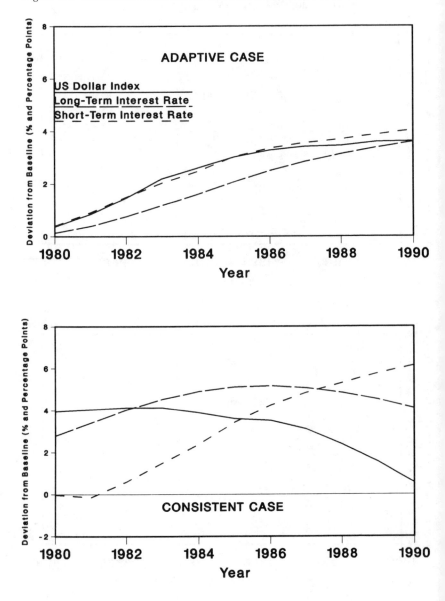

money supply is the same under the two alternative patterns of government spending.

The results based on model-consistent expectations, combined with the assumption that the fiscal expansion was foreseen, suggest that the 1986 fiscal deficit was 3.3 percent of GNP larger (about $140 billion), and the current account deficit 1.3 percent of GNP larger (about $55 billion) than they would have been without the fiscal expansion. As the figures show, the current account effects continue to rise through the decade, as the foreign debt share continues to build up. Because future increases in government spending are foreseen at the beginning of the decade, there are immediate increases in the external value of the dollar[17] and in long-term interest rates, which almost completely crowd out the income-increasing effects of government spending.[18]

Under adaptive expectations, the future effects of fiscal expansion are not foreseen, and the increases in the value of the dollar and in long-term interest rates are much less. As a result, increases in income are larger, and government deficit increases are generally smaller. The external deficit comparison is more ambiguous. Under adaptive expectations, higher income means higher real imports, which tend to make the current account effects larger. However, there is much less increase in the value of the dollar, and hence much less reduction in real net exports via that channel. However, the nominal current account is less rapidly affected by these relative price effects, because the dollar cost of U.S. imports falls when the dollar is stronger, as it is under consistent expectations. As time progresses, the external deficit effects become much larger, especially under consistent expectations, when the J-curve effects have time to work themselves through.

A striking feature of the results, under both adaptive and consistent expectations, is the build-up of government and external debt and the growing importance of debt service charges. By the end of 1989, under consistent expectations, net foreign debt is $500 billion higher than it would have been without fiscal expansion, and government debt is $1,000 billion higher.[19] As a result of the accumulation of foreign debt, a substantial wedge is created between real output (GDP, or value-added within the United States) and real income (GNP, or real income accruing to U.S. residents), equal to the reduction of net interest and dividend income from foreigners. By 1989, real GNP has fallen by more than 1 percent relative to GDP, representing the net cost of servicing the foreign debt.

The numbers used in this section are not intended as precise estimates, since they come from only one of many models[20] and, more importantly, because we cannot know to what extent the fiscal expansion of the 1980s was foreseen, and hence how much of the higher interest rates and higher exchange value of the dollar can be attributed to it.[21] Nevertheless, the evidence from a substantial number of models, and from several alternative approaches, suggests that U.S. fiscal policy in the first half of the 1980s was responsible for about half of the buildup of the external deficit, and that cumulated foreign debt is now about half a trillion dollars higher than it would have been without the fiscal expansion.

If U.S. fiscal policy was not responsible for more than half of the growth of the external deficit in the 1980s, what are the factors responsible for the rest of the growth? One frequent candidate is tighter U.S. monetary policy, which helped to raise the value of the dollar and to crowd out real net exports. However, when the multi-country models are simulated under tighter U.S. monetary policy, they typically show very little net effect on the external deficit. For example, Table 3.1 of Bryant, Helliwell and Hooper (1989) shows that a 1 percent U.S. monetary expansion lowers the value of the U.S. dollar by about 1 percent, on average, but has no net effect on the current account, since the relative price effects are offset by the increased imports caused by the higher levels of U.S. final demand.

Another widely studied explanation for the growth of the external deficit in the 1980s is that the exchange market overvalued the U.S. dollar in the mid-1980s, independent of the induced effects of the monetary and fiscal polices of the time, and that this added to the external deficit. The multicountry models show that on average each 1 percent increase in the value of the dollar that is not caused by fiscal or monetary policy changes worsens the U.S. current account, in the third year, by somewhat less than $1 billion.[22]

There is also the possibility, noted by Genberg (1988) and others, that abnormal increases in private investment spending, whether based on changes in the tax rules and rates applicable to investment spending (which have not been explicitly incorporated in the fiscal policy assessments in this paper), or on changes in business confidence, could have contributed to the increase in the current account deficit, at least during the period when the new capacity had not been fully brought on stream.

Finally, there is the role of fiscal contraction in countries outside North America. The G-7 countries outside North America followed generally restrictive fiscal policies during the first half of the 1980s, by amounts averaging about 2.5 percent of their GNP (Helkie and Hooper 1988, Table 2-17). Figure 1.7 shows INTERMOD estimates of the link-

Figure 1.7. THIRD-YEAR EFFECTS OF FISCAL EXPANSION: CONSISTENT EXPECTATIONS

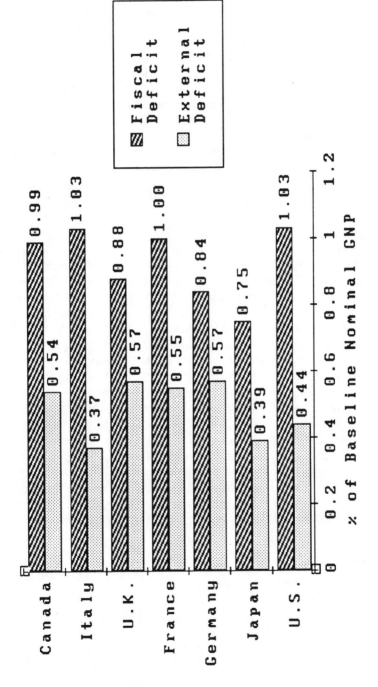

ages between the fiscal and external deficit consequences of separate fiscal expansions (with spending increased by amounts equal to 1 percent of GDP) in each of the G-7 economies. The countries are shown in ascending order of size from top to bottom. All seven countries show substantial linkages between the external and fiscal deficits, with the effects of fiscal expansion on the external deficit being slightly greater for the smaller and more open economies. Italy provides a slight exception, mainly due to the high private savings rate there, an often noted feature of the Italian economy.[23]

A precise calculation of the impact of foreign fiscal policy on the U.S. current account would require looking at each country's policy separately, since each of the G-7 countries has different trading links with the United States. However, a reasonable approximation can be provided by using the evidence for changes in government spending among the non-U.S. members of the OECD, referred to as the "rest of the OECD" or ROECD. This evidence was presented at the 1986 Brookings conference on Empirical Macroeconomics for Interdependent Economies (Bryant, Henderson et al. 1988). Using this evidence, Helkie and Hooper (1988, Table 2-17) estimate that tighter fiscal policy in the ROECD contributed an additional $25 billion to the U.S. external deficit in 1986.

Combining the model-based evidence of the impact of U.S. and foreign fiscal policy on the U.S. external deficit, together with other factors leading to dollar appreciation in the 1980s, Helkie and Hooper (1988, Table 2-17) estimate that about $135 billion of the 1986 U.S. current account deficit is explainable.[24] The aim of this paper is not to explain fully the evolution of the U.S. current account, which raises a number of larger issues, but to spell out the evidence linking U.S. fiscal policy to the external deficit. This evidence is perhaps best summarized by a 50 percent rule of thumb: that in the macroeconomic environment of the 1980s, an increase in the fiscal deficit arising from changes in government spending is likely to have been accompanied by about half as large an increase in the external deficit.

IMPLICATIONS FOR THE 1990s

This paper has summarized the model-based evidence of the linkage between fiscal policy and the external deficit in the 1980s. The experiments used were based on the analysis of changes in the current and future levels of government spending, where (at least in the models with consistent or forward-looking expectations) the proposed changes in future spending were fully credible to all participants. However, the real world is more complicated than this in at least two important ways. First, the political process does not operate so as to provide a close link between currently announced objectives and actual future policy. Thus, any announcement of future policy is bound to be at least partially discounted in the minds of market participants.[25] Second, given the uncertainty about institutions, behaviour, and future events, policies are better analyzed in terms of the reactions of policymakers to unfolding events. More and more researchers are using models to evaluate alternative policy rules in this way,[26] but so far there is no evidence available on the design and consequences of alternative deficit reduction strategies within this more general framework. In any event, benchmark estimates of the type examined in this paper will remain relevant to more complex studies of policy strategies.

To what extent is the evidence presented in this paper transferable to the 1990s? Several of the experiments discussed in this paper were based on the effects of reductions in U.S. government spending starting in 1987 or 1988 and extending into the 1990s. Thus, these results largely incorporate the accumulated debt levels of this period, and the broad features of the results are likely to be relevant for assessments covering the first half of the 1990s. Therefore it is likely that in the 1990s, to the extent that the models assessed come close to capturing the main elements of macroeconomic linkages, reductions in the fiscal deficit will, on their own, contribute to a reduction in the external deficit about half as great. This arises from the combined effects of the lower domestic final demand and the higher foreign demand, spurred by the lower real value of the dollar. The lower real value of the dollar is partly the result of a lower nominal value and partly the result of a lower U.S. inflation rate.

What effect will other factors have on the external deficit? Monetary expansion, whether intended to offset the temporary contractionary effects of fiscal deficit reduction[27] or to lower the value of the dollar to help encourage net exports, has almost no net effect on the external deficit, despite a very large effect on the value of the dollar.[28]

Drops in the value of the dollar coming from sources other than changes in fiscal and monetary policies are estimated, with much imprecision, to have only a slight net effect on the external deficit. Thus the link between the exchange rate and the external deficit depends critically on what is making the exchange rate change. According to the evidence surveyed here, a lower value of the dollar only has a material effect on the external deficit when it is caused by a change in domestic final spending. Thus, to the extent that reducing the external deficit should become a focus of macroeconomic policy, reductions in the fiscal deficit provide the policy instrument.

Since the fiscal and external deficits are siblings rather than twins, domestic policy alone is not likely to remove the external deficit entirely, especially in the short-run. Higher real growth in countries outside North America, as implied by their continuing convergence toward North American levels of real income and productivity, is likely to be a welcome partner to U.S. domestic fiscal policy in obtaining and maintaining U.S. fiscal and external balance. If internal balance and sustainability of the external position were to be achieved, however, there would seem little further reason why the external deficit or surplus should be a focus of special policy attention, beyond being an interesting record of the international pattern of saving and investment.

Notes

The research underlying this paper was greatly aided by the research collaboration of Alan Chung under the financial support of the Social Sciences and Humanities Research Council of Canada. In revising this paper, I have been much aided by the comments and suggestions of Jacob Frenkel and John Williamson.

1. In 1979 the federal fiscal deficit was $16 billion, more than offset by a state and local surplus of $28 billion (*Economic Report of the President*, January 1989, Table B-79). In the same year, there was a merchandise trade deficit of $27 billion, more than offset by net investment income of $31 billion and a small surplus on other services, to give a positive balance of $5 billion on the goods and services account. This surplus was in turn mostly offset by net unilateral transfers, to give a current account of the balance of payments of less than $1 billion (*Economic Report*, Table B-102).

2. *Economic Report*, Tables B-79 and B-102. The total government sector had a $15 billion surplus in 1979 and a peak deficit of $144 billion in 1986.

3. For example, the U.S. current account blocks of the six multicountry models whose properties are surveyed by Bryant, Holtham and Hooper (1988, 133) show long-run income elasticities averaging 1.87 for non-oil imports and 1.27 for goods exports.

4. See, for example, Branson and Marston (1989), Froot and Klemperer (1988), Krugman (1987), Mann (1986), and Marston (1989).

5. For example, five of the six multicountry models analyzed by Bryant, Holtham

and Hooper (1988, 113), have U.S. current account blocks that show a first-year worsening of the nominal current account by an amount averaging, for the five models, 0.37 percent of GNP, from a 20 percent decline in the nominal value of the U.S. dollar. In four of these five models, the current account effect becomes positive by the second year. In the fifth model, the negative section of the "J-curve" lasts until the third year.

6. The model with perfect capital mobility and static expectations was first presented by Mundell (1963) as a special case of the model with imperfect capital mobility developed earlier by Mundell and also by Meade (1951) and Fleming (1962). The model, especially the version with perfect capital mobility, is often referred to as the Mundell-Fleming model, with subsequent uses and developments surveyed by Frenkel and Razin (1987b).

7. Under a certain configuration of preferences, Frenkel and Razin (1988a, 313) show that a deficit caused by a fall in taxation of consumption or on foreign borrowing tends to worsen the current account, while lower income taxation tends to improve it.

8. Barro (1989, 40) notes that Ricardian equivalence and the lack of relation between budget deficits and the current account, apply only to deficits created by changing the pattern of taxes for a given flow of government expenditures. However, the empirical evidence he reports relates to correlations between government deficits and the current account, without reference to the source of the government deficits.

9. The conferences and models involved are described in more detail in Bryant, Helliwell and Hooper (1989).

10. The data were prepared in comparable form and reported in Bryant, Helliwell and Hooper (1989). The sample of ten models reported here is the BHH twelve-model sample minus two models for which some of the series reported in this paper were not available. Table 1.4 (for all tables see the appendix, p. 51) reports the primary data for a larger sample of eighteen "models" (some of which are different versions of the same model), which in turn is the full twenty-model sample used by BHH less two models for which not all the series were available. Most of the model runs used a decrease in U.S. federal spending, and all of the results were converted to that basis, assuming approximate linearity of responses for the experiments reported in BHH. For this paper, the results are reported as though the expenditure changes were increases in government spending, so as to make the evidence more easily applicable to explaining the increasing fiscal and external deficits of the 1980s.

11. Each of the models integrates all of the partial approaches listed earlier in this paper, with relative importance that differs somewhat from one model to the next.

12. A strict interpretation of these standard deviations would require that the observed properties were based on samples from a population of models with normally distributed properties. The models could be considered to differ by being different estimates of the properties of an underlying "true" model of the economy, or by being representative of the variety of models actually used by those forming expectations of the effects of policies. The observations are in fact neither independent nor random, as some models have been excluded on the basis of implausible properties, some of the results are from slightly different versions of the same model, and some of the models are intentionally similar to one another. In addition, the distributions are not normal, especially in the 18-model sample, where, especially in the later years, the distributions are skewed by one or two implausible outliers, as is apparent from the results for individual models reported in table 1.4.

13. The means and standard deviations plotted in figures 1.1 and 1.2 are reported in table 1.1.

14. Although these models have fully forward-looking expectations, they still have substantial fiscal multipliers, partly because of wage setting by staggered contracts,

and partly because both consumption and investment spending are estimated to be significantly affected by current incomes, even in those models where crowding-out is complete over the longer term.

15. The model was developed in the Canadian Federal Department of Finance, based on the 1988 version of the IMF's MULTIMOD (Masson et al. 1988), and was extended to include separate country blocks for each of the G-7 economies. It was prepared in both mainframe and PC versions, as described in Helliwell, Meredith, Durand and Bagnoli (1990). The simulations reported here use version 1.2, which differs from the earlier version by implementing a monetary policy that holds the money supply unchanged in response to fiscal changes, instead of the earlier monetary policy reaction function that dampened the interest rate effects of fiscal policy changes. Version 1.2 has a monetary sector with properties similar to the average of those of the multicountry models surveyed by Helliwell, Cockerline and Lafrance (1988).

16. This is to avoid the possibility of unstable long-term solutions of the models with forward-looking expectations. In these models, an unsustainable fiscal policy is foreseen by financial markets, so that the future fiscal policy must be consistent with the models' portfolio equilibrium conditions. The fiscal expansion is reduced by 20 percent of the annual declining balance in each year following 1990. This has no effect on the 1980s results for models with adaptive expectations, since policies expected to be introduced after 1990 have no explicit effects on 1980s behaviour in these models.

17. The importance of expected future budget deficits in determining the value of the dollar has been widely studied and emphasized. See, for example, Feldstein (1986).

18. As shown in Figure 4.1 of Bryant, Helliwell and Hooper (1989), when expected future increases in government spending are announced they can lower aggregate spending. This is because the crowding-out effects of the exchange rate and long-term interest rates appear immediately, while the demand-expanding effects of government spending appear only later. Similar effects of anticipated future spending are shown by other researchers using model-consistent expectations, e.g., by Masson and Blundell-Wignall (1985), Haas and Masson (1986), and McKibbin and Sachs (1989, Table 6).

19. Under adaptive expectations, where the expansionary effects of fiscal policy are larger, the debt build-up is smaller: $400 billion in external debt and $800 billion in government debt.

20. The debt accumulation results are not available for a wider variety of models. Not all of the multicountry models fully account for the interactions between debt accumulation, both domestic and foreign, and the resulting debt service payments.

21. In addition, the interaction between deficits and debt is strong enough that the baseline matters. The INTERMOD estimates of the effects of U.S. fiscal policy on the external deficit would be slightly smaller if the experiments were run on a baseline that excluded the policies. On the other hand, INTERMOD and MULTIMOD both have an endogenous tax policy that comes into play to guarantee that the debt/GNP ratio does not become explosive, and this plays a role in limiting the estimates of the induced fiscal deficit, and hence debt, in the latter half of the 1980s.

22. A gradual depreciation of the dollar, totaling just under 25 percent by the fourth year, improves the U.S. current account in that year by about $19 billion, as reported for an average of 11 models in Bryant, Henderson et al. (1988, Supplemental Volume, Table F, 100).

23. The data are drawn from Tables A1 and A3-A8 of Helliwell, Meredith et al. (1990). It should be noted that the three savings rates (private, government and foreign) do not sum to zero as a percentage of baseline nominal GNP, but to the change in nominal investment, also measured as a share of baseline GNP. Thus, international differences

in the extent to which private investment is induced or crowded out by fiscal expansion can also play a role in mediating the differences between the external and fiscal deficit effects. All of the G-7 countries show induced investment, averaging about the same as Italy's .6 percent of baseline GNP, while Italy's personal savings, at 1.25 percent, is among the highest.

24. Subsequent refinements of these estimates are reported in Hooper and Mann (1989).

25. This may have the effect of making the actual effects of policies fall in between the paths predicted by models with adaptive and rational (i.e. model-consistent) expectations. This is by no means sure, however, as it depends on the structure and diversity of the processes actually used by market participants to form their expectations about future policy, as well as on their beliefs about the structure of the economy itself.

26. Current examples of the evaluation of alternative monetary policy rules, including the implications for policy coordination, include Frenkel, Goldstein and Masson (1989) and Taylor (1989). Evaluation of policy rules in a stochastic environment is the focus of continuing collaborative research among users of multicountry models, with a workshop to be held in Washington in the spring of 1990.

27. Almost all of the multicountry models surveyed show that there is complete or nearly complete crowding out (or crowding in, in the case of fiscal contraction) of real private spending and net exports in the medium term, in response to changes in government spending. Thus, the real GNP effects of budget reductions are temporary, although spread over years rather than months. The models with forward-looking expectations also show that credibly announced future changes in fiscal policy have much smaller real GNP effects, since the exchange rates and long-term interest rates move quickly so as to accelerate the substitution of private expenditures for public ones.

28. Bryant, Henderson et al. (1988, Supplemental volume, Table E, 87). The inflationary effects of the monetary expansion combine with the expenditure-increasing effects to offset the increases in net exports that might otherwise be expected to follow from a reduction in the value of the dollar.

References

Barro, Robert J. 1989. "The Ricardian Approach to Budget Deficits." *Journal of Economic Perspectives* 3 (Spring):37–54.

Barro, R. 1974. "Are Government Bonds Net Wealth?" *Journal of Political Economy* 82 (November/December):1095–1117.

Branson, William H. and Richard C. Marston. 1989. "Price and Output Adjustment in Japanese Manufacturing." *NBER Working Paper* 2878 (March).

Bryant, Ralph C., John F. Helliwell and Peter Hooper. 1989. "Domestic and Cross-Border Consequences of U.S. Macroeconomic Policies." In *Macroeconomic Policies in an Interdependent World*, edited by R.C. Bryant, D.A. Currie et al., 59–115. Washington: International Monetary Fund.

Bryant, Ralph C., Dale W. Henderson, Gerald Holtham, Peter Hooper, and Steven A. Symansky, eds. 1988. *Empirical Macroeconomics for Interdependent Economies.* Washington, D.C.: Brookings Institution.

Bryant, Ralph C., Gerald Holtham, and Peter Hooper, eds. 1988. *External Deficits and the Dollar: The Pit and the Pendulum.* Washington, D.C.: Brookings.

Dornbusch, R. 1989. "The Adjustment Mechanism: Theory and Problems." In *International Payments Imbalances in the 1980s,* edited by Norman S. Fieleke. Boston: Federal Reserve Bank of Boston.

Feldstein, Martin S. 1986. "The Budget Deficit and the Dollar." In *NBER Macroeconomics Annual 1986,* edited by S. Fischer, 355–392. Cambridge, MA: MIT Press.

Feldstein, Martin S. and C. Horioka. 1980. "Domestic Saving and International Capital Flows." *Economic Journal* 90 (June): 314–329.

Fleming, J.M. 1962. "Domestic Financial Policies Under Fixed and Under Floating Exchange Rates." *IMF Staff Papers* 9 (November): 369–379.

Frenkel, Jacob A., Morris Goldstein and Paul R. Masson. 1989. "Simulating the Effects of Some Simple Coordinated versus Uncoordinated Policy." In *Macroeconomic Policies in an Interdependent World,* edited by R.C. Bryant, D.A. Currie et al., 203–239. Washington: International Monetary Fund.

Frenkel, Jacob A. and Assaf Razin. 1988a. "Budget Deficits Under Alternative Tax Systems." *IMF Staff Papers* 35:297–315.

Frenkel, Jacob A. and Assaf Razin. 1988b. *Spending, Taxes and Deficits: International-Intertemporal Approach.* Princeton: Princeton Studies in International Finance No. 63.

Frenkel, Jacob A. and Assaf Razin. 1987a. *Fiscal Policies and the World Economy: An Intertemporal Approach.* Cambridge: MIT Press.

Frenkel, Jacob A. and Assaf Razin. 1987b. "The Mundell-Fleming Model a Quarter Century Later." *IMF Staff Papers* 34:567–620.

Froot, Kenneth A. and Paul Klemperer. 1988. "Exchange Rate Pass-Through When Market Share Matters." *NBER Working Paper* No. 2542 (March).

Genberg, Hans. 1988. "The Fiscal Deficit and the Current Account: Twins or Distant Relatives?" *Research Discussion Paper* 8813. Sydney: Reserve Bank of Australia.

Haas, Richard and Paul R.Masson. 1986. "MINIMOD: Specification and Empirical Results." *IMF Staff Papers* 33 (December): 722–767.

Helkie, William L. and Peter Hooper. 1988. "An Empirical Analysis of the External Deficit, 1980–86." In *External Deficits and the Dollar,* edited by Bryant, Holtham and Hooper, 10–56.

Helliwell, John F., Jon Cockerline, and Robert Lafrance. 1988. "Multicountry Modelling of Financial Markets." *NBER Working Paper* 2736 (October).

Helliwell, John F., Guy Meredith, Yves Durand and Philip Bagnoli. 1990.

"INTERMOD 1.1: A G-7 Version of the IMF's MULTIMOD." *Economic Modelling* 7 (January): 3–62.

Hooper, Peter, and Catherine Mann. 1989. "The U.S. External Deficit: Its Causes and Persistence." In *The U.S. Trade Deficit: Causes, Consequences and Cures*, the proceedings of the 12th Annual Economic Policy Conference of the Federal Reserve Bank of St. Louis, edited by Albert E. Burger 3–105 (Boston: Kluwer Academic Publishing).

Krugman, Paul R. 1988. "Sustainability and the Decline of the Dollar." In *External Deficits and the Dollar*, edited by Bryant, Holtham and Hooper, 82–100.

Krugman, Paul R. 1987. "Pricing to Market When the Exchange Rate Matters." In *Real-Financial Linkages among Open Economies*, edited by S.W. Arndt and J.D. Richardson, 49–70. Cambridge: MIT Press.

Marris, Stephen. 1987. *Deficits and the Dollar: The World Economy at Risk*. Policy Analyses in International Economics 22, revised edition. Washington: Institute for International Economics.

Mann, Catherine L. 1986. "Prices, Profit Margins, and Exchange Rates." *Federal Reserve Board Bulletin* 72 (June): 366–379.

Marston, Richard C. 1989. "Pricing to Market in Japanese Manufacturing." *NBER Working Paper* 2905 (March).

Masson, Paul R., and A. Blundell-Wignall. 1985. "Fiscal Policy and the Exchange Rate in the Big Seven: Transmission of U.S. Government Spending Shocks." *European Economic Review* 28 (May):11–42.

Masson, P., S. Symansky, R. Haas and M. Dooley. 1988. "MULTIMOD: A Multi-Region Econometric Model." *Staff Studies for the World Economic Outlook* (July):50–104. Washington: International Monetary Fund.

McKibbin, W.J. and J.D. Sachs. 1989. "The McKibbin-Sachs Global (MSG2) Model." *Brookings Discussion Papers in International Economics* 78.

Meade, J.E. 1951. *The Theory of International Economic Policy*. London: Oxford University Press.

Mundell, Robert A. 1963. "Capital Mobility and Stabilization Policy Under Fixed and Flexible Exchange Rates." *Canadian Journal of Economics and Political Science* 29, (November):475–85.

Taylor, John B. 1989. "Policy Analysis with a Multicountry Model." *NBER Working Paper* 2881 (March).

Williamson, J. 1985. *The Exchange Rate System*. Washington: Institute for International Economics.

Williamson, J. and M. Miller. 1987. *Targets and Indicators: A Blueprint for International Coordination of Economic Policy*. Washington: Institute for Policy Analysis.

Part One

APPENDIX

Tables: GUIDE TO MODEL MNEMONICS

EP(1988FR)	EPA: World Econometric Model of the Japanese Economic Planning Agency.
EPA (EMIE)	"
MC(1988FR)	MCM: Multicountry Model of the US Federal Reserve Board.
MCM (EMIE)	"
NI(1988FR)	GEM: Global Economic Model of the National Institute of Economic and Social Research of the United Kingdom.
OE(1988FR)	OECD: Interlink model system of the Economics and Statistics Department of the OECD.
OECD(EMIE)	"
LI(1988FR)	LINK: Project Link model.
LINK(EMIE)	"
MP(1988FR)	MPS: Federal Reserve Board MPS model.
MU	MULTIMOD: MULTI-region econometric MODel of the IMF.
INY	INTERMOD: Adaptive case.
INZ	INTERMOD: Consistent case.
LIV (EMIE)	LIVERPOOL: The Liverpool model built by Patrick Minford and associates at the University of Liverpool.
DRI (EMIE)	DRI: International Model of Data Resources Incorporated.
EEC (EMIE)	COMPACT: developed by the staff of the EC Commission.
MCK (EMIE)	MSG: McKibbin-Sachs Global model developed by Warwick McKibbin and Jeffrey Sachs at Harvard University.
MINI(EMIE)	MINIMOD model constructed by Richard Haas and Paul Masson at the International Monetary Fund.

Notes:

EMIE refers to the conference "Empirical Macroeconomics for Interdependent Economies." It was held at Brookings in March 1986, the proceedings are published as Bryant, Henderson et al., eds, (1988).
1988FR refers to the Federal Reserve Board Conference, May 1988.

Table 1.1 EFFECTS OF A CHANGE IN GOVERNMENT EXPENDITURES EQUAL
          TO 1% OF GNP

Means and Standard Deviations for 10-Model Sample						
Year	1	2	3	4	5	6
(a) ugnpv mn	1.401	1.400	1.123	0.894	0.693	0.486
sd	0.317	0.426	0.373	0.315	0.340	0.412
(b) ucurdef/ mn	0.250	0.346	0.387	0.434	0.485	0.551
ugnp sd	0.091	0.091	0.095	0.116	0.164	0.218
(c) ugdef/ mn	0.615	0.643	0.850	1.013	1.161	1.321
ugnp sd	0.212	0.210	0.210	0.316	0.443	0.568
(d) ucurdef/ mn	0.484	0.639	0.490	0.459	0.456	0.457
ugdef sd	0.322	0.392	0.211	0.167	0.172	0.174

Units: (a) Percent deviation from baseline
            (b),(c) Deviation from baseline as percent of
            nominal baseline GNP
            (d) Ratio of deviation from baseline
            (s-c)/(s-c)

Mnemonics: mn = Mean, sd = Standard Deviation
            ugnpv = US real gross national product
            ugnp = US nominal gross national product
            ucurdef = US current account deficit
            ugdef = US government deficit

10-model sample: MC, OE, MU, INY, INZ, MCM, DRI, EEC, MINI, OECD

continued

Table 1.1. (*Continued*)

Correlation Matrix for 10-Model Sample			
Year 1			
(a) 1.000			
(b) 0.227	1.000		
(c) -0.726	0.133	1.000	
(d) 0.830	0.434	-0.774	1.000
(a)	(b)	(c)	(d)
Year 2			
1.000			
0.603	1.000		
-0.663	-0.452	1.000	
0.786	0.808	-0.877	1.000
Year 3			
1.000			
0.493	1.000		
-0.443	-0.196	1.000	
0.580	0.769	-0.745	1.000
Year 4			
1.000			
0.297	1.000		
-0.354	0.125	1.000	
0.486	0.619	-0.654	1.000
Year 5			
1.000			
0.174	1.000		
-0.351	0.177	1.000	
0.415	0.559	-0.653	1.000
Year 6			
1.000			
0.030	1.000		
-0.396	0.174	1.000	
0.291	0.606	-0.590	1.000

Table 1.2. MEANS AND STANDARD DEVIATIONS FOR 18-MODEL SAMPLE

		Year	1	2	3	4	5	6
(a) ugnpv	mn		1.328	1.323	1.086	0.867	0.615	0.268
	sd		0.373	0.576	0.561	0.419	0.485	1.352
(b) ucurdef/	mn		0.247	0.349	0.389	0.421	0.454	0.497
ugnp	sd		0.117	0.143	0.172	0.205	0.271	0.361
(c) ugdef/	mn		0.578	0.583	0.766	0.941	1.104	1.281
ugnp	sd		0.249	0.249	0.258	0.346	0.454	0.634
(d) ucurdef/	mn		1.176	0.887	0.685	0.639	0.651	0.652
ugdef	sd		3.077	1.026	0.846	0.909	1.065	1.097

Units: (a) Percent deviation from baseline
                  (b),(c) Deviation from baseline as percent
                  of nominal baseline GNP
                  (d) Ratio of deviation from baseline
                  (s-c)/(s-c)

Mnemonics: mn = Mean, sd = Standard Deviation
                  ugnpv = US real gross national product
                  ugnp = US nominal gross national product
                  ucurdef = US current account deficit
                  ugdef = US government deficit

18-model sample: EP, MC, NI, OE, LI, MP, MU, INY,
                 INZ, EPA, LIV, MCM, DRI, EEC, LINK, MCK,
                 MINI, OECD

continued

Table 1.2. (*Continued*)

Correlation Matrix for 18-Model Sample			
Year 1			
(a) 1.000			
(b) -0.027	1.000		
(c) -0.525	-0.120	1.000	
(d) -0.138	0.412	-0.598	1.000
(a)	(b)	(c)	(d)
Year 2			
1.000			
0.344	1.000		
-0.400	-0.401	1.000	
0.062	0.725	-0.696	1.000
Year 3			
1.000			
0.155	1.000		
-0.223	-0.298	1.000	
-0.118	0.690	-0.662	1.000
Year 4			
1.000			
0.178	1.000		
-0.133	-0.095	1.000	
-0.129	0.534	-0.609	1.000
Year 5			
1.000			
0.562	1.000		
-0.230	-0.060	1.000	
0.097	0.428	-0.580	1.000
Year 6			
1.000			
0.618	1.000		
-0.517	-0.178	1.000	
0.171	0.395	-0.514	1.000

Table 1.3. MEANS FOR ADAPTIVE AND CONSISTENT EXPECTATIONS MODELS

Year	1	2	3	4	5	6
Adaptive Models: MC, OE, INY, MCM, DRI, EEC, OECD						
(a) ugnpv	1.517	1.530	1.178	0.920	0.713	0.504
(b) ucurdef/ugnp	0.292	0.368	0.403	0.438	0.479	0.535
(c) ugdef/ugnp	0.588	0.601	0.853	1.037	1.203	1.392
Consistent Models: MU, INZ, MINI						
(a) ugnpv	1.130	1.098	0.997	0.834	0.646	0.446
(b) ucurdef/ugnp	0.152	0.295	0.349	0.424	0.500	0.588
(c) ugdef/ugnp	0.677	0.742	0.843	0.957	1.065	1.157

Note: Reported numbers are means.

Units: (a) Percent deviation from baseline
              (b),(c) Deviation from baseline as percent of
              nominal baseline GNP

Mnemonics: ugnpv = US real gross national product
              ugnp = US nominal gross national product
              ucurdef = US current account deficit
              ugdef = US government deficit

Table 1.4. RESULTS FROM INDIVIDUAL MODELS

UGNP (percent deviation from baseline)

	1	2	3	4	5	6
EP	1.406	1.111	1.118	1.034	0.917	0.809
MC	1.565	1.773	1.552	1.429	1.366	1.212
NI	1.150	0.850	0.250	0.050	0.175	0.300
OE	1.012	0.907	0.578	0.476	0.339	0.136
LI	1.030	0.660	0.450	0.490	0.530	0.480
MP	2.031	2.838	2.601	1.612	-0.648	-4.822
MU	1.064	1.232	1.188	1.040	0.846	0.616
INY	1.550	1.760	1.550	1.260	0.990	0.760
INZ	1.220	1.110	1.050	0.910	0.740	0.550
EPA	1.578	1.710	1.605	1.575	1.604	1.916
LIV	0.653	0.573	0.523	0.498	0.471	0.447
MCM	1.564	1.838	1.434	0.936	0.522	0.057
DRI	2.049	2.103	1.444	0.980	0.853	0.957
EEC	1.340	1.245	1.049	0.850	0.645	0.446
LINK	1.247	1.219	0.983	0.709	0.474	0.282
MCK	0.811	0.855	0.780	0.703	0.621	0.552
MINI	1.106	0.953	0.753	0.552	0.353	0.173
OECD	1.536	1.082	0.637	0.510	0.275	-0.043

UGDEF/UGNP (deviation from baseline as percent of baseline nominal GNP)

	1	2	3	4	5	6
EP	0.550	0.639	0.673	0.730	0.809	0.865
MC	0.414	0.386	0.558	0.683	0.779	0.908
NI	0.749	0.465	0.898	1.355	1.400	1.134
OE	0.820	0.746	0.937	1.159	1.330	1.521
LI	0.031	0.136	0.188	0.172	0.152	0.161
MP	0.402	0.377	0.589	0.977	1.602	2.660
MU	0.766	0.817	0.914	1.033	1.147	1.236
INY	0.700	0.760	0.880	1.010	1.150	1.270
INZ	0.720	0.880	1.030	1.200	1.360	1.500
EPA	0.302	0.263	0.590	0.971	1.363	1.692
LIV	0.978	0.992	1.031	1.066	1.098	1.155
MCM	0.382	0.320	0.599	0.912	1.188	1.475
DRI	0.218	0.408	0.896	1.214	1.382	1.466
EEC	0.832	0.764	0.887	0.635	0.507	0.511
LINK	0.493	0.384	0.387	0.454	0.567	0.697
MCK	0.757	0.811	0.944	1.093	1.273	1.476
MINI	0.545	0.528	0.585	0.638	0.688	0.734
OECD	0.752	0.826	1.211	1.644	2.082	2.590

continued

Table 1.4. RESULTS FROM INDIVIDUAL MODELS (Continued)

UCURDEF/UGNP (deviation from baseline as percent of baseline nominal GNP)

EP	0.076	0.290	0.363	0.441	0.529	0.630
MC	0.283	0.419	0.471	0.523	0.583	0.636
NI	0.140	0.105	0.146	0.196	0.177	0.141
OE	0.364	0.356	0.369	0.416	0.450	0.483
LI	0.417	0.618	0.740	0.720	0.732	0.794
MP	0.304	0.477	0.337	0.162	-0.037	-0.323
MU	0.234	0.302	0.343	0.398	0.450	0.519
INY	0.210	0.260	0.300	0.350	0.410	0.480
INZ	0.120	0.380	0.440	0.550	0.660	0.780
EPA	0.211	0.491	0.604	0.679	0.758	0.855
LIV	0.168	0.166	0.141	0.125	0.103	0.104
MCM	0.253	0.396	0.524	0.657	0.818	0.993
DRI	0.272	0.522	0.519	0.463	0.473	0.569
EEC	0.281	0.281	0.289	0.275	0.234	0.198
LINK	0.130	0.156	0.145	0.124	0.104	0.093
MCK	0.498	0.523	0.649	0.795	0.961	1.142
MINI	0.101	0.204	0.265	0.324	0.389	0.466
OECD	0.382	0.341	0.349	0.382	0.384	0.384

UCURDEF/UGDEF (ratio of deviation from baseline (s-c)/(s-c))

EP	0.138	0.454	0.539	0.604	0.654	0.728
MC	0.684	1.085	0.844	0.766	0.748	0.700
NI	0.187	0.226	0.163	0.145	0.126	0.124
OE	0.444	0.477	0.394	0.359	0.338	0.318
LI	13.452	4.544	3.936	4.186	4.816	4.932
MP	0.756	1.265	0.572	0.166	-0.023	-0.121
MU	0.305	0.370	0.375	0.385	0.392	0.420
INY	0.300	0.342	0.341	0.347	0.357	0.378
INZ	0.167	0.432	0.427	0.458	0.485	0.520
EPA	0.699	1.867	1.024	0.699	0.556	0.505
LIV	0.172	0.167	0.137	0.117	0.094	0.090
MCM	0.662	1.237	0.875	0.720	0.689	0.673
DRI	1.248	1.279	0.579	0.381	0.342	0.388
EEC	0.338	0.368	0.326	0.433	0.462	0.387
LINK	0.264	0.406	0.375	0.273	0.183	0.133
MCK	0.658	0.645	0.687	0.727	0.755	0.774
MINI	0.185	0.386	0.453	0.508	0.565	0.635
OECD	0.508	0.413	0.288	0.232	0.184	0.148

COMMENTS ON "THE FISCAL DEFICIT AND THE EXTERNAL DEFICIT: SIBLINGS BUT NOT TWINS"

John Williamson

This paper fulfills its mandate admirably. I particularly enjoyed the later part, where the author employs the multicountry models to whose evolution he has contributed so much. It is in asking questions like the extent to which we can attribute the external deficit to domestic fiscal policy that these large multicountry macroeconometric models really prove their utility.

I was particularly pleased to discover the author's 50 percent rule of thumb: that 50 percent of an increase in the federal deficit gets translated into an increased external deficit. It happens that I presented exactly the same rule of thumb in congressional testimony in February 1989. Obviously these are not completely independent observations, any more than the different models that John uses are totally independent: we looked at much the same set of econometric evidence, primarily that revealed by the Brookings Institution's series of simulations. But it is reassuring to find that when an expert looks at that evidence he comes up with the same conclusion that I did.

This evidence helps explain the sharp difference of view between Fred Bergsten and myself about the desirable target current account deficit for the United States. In Bergsten's *America in the World Economy* (Washington, D.C.: Institute for International Economics, 1988), he urged the United States to aim at eliminating the current account deficit by 1992. I have taken the view that the objective should be to get the deficit down to something that is safely sustainable, meaning perhaps one percent of GNP. One of the reasons I have argued against the target of zero is my skepticism concerning the ability of the U.S. political system to generate the budget surplus of over $100 billion that this 50 percent rule of thumb implies would be necessary. We are as likely to see that as to see the communist system suddenly start to generate economic prosperity.

Early in his paper, Helliwell presents a useful taxonomy of the different variants of the savings-investment approach to analyzing the relationship between the [fiscal] and external deficits.

(1) He attributes what he calls the twin deficit view to the New Cambridge school, which is now pretty much defunct. However, this view is still very much with us in the work of Ronald McKinnon.

(2) The Feldstein-Horioka view argues that domestic investment reflects national savings. This is what I think of as a pre-Donald Regan view of the world. Before Ronald Reagan's secretary of the treasury, Donald Regan, came on the scene, it was taken for granted that governments (at least of larger countries) would aim for current account outcomes not too different from zero. I have long assumed that Donald Regan's ambition in life must have been to be the world's biggest bond salesman, for I can think of no rationale for his lack of concern for the developing external deficit other than the desire to be able to sell a lot of bonds to foreigners.

(3) The world of integrated capital markets analyzed by Jacob Frenkel and Assaf Razin argues that the current account deficit is a result of forward-looking investment, private consumption, and government spending, all of which are assumed to be determined in a rational manner with due account taken of their intertemporal consequences and with everyone acting optimally. The theory of Ricardian equivalence is a special case of this approach.

(4) Helliwell's final category involves the sustainability concerns of Paul Krugman and my colleague Stephen Marris. The latter may have been a little dogmatic on the timing of some of the disasters that were to befall the world, but his fundamental insights and concerns were also very much about sustainability.

My own work on fundamental equilibrium exchange rates was also concerned with that issue. The fundamental equilibrium exchange rate reflects an external balance target. This is essentially a current account target, where in principle the target current account should transfer what would be intertemporally optimal, but is qualified by sustainability constraints and shorn of faith that anything that private markets do must of its nature be optimal. I see no reason to suppose that market participants are well placed to think through questions of collective intertemporal optimality and sustainability. I do believe it is sensible to try to get governments to think about those issues—about what appears to be implied by national savings propensities and investment opportunities, taking account of creditworthiness constraints, which may limit the extent to which countries can borrow.

When I was one page from the end of the paper, I was worried that I was not going to be able to say anything much except "amen." At that point I began to wonder whether John had recognized my problem, and therefore had deliberately tried to provoke me in the final page.

The first remark that might have been intended to be provocative was that a "lower value of the dollar only has a material effect on the external deficit when it is caused by [lower] domestic final spending." I am not sure this squares with the evidence in the Helkie/ Hooper paper that he cites. Of the $135 billion deterioration in the U.S. current account that Helkie and Hooper explain, they get $95 billion out of fiscal changes ($70 billion from changes in domestic fiscal policy and another $25 billion from changes in foreign fiscal policy), plus another $40 billion out of the unexplained appreciation of the dollar—what we think of as the speculative bubble part of the dollar appreciation. Because $40 billion is quite a big swing, it is an overstatement to say that the exchange rate does not have any effect unless it is caused by lower domestic spending.

Even to the extent that the proposition is true, it can be phrased another way: a lower dollar must be accompanied by lower domestic spending if it is to yield a balance of payments improvement rather than simply more inflation (under conditions of full employment). This statement is equivalent to John's, but perhaps the latter tends to suggest a more important role for exchange rate policy.

The author's other attempt to provoke me comes in the very last sentence of the paper, where he says that "once internal balance and sustainability of the external position seem secure . . . there seems little reason why the external deficit or surplus should be a focus of special policy attention. . . " I agree that sustainability is the principal reason why the current account should be a focus of policy attention. But sustainability is not something that can be secured once and for all, so that thereafter we can forget about the current account. True, it is not necessary to monitor or control the current account very closely. I certainly do not regard it as desirable to try to secure current account balance in every year, or even a current account balance equal to the long-run underlying capital flow in any particular year. On the contrary, it is useful to allow the current account to vary as a shock absorber. Furthermore, it is sensible to allow the current account to change before policy adjustments are brought into play, because at times current account changes may tell us something about what is intertemporally optimal.

Nevertheless, I am convinced that prudence demands continual checks for sustainability, because at times we do see unsustainable current account positions emerging, and sooner or later they lead to disaster. The fact that this has not yet happened in the case of the United States does not imply that it is never going to happen. On the contrary, disaster becomes progressively more likely as the outstanding stocks of debt build up.

COMMENTS ON "THE FISCAL DEFICIT AND THE EXTERNAL DEFICIT: SIBLINGS BUT NOT TWINS"

Jacob A. Frenkel

I am impressed with the breadth of this paper and I am provoked by its final pages. I will make a few remarks on the analytical section of the paper, a very few remarks on the empirical section, and concentrate on the policy part.

I agree completely with the general premise that we are not going to understand current accounts, budget deficits and, more importantly, the interactions between them using a partial model that does not link export equations and import equations with other macroeconomic forces. John Helliwell clearly describes the various alternative approaches to macroeconomic modeling. All alternatives, with different degrees of complexity, have one thing in common. That is, they cannot be used to fully analyze an important sector of the economy without the existence of considerable analytic and empirical information regarding some other sectors of the economy. The degree of complexity chosen depends on how refined you wish to be. And here I have relatively strong views on the nature of the "proper model." The question relates to how one recognizes the links that operate.

When we ask how a government policy change affects the economy, we always need to have first, a detailed description of the government's policies, and second, a theory of how the private sector responds to these policies. Then we have to put the two parts together to determine the net economic impact. Therefore, when somebody tells me that the government increases its budget deficit, that says little unless I know whether the deficit increase is caused by a rise in spending or a fall in taxes. And if somebody tells me that a rise in spending takes place, that says little unless I know what type of spending is increased. This is especially important if the real exchange rate plays an important role in the economy, because then it is crucial to know whether the increased government spending is on tradeable goods or on nontradeable goods. Furthermore, since the models estimate effects on interest rates, the present is linked to the future. Therefore it is crucial to know if government spending is increased today only, tomorrow only, permanently, or transitorily. Turning to taxes, it is again essential to know whether the government finances its spending through an income tax which may have profound implications for the supply of labor, or a capital tax or some other type of tax. These are not merely refinements of the model, because we know from theory that different types and different timings of spending or tax policies have very different effects.

Put another way, the nature of the linkage between budget deficits and current account deficits may seem elusive only because the policy changes that we wish to examine have not been described in sufficient detail. One can only justify referring to uninformative aggregates such as budget deficits and current accounts if, as a rule of thumb, they are driven by some stylized regularity. If they are not, the analysis requires much more detailed information. In a recent study of these matters, which I conducted jointly with Assaf Razin, we concluded that "A proper analysis of the effects of fiscal policies on the world economy cannot be carried out on the basis of a single aggregate measure of the fiscal stance such as the budget deficit. It must be based on more detailed and specific information on government spending and taxes. On the spending side, such information must specify the distribution of spending between tradeable and nontradeable goods and its intertemporal allocation. On the revenue side, the information must specify the characteristics of the tax system, including the timing of taxes and the types of taxes used to finance the budget."* I fully stand by this statement today.

Let me now turn to the issue of sustainability. John Helliwell considers the sustainability issue within the context of a so-called "irrational" group of models. The models are not truly irrational, but they assume that economic actors do not understand that current conditions are not sustainable. This can obviously happen, but eventually markets wake up. And as they wake up, sustainability becomes an issue. And therefore I would view the sustainability analysis as somewhere in between the modeling that assumes that people ignore the future completely and the modeling that assumes that people forecast the future perfectly. That is to say, people ignore the problem for a time, but then they wake up and suddenly recognize the reality of the situation.

---

*See Frenkel, Jacob A. and Assaf Razin. 1988. "Spending, Taxes and Deficits: International-Intertemporal Approach." Princeton: Princeton Studies in International Finance 63 (Decémber).

Let me make one remark on Helliwell's empirical results. One has to feel a little bit uneasy regarding the model's linkage between the current account and budget deficits, because the model also suggests that the dollar's effective exchange rate appreciates by only four percent in response to the increased budget deficits. But the fact is that from the trough of 1979 to the peak of 1985, the dollar appreciated by 50 percent. Does this mean that there is some problem in the model? If not, it may be that this significant appreciation did not affect the current account for many other reasons still to be explored. Another reason for regarding the empirical results with a grain of salt is that the simulations all assume that a rise in government spending caused the budget deficit in the United States. But, in fact, much of the deficit arose from a fall in taxes. If you believe that the source of the deficit matters significantly, additional analysis may be merited.

Let me turn now to the policy discussion. The paper makes two key policy statements. First, domestic policy alone is not likely to remove the external deficit entirely, and therefore higher growth in countries outside of North America is required. Because the simulations suggest that monetary policy has little effect on growth, presumably it is fiscal stimulus that is required. Up to two years ago, or even a year ago, the strategy of G-7 coordination, at least in terms of some of the pronouncements, could be called the "tango principle." Namely, as the U.S. decreases its budget deficit, surplus countries like Germany and Japan should increase their spending or budget deficit to prevent the world spinning into a big recession. As one foot goes back it makes room for the other foot to step in and the tango continues. This is the rationale for the view that "as we withdraw, they must expand."

This leads to two concerns. The first and foremost is whether this is what the world needs today. The world is now operating close to full capacity, and the most serious problems are the shortage of global savings and the threat of inflation. It is not by chance that the G-7 are no longer talking about the tango principle. Now, they talk instead about joint action. This means that as the U.S. brings down its budget deficit, surplus countries are using the momentum of coordination to carry out actions that are in their own interests, such as structural reforms. The need to promote global world savings is based on the recognition that the debt situation as well as the emerging developments in Eastern Europe call for additional financial resources if investment is not to be crowded out.

Second, the tango principle presumes a tremendous degree of flexibility in fiscal policy. If there is one lesson from the past few years, it is that fiscal policy is not a flexible instrument that can be used as precisely as dancing the tango. Typically, if you try to use it you will probably find yourself fighting the previous war because there are significant lags between the time of recognition that a fiscal action is needed and the time that the fiscal action is implemented. Furthermore, the effects of fiscal policy on the economy work only after long lags. Maybe this is a good thing, because if fiscal policy were a much more flexible policy instrument we might have been tempted to do too much fine tuning, which usually turns out badly. Fiscal policy must be framed in the medium term and not focused on the very short run.

The other policy question raised by the paper is whether we should focus on the current account in coordinating policy. The author's answer is yes for now, but once the sustainability of the external position has been established the focus on the current account should be diminished. Here John Helliwell is scratching the surface of a deeper question that I want to touch upon: "What is wrong with current account imbalances?" First, are they something we should worry about, and second, should we put them on the same footing as budget deficits? Or do we feel that budget deficits are more of a policy issue than current account imbalances?

I believe that we had better always watch the current account deficit, whether it is sustainable or not, because it may get out of line. But there is another reason to watch the external deficit. The rationale for international coordination is related to current accounts. If it were not for the effects of one nation's policies on others, then the admonishment to "Keep your own house in order" would provide all of the policy guidance necessary. The interests of each country must be determined by asking what effect it has on the rest of the world and what is the effect of the rest of the world on it. As we go from one stock market crash to another, we recognize again and again that world capital markets are highly integrated and that we are all in the same boat.

When John raised the question of whether current accounts are an issue, I thought he might be agreeing with Nigel Lawson, the former Chancellor of the Exchequer of the United Kingdom, who has argued that even though the U.K. may have a very large external deficit, it is not a public policy problem because the government's budget is in good shape. He views the current account deficit as reflecting a private sector deficit, and feels that if the private sector decides to spend more, so be it. I want both to sympathize and take issue with the Chancellor's perspective, which may also underlie Helliwell's remarks that suggest that the current account is not a policy issue. I sympathize with this perspective because we all have the generally good instinct that private sectors in their autonomous decisions are to be respected more than the public sector. On the other hand, in the 1970s, when people were asking whether it was possible that banks were lending too much to some Latin American borrowers, I remember I was told, "Don't worry, when two consenting adults are involved it's a non-issue." And that is a perfectly fine answer as long as the decisions of these two consenting adults do not have negative implications for the rest of us. So the very fact that the private sector is doing something does not imply that it is right. One needs to go one step further and ask if the private sector operates under the right incentives and if it is generating some externalities. The answers may imply that we do indeed have a policy issue.

Let me add a footnote concerning another issue in the paper—the Ricardian equivalence. Yes, one can say that under certain assumptions a change in the timing of taxes does not affect the real equilibrium because the present value of taxes remains constant if governments are to remain solvent and maintain the level of their spending. That is correct provided that there are no distortions. Ricardian equivalence is a statement about the wealth effects of taxes but as we know, lump sum taxes, non-distorting taxes, are only the invention of the analyst and are not often found in practice. Most taxes are distortionary; therefore, the timing of taxes may have an important effect whether you are a Ricardian or not.

I conclude by raising an additional point about the budget and the current account. It is related to regional issues. At the same time as we hear the Chancellor of the Exchequer saying that private sector deficits are not a problem, we also hear that all of West Germany's current account surplus is bottled within Europe and is therefore not an issue for the rest of the world, outside Europe. I think that this is also a fallacy, because it is not proper to analyze current account imbalances on a bilateral basis. It does not matter for the public policy of the U.S. whether its current account deficit is with respect to Japan or other countries. This is determined by real exchange rates and other considerations. By and large, the macro question of differences between national income and national spending is the same independent of where the difference goes. Therefore, the fact that the West German surplus today is bottled within Europe does not necessarily carry implications for the macroeconomic policies of West Germany.

One should keep in mind that in an interdependent model, all deficits are, of course, interrelated. But let us not fall into the fallacy of concluding that since there has been some correlation between two endogenous variables, these correlations are part of the structure of our world. The whole rationale for examining the policies that underlie the deficit—spending and taxes and their timing and composition—is that these correlations are not robust.

Part Two

THE EFFECTS OF FEDERAL BUDGET DEFICITS ON INTEREST RATES AND THE COMPOSITION OF DOMESTIC OUTPUT

THE EFFECTS OF FEDERAL BUDGET DEFICITS ON INTEREST RATES AND THE COMPOSITION OF DOMESTIC OUTPUT

James R. Barth, George Iden, Frank S. Russek, and Mark Wohar

INTRODUCTION

Large federal budget deficits have been a feature of the U.S. economy for almost a decade. The impact of these deficits on interest rates and on general economic conditions has been a major concern of policymakers for almost as long. Lately, however, some complacency seems to have developed. The federal deficit—both in absolute terms and relative to the size of the economy—has peaked and somewhat declined. Some of the dire scenarios some predicted would result from these large deficits have not taken place: domestic recovery has not been prematurely terminated, the inflation rate has not become intolerable, and the nation is not in a financial crisis.

Is this recent complacency justified? What domestic economic effects of large government deficits should policymakers be concerned about? The conventional view is that large government deficits of the kind experienced in the 1980s drive up interest rates and exchange rates, and shift the composition of output toward consumption and away from investment and net exports. To the extent that these developments occur, the long-run effect of deficits is to reduce future living standards.

This conventional view, however, has been challenged by those who argue that government deficits have no real economic effects. According to the "Ricardian equivalence" proposition, individuals see through the veil of government finance and hence are indifferent to changes in the mix between taxes and government borrowing. Government borrowing merely postpones taxes that must be paid, and economic agents adjust their saving accordingly. Therefore, interest rates do not rise because overall national saving is unaffected by government deficits.

Based upon the sizable amount of research on this question, one might think that this issue would have been settled by now and that policymakers would have some conclusive answers. But this is not the case. The 1980s economy exhibited some symptoms associated with the conventional view about the effects of large federal deficits—high real interest rates, a low national saving rate, and a massive trade deficit. Nevertheless, more detailed statistical evidence of these effects remains inconclusive. If government deficits have no deleterious effects, then reducing them should not be a serious concern. However, the potential economic costs of being wrong, when deficits do have an adverse effect, may be too high a risk to incur.

The purpose of this paper is to review and examine systematically several empirical studies on the effects of federal deficits on interest rates and the composition of domestic output. The conclusion reached is that it is difficult to reject outright any of the main competing views. Not only are the empirical results mixed, but they are not always robust. Policymakers, therefore, should be cautious when relying upon any particular study to support a given position.

This paper is divided into five main parts and a conclusion. The first part presents the historical record on federal deficits and debt and examines data on interest rates and on the composition of output. The second part outlines the main competing views about the effects of federal deficits on the economy. The third part examines some empirical issues that arise when estimating the effects of government deficits on interest rates. The next part surveys the empirical evidence on the domestic economic effects of federal deficits, and the last part analyzes in detail the empirical findings of several recent studies dealing with the effect of deficits on interest rates and on the composition of output.

Alternative Federal Deficit Measures

The unified federal budget deficit is the difference between total government receipts and total government outlays, including the operations of trust funds such as Social Security. In general, the deficit excludes the operations of off-budget agencies, such as the Federal National Mortgage Association. The budget deficit includes the net lending activities of government agencies but not the costs of credit guarantees, unless the guarantees come due.[1] The deficit also reflects sales of government assets.

For purposes of analysis, economists frequently use the National Income and Product Accounts (NIPA) measure of the federal deficit, sometimes augmented by including the state and local sector. This measure excludes purely financial transactions, such as the sale of financial assets and net lending by federal agencies. The NIPA measure also records some revenues on an accrual rather than on a cash accounting basis and records some purchases on a delivery rather than on a progress payment basis.

Several specially constructed analytic measures of the federal deficit (generally based upon NIPA) deserve mention. These include: the "cyclically adjusted" deficit, the "inflation-adjusted" deficit, and the "primary" deficit. The cyclically adjusted deficit is a calculation of what federal revenues and expenditures would be when measured at some benchmark level of output and unemployment. In other words, it is a measure of the federal deficit purged of business-cycle effects. The inflation-adjusted deficit is a calculation that subtracts from the federal deficit the decline in the real value of outstanding federal debt due to inflation. This measure indicates increases or decreases in the real value of federal debt. The primary deficit is the federal deficit calculated without net interest payments. Thus it excludes the direct effect of interest rate changes on the federal deficit.

The growth in publicly held federal debt is, of course, closely related to the federal budget deficit. Any differences are due to movements in government cash balances. The term "publicly held" is defined to include not only the debt held by the private sector (households, businesses, state and local governments, and foreigners), but also the debt held by the Federal Reserve. However, the term does not include the federal debt held by federal agencies. Increases in this "agency-held" federal debt are not reflected in the federal budget deficit.[2]

THE HISTORICAL RECORD

The history of federal budget deficits and publicly-held federal debt since 1789 is summarized in figures 2.1 and 2.2. Relative to the gross national product (GNP), most deficits—and especially large ones—have been associated with recessions and wars. Besides the depression years, the major exception is the 1980s, when the deficit reached about 6 percent of GNP. Peacetime deficits became considerably more frequent during the post-World War II period. While deficits

Figure 2.1. FEDERAL DEFICIT AS A PERCENTAGE OF GNP (1789–1988)

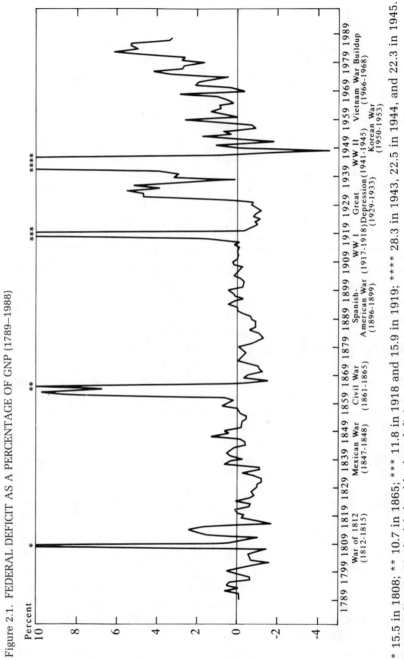

* 15.5 in 1808; ** 10.7 in 1865; *** 11.8 in 1918 and 15.9 in 1919; **** 28.3 in 1943, 22.5 in 1944, and 22.3 in 1945.

Note: Deficit = Unified federal budget deficit.

Figure 2.2. PUBLICLY HELD FEDERAL DEBT AS A PERCENTAGE OF GNP (1789–1988)

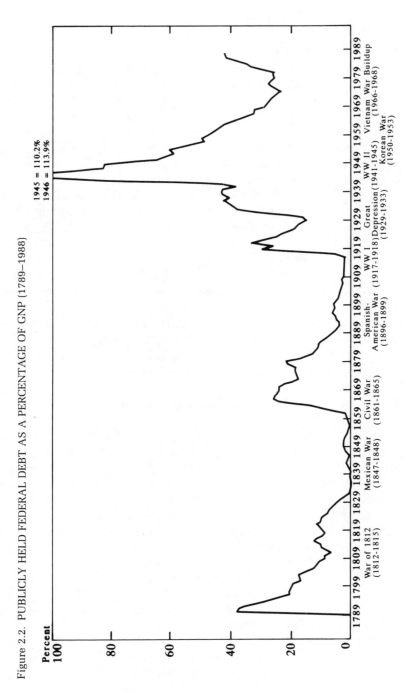

occurred in only 45 of the 142 years before 1931 (32 percent of the time), the budget has been in deficit 34 out of 42 years since 1946 (81 percent of the time).

Although changes in the federal debt relative to GNP need not exactly match movements in the federal deficit relative to GNP, figure 2.2 does resemble figure 2.1. Publicly-held federal debt rose relative to GNP during wartime and then declined gradually during peacetime. Recessions and recoveries also correspond with movements in this ratio. Again, the depression years and the 1980s stand out as the only peacetime periods of very large ratios of debt-to-GNP.[3]

Post-war trends in the ownership of publicly held federal debt are shown in figure 2.3. In panel A, relative to GNP, the holdings of the domestic private sector fell substantially until the mid-1970s and rose substantially thereafter, reflecting movement in the total publicly held federal debt. Although relatively stable, the holdings of the Federal Reserve have declined since the mid-1970s, while the holdings of foreigners increased somewhat during the 1970s. In panel B a similar pattern applies to these holdings measured as percentages of the total publicly held federal debt. The portion held by the Federal Reserve increased during the 1960s and early 1970s, but has declined gradually since then. The portion held by foreigners increased in the 1970s, but then declined slowly during the first half of the 1980s. Since the mid-1980s, the foreign share has increased slightly.

Trends in Interest Rates and the Composition of Output

Trends in interest rates since 1950 are summarized in figure 2.4. Three prominent features emerge. First, interest rates were unusually high in the 1980s, although they have come down somewhat in recent years. Second, nominal interest rates were on an upward trend from 1950 to the early 1980s, when they reached a peak. Third, as shown in panel B, the pattern of real rates—measured by the three-month Treasury bill rate minus inflation—was substantially different from the pattern of nominal rates. Although real rates fluctuated sharply, they dropped below zero in the mid-1970s before rising steadily to relatively high levels in the early 1980s. Since 1984, the real rate has dropped to about the same range as during the 1960s.

The conventional view is that large government deficits of the kind experienced during the 1980s raise interest rates and consumption, and reduce national saving, investment, and net exports. The trends in the reported data for the 1980s, in general, are consistent with these predictions, although such "trends" do not demonstrate caus-

Figure 2.3. OWNERSHIP OF PUBLICLY HELD FEDERAL DEBT

Panel A -- As Percentage of GNP

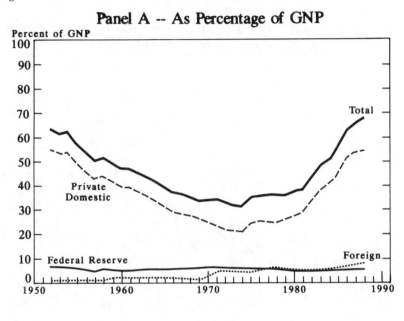

Panel B -- As Percentage of Total Publicly Held Federal Debt

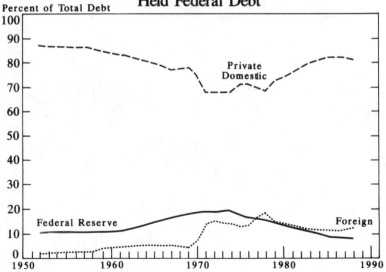

Figure 2.4. TRENDS IN INTEREST RATES FROM 1950 TO PRESENT
(QUARTERLY)

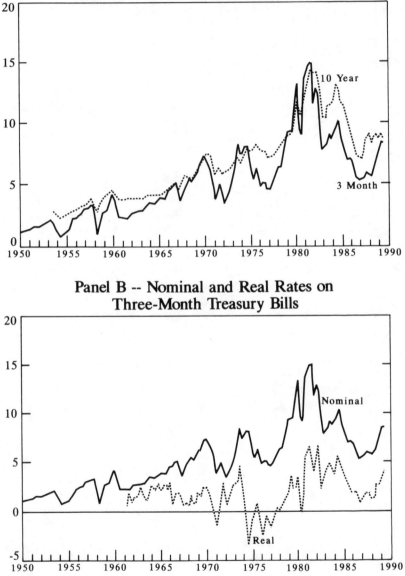

Panel A -- Nominal Rates on Ten Year Government Securities
and on Three-Month Treasury Bills

Panel B -- Nominal and Real Rates on
Three-Month Treasury Bills

Note: Real rate calculated using Consumer Price Index, excluding food,
energy and used cars.

ation. Furthermore, some of the trends in the data do not fit this view.

Several characteristics of the economy during the 1980s are at least consistent with the conventional view. First, interest rates were unusually high, although they have declined somewhat in recent years (figure 2.4). Second, and probably more reason for concern, the nation's net saving rate was dramatically low during the last decade (table 2.1 and figure 2.5). Net saving averaged only about 3 percent of Net National Product (NNP) during the 1980s, compared with approximately 8 percent during the prior 30 years. The overall decline in the saving rate is associated both with a decline in the government saving rate and with a decline in the private saving rate. Third, net investment as a share of NNP was also lower, although the decline is considerably less than for net saving. Fourth, the difference between the behavior of the saving rate and the investment rate has been financed by a dramatic rise in net foreign investment. Finally, the consumption share, or personal consumption relative to GNP, averaged several percentage points higher in the 1980s than in the previous 30 years (table 2.2, column 6).

The significance and causes of these trends can be challenged, but the pieces of the puzzle about recent trends in the composition of output seem to fit together. The patterns are consistent with the conventional view. While there are alternative explanations for the behavior of individual series, a unified alternative explanation of the growth of the trade deficit, the decline in the national saving rate, and the weakness in net investment does not seem to be currently available.

With respect to the decline in saving, some analysts argue that the NIPA measured rate does not accurately measure saving. If the change in wealth is used as a measure of saving, the saving rate may still have declined, according to some (Poterba and Summers 1987), though others find that it has not (Barro 1989). A wealth-based measure of saving may be more appropriate for evaluating household behavior. But the NIPA definition of saving seems more appropriate as a measure of current production available for capital formation and, therefore, for economic growth. In addition, gross saving rates as measured by NIPA have not declined as much as net saving rates. Some analysts argue that the gross measures are more accurate.[4]

With respect to investment, most measures of gross investment do not show a decline during the 1980s, particularly if measured in real terms (table 2.2 and figure 2.6). The measure of investment on which one should focus is a hotly debated issue. Net investment is impor-

Table 2.1 NET NATIONAL SAVING, NET DOMESTIC INVESTMENT, AND NET FOREIGN INVESTMENT AS PERCENTAGES OF NET NATIONAL PRODUCT

	(1) Personal Saving	(2) Retained Earnings	(3) Net Private Saving (1) + (2)	(4) State/ Local Surplus	(5) Federal Surplus	(6) Government Surplus (4) + (5)	(7) Net National Saving (3) + (6)	(8) Net Domestic Investment	(9) Net Foreign Investment (7)–(8)*
1950–1959	5.2	3.0	8.2	−0.2	0.1	−0.1	8.1	8.2	0.1
1960–1969	5.1	3.8	8.9	0.0	−0.3	−0.3	8.6	7.7	0.7
1970–1979	6.2	2.7	8.9	0.9	−1.9	−1.1	7.9	7.6	0.3
1980–1988	4.3	2.0	6.3	1.4	−4.4	−2.9	3.4	5.2	−1.8
1980	5.6	1.6	7.2	1.1	−2.5	−1.4	5.8	5.5	0.5
1981	5.9	1.6	7.5	1.3	−2.3	−1.1	6.4	6.2	0.4
1982	5.5	0.7	6.3	1.3	−5.2	−4.0	2.3	2.3	0.0
1983	4.3	2.1	6.5	1.6	−5.9	−4.3	2.2	3.5	−1.1
1984	4.9	2.8	7.7	1.9	−5.0	−3.1	4.6	7.4	−2.7
1985	3.5	2.9	6.4	1.8	−5.5	−3.7	2.7	5.8	−3.2
1986	3.3	2.2	5.6	1.7	−5.5	−3.8	1.7	5.3	−3.6
1987	2.5	1.9	4.4	1.3	−4.0	−2.7	1.7	5.3	−3.7
1988	3.3	1.8	5.1	1.1	−3.3	−2.2	2.9	5.4	−2.7

Source: U.S. Department of Commerce, Bureau of Economic Analysis; and authors.
*Figures in column (9) do not exactly equal the difference between columns (7) and (8) due to statistical discrepancy and rounding.
Note: Columns may not agree exactly, due to rounding.

Figure 2.5. NET SAVING, NET DOMESTIC INVESTMENT, AND NET FOREIGN
INVESTMENT AS PERCENTAGES OF NET NATIONAL PRODUCT

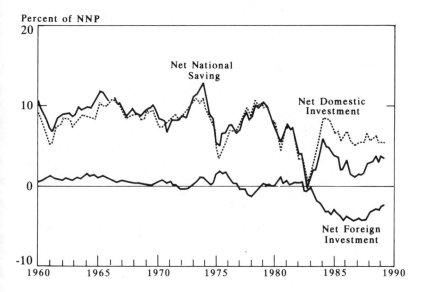

tant for economic growth, because it represents increases in the capital stock. However, there are serious problems in estimating depreciation, not to mention problems of valuation over time (notably, computers). Also, new technology is embedded in gross investment. In any case, gross investment—particularly gross business fixed investment—was not especially weak during the 1980s; by some measures, investment was relatively strong.[5]

The conclusions about the 1980s, as a whole, are generally in accord with comparisons of the current recovery/expansion cycle and earlier business cycles. Such comparisons suggest that investment was relatively strong during the first two years of the recovery, but then became more typical of earlier expansions as time passed.[6] With respect to other components, federal government purchases and personal consumption seemed to be about average. Net exports seem to be the only major sector that stood out as being unusually weak during the most recent recovery. Despite the weakness in net exports, the performance of manufacturing as a whole was not obviously affected in the early phases of the recovery (Congressional Budget Office 1985a and 1985b).

In addition to the question of whether the budget deficit is a cause

Table 2.2 GROSS INVESTMENT, GROSS SAVING, AND PERSONAL CONSUMPTION AS PERCENTAGES OF GNP

	(1) Total Gross Investment	(2) Business Fixed Investment	(3) BFI Real*	(4) Gross Saving	(5) Gross Private Saving	(6) Personal Consumption
1950–1959	16.2	9.6	9.9	16.0	16.2	63.7
1960–1969	15.5	9.9	10.3	16.3	16.6	62.7
1970–1979	16.4	10.7	11.1	16.7	17.6	62.7
1980–1988	15.8	10.9	11.9	14.1	16.7	65.0
1980	16.0	11.8	11.9	16.2	17.5	63.4
1981	16.9	12.1	12.2	17.1	18.0	62.7
1982	14.1	11.6	11.6	14.1	17.6	64.8
1983	14.7	10.5	11.0	13.6	17.4	65.6
1984	17.6	11.0	12.1	15.1	17.9	64.4
1985	16.0	11.0	12.5	13.3	16.6	65.5
1986	15.6	10.3	11.8	12.4	15.8	66.1
1987	15.5	9.8	11.8	12.2	14.7	66.6
1988	15.4	10.0	12.3	13.2	15.1	66.3

Source: U.S. Department of Commerce, Bureau of Economic Analysis; and authors.
*Real business fixed investment as a percent of real GNP. (The other columns pertain to current prices.)

Figure 2.6. GROSS DOMESTIC INVESTMENT AND BUSINESS FIXED
INVESTMENT AS PERCENTAGES OF GROSS NATIONAL PRODUCT

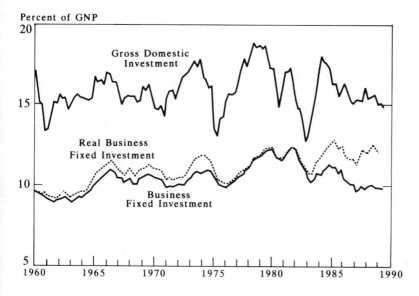

of the trade deficit, there is the issue of whether the large trade deficit
and associated capital inflows have affected interest rates and the
composition of output during the 1980s. According to conventional
views, without the net foreign investment interest rates would have
been even higher in the United States and investment significantly
lower (Penner 1989). In any event, the high dollar in foreign exchange
markets caused severe problems of competition in selected manufacturing industries such as iron and steel (Congressional Budget
Office 1985c). In turn, the severe pressures on particular industries
caused extremely high unemployment in some geographic areas,
particularly in the Midwest, where there is a high concentration of
smokestack industries.

According to many, the massive trade deficit should have caused
a discernable shift in the composition of output away from tradable
goods and toward services. However, the effect of the trade deficit
on the composition of output is difficult to identify (table 2.3). One
reason is that the Economic Recovery Tax Act of 1981 contained
major new investment incentives that helped blunt the effects of an
increase in real interest rates. A second reason is that the buildup
in defense during the early years of the Reagan administration brought

Table 2.3 MAJOR TYPES OF PRODUCT AS PERCENTAGES OF GNP

	(1) Goods	(2) Services	(3) Structures	(4) Goods Real*
1950–1959	53.6	34.2	12.2	45.7
1960–1968	48.6	40.1	11.3	43.3
1970–1979	44.7	44.3	10.9	42.3
1980–1988	41.2	48.9	9.9	42.7
1980	43.0	46.3	10.7	42.2
1981	43.3	46.4	10.3	42.7
1982	41.7	48.9	9.5	41.7
1983	41.0	49.4	9.6	41.7
1984	41.9	48.1	10.0	43.1
1985	40.9	49.0	10.1	42.9
1986	39.9	50.1	10.1	42.8
1987	39.5	50.9	9.6	43.3
1988	39.6	51.2	9.2	44.0

Source: U.S. Department of Commerce, Bureau of Economic Analysis; and authors.
*Goods as a percent of GNP, with both series measured in constant, 1982 prices.

about a surge in federal procurement of goods, notably weapons systems. The third reason is that economic growth was relatively strong in the first two years of the recovery, although only about average for a recovery period. As a result, the improvement in the economy may have masked the effects of the increased trade deficit on the composition of output.

Another reason that effects of the trade deficit on output composition are difficult to identify is that no current data exist on gross product originating in manufacturing. The old methodology used to construct these data showed no decline in manufacturing output as a share of GNP during the 1980s. This was cited by some analysts as evidence that the United States was not deindustrializing. However, the methodology used to construct the manufacturing output series has been criticized on several grounds. Plausible alternative assumptions to construct the series could show a substantial decline in the manufacturing share (Mishel 1989 and Young 1989). In any case, the methodology is being reviewed by the Bureau of Economic Analysis, with a new series expected in 1990.

Based on employment data, the manufacturing sector seems to have been stronger than normal during the first two years of the recent recovery. In the third and fourth years of the recovery expansion, however, the economy slowed considerably and the industrial sector slowed even more. Payroll employment data suggest that the recovery in manufacturing may still be incomplete after almost seven years of continuous expansion in the economy (see figure 2.7).

The effect of changes in net exports on the composition of employment over the period 1979 to 1984 was examined recently using input-output analysis. The conclusion reached was that "Had trade effects remained neutral between 1979 and 1984, there would have been 1.7 million more manufacturing jobs in 1984 and 116,000 more farming jobs. Trade and service employment would have been correspondingly lower" (Stone and Sawhill 1989, p. 18).

THE COMPETING VIEWS ABOUT DEFICIT EFFECTS

Two viewpoints dominate most analyses of the effects of federal deficits on interest rates and other macroeconomic variables. The conventional view maintains that changes in taxes and spending have real economic effects, including effects on real interest rates. The Ricardian equivalence proposition, on the other hand, argues that shifts in the method of financing government expenditures have no significant macroeconomic effect. In addition, a third view has also received some attention—the new classical view. We now discuss these views in some detail.

The Conventional View

According to the conventional view, deficits increase interest rates when an increase in the government deficit results from a tax reduction, because the latter raises income and wealth and thereby stimulates consumption and hence aggregate demand. Interest rates rise because the demand for credit increases along with the increase in aggregate demand.[7] The increase in wealth is due to the government bonds sold to finance the deficit, which are considered a component of household wealth. An increase in the deficit that results from an increase in government purchases is viewed as even more stimulative because it has a more direct impact on aggregate demand. What happens to the composition of output then depends on how long the deficit persists and on how much slack there is in the economy, but eventually the higher interest rates crowd out investment.

Open economy considerations complicate matters somewhat, but the basic story associated with the conventional view remains intact.

Figure 2.7. PAYROLL EMPLOYMENT IN MANUFACTURING AND THE PRIMARY
METALS INDUSTRY (in thousands)

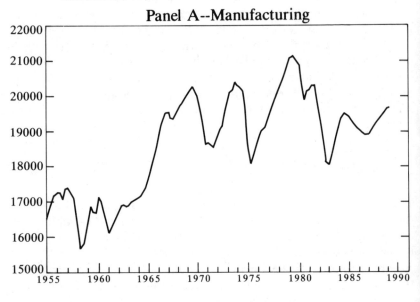

Panel A--Manufacturing

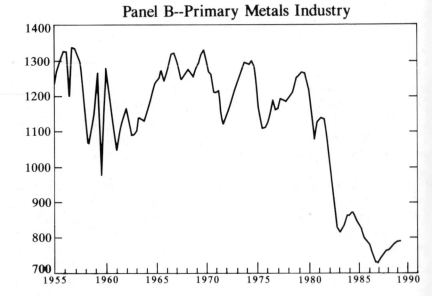

Panel B--Primary Metals Industry

The increase in domestic interest rates establishes a differential over interest rates abroad, thus affecting foreign capital flows into the U.S. If international capital markets work efficiently, the rise in interest rates might be very small, which would make an interest rate effect very difficult to detect. In the case of a large economy and a large government deficit, however, world capital markets would be affected to some degree, and both domestic and foreign interest rates would therefore be higher (Tanzi 1985b). In any case, the effect of government deficits on domestic investment would be muted due to capital inflows, making that particular effect hard to detect. But the fact that investment may suffer little, at least for a while, does not necessarily imply that deficits are harmless. Transfer of wealth from domestic to foreign ownership—the effects of which might be scarcely noticeable at first— may in time result in deleterious effects. The extent to which foreign wealth holders eventually become saturated with the assets of the country running the government deficits and then begin to demand larger returns may also lead to harmful effects. Moreover, like eating too much at a party, the feeling of saturation might come suddenly, in this case with attendant financial disruptions.

Within this conventional framework, there is clearly quite a range of views about the magnitude of deficit effects, and therefore their importance. Some economists argue that due to well-developed international capital markets, the supply of capital is so elastic with respect to interest rates that for all practical purposes government deficits have a negligible effect on interest rates. In addition, some economists argue that the total amount of assets in the U.S. or in the world is so large that even a hundred billion dollar federal deficit is like a drop in the bucket. Furthermore, some argue that capital inflows support greater investment activity, which, in turn, will generate enough economic growth to repay foreign indebtedness as well as produce a higher standard of living.

The Ricardian Equivalence Proposition

The Ricardian equivalence proposition, as developed by Barro (1974), among others, has challenged the conventional view. This proposition maintains that (holding government purchases constant) federal deficits do not raise interest rates or have any of the other major adverse effects described by the conventional view. In this framework, the substitution of debt for tax financing of government spending does not raise private sector income or wealth, because individuals assume that a current deficit implies higher taxes in the future to service and repay the additional debt. As a result, the current generation increases its saving by the amount of the additional debt in anticipation of the future tax increases. Thus, the increase in federal debt is not viewed as an increase in wealth, because the tax reduction or transfer increase underlying the deficit is viewed as temporary.[8] Consequently, there is no income or wealth effect on consumption and aggregate demand, and no effect on the national saving rate or interest rates—and no effect on exchange rates or the trade deficit either.[9]

According to Barro (1980), a distinction should be made between systematic (anticipated) and nonsystematic (unanticipated) increases in federal debt, and between temporary and permanent increases in government purchases. In contrast to anticipated increases, unanticipated increases in government debt have real economic effects. A temporary increase in government purchases can also raise interest rates (Barro 1981b), unless the purchases are perfect substitutes for private purchases.[10]

The Ricardian equivalence proposition is based on a number of important assumptions. First, it assumes that each generation derives utility from all future offspring as well as from its own lifetime consumption. This assumption connects the utility functions of all generations, and implies that the current generation adjusts its saving to offset any fiscal actions that have effects beyond its own lifetime. Second, it is also assumed that the present value of government spending equals the present value of taxes. This intertemporal budget constraint imposes a constraint on the growth of government debt. In other words, securities that are issued in the current period to finance a deficit are matched by future taxes to service and repay the debt. Without the first assumption, a tax reduction would cause the current generation to increase consumption, thus shifting the burden of government debt entirely onto future generations. Without the second assumption, no person would have any reason to believe that deficits are a temporary phenomenon or that government debt would not grow without limit.[11]

Some additional comments may help to clarify the scope and limitations of the debt-neutrality proposition.[12] First, this proposition applies to debt-financed decreases in taxes or increases in transfers, but not to debt-financed increases in government purchases. It does not rule out an increase in interest rates due to an increase in debt-financed government purchases unless government purchases are a perfect substitute for private consumption.[13] Barro (1981b) has argued that a permanent change in government expenditures financed by taxes has little or no effect on the real rate of interest, while a temporary change in government expenditures financed by debt induces an increase in current prices relative to expected future prices, and therefore an increase in the real interest rate. A temporary increase in government purchases may be debt financed so as to avoid intertemporal fluctuations in tax rates. In this case, one could find a positive correlation between changes in the debt and changes in real interest rates that is consistent with the Ricardian equivalence proposition that there is no effect on real interest rates resulting from permanent changes in government purchases, whether financed by debt or taxes.[14]

The second assumption of the Ricardian equivalence proposition is that tax changes are of the lump-sum variety. It does not rule out macroeconomic effects from tax rate changes. Any fiscal action that alters relative prices has the potential to change work-leisure choices and capital stock decisions. Therefore, only certain types of deficits, those that result from lump-sum changes in taxes or transfer payments, fail to generate real economic effects.

The Ricardian equivalence proposition also assumes away the possibility of permanent deficits that cause federal debt to grow without limit (relative to national income in an expanding economy).[15] Most economists would agree that such deficits produce adverse effects by increasing the likelihood that the government will default on its debt or by causing the monetary authority to monetize ever increasing proportions of deficits. If such a situation were to develop, it would negate a basic assumption of the Ricardian equivalence proposition.

The New Classical View

In addition to the two main views, there is a new classical view, which is attributed to the work of Lucas (1976), among others. It suggests that if policy induced movements in the deficit are unanticipated, they may have real effects. This result comes about because of two assumptions. First, agents collectively use all available information to form rational expectations of the future path of economic variables, so that there is no systematic error. Second, prices are flexible enough to clear all markets at all times. Given a stable policy regime known by the public, the public conditions its behavior on *anticipated* fiscal actions. When the fiscal action actually occurs, there is no effect since such movements have already been reflected in equilibrium prices. Thus, fiscal actions can only affect output in the short run if they are unexpected.[16]

These considerations have led some economists to question the relevance of the findings from studies examining the effects of current and past deficits on interest rates. Instead, this view suggests that the focus should be on the unexpected component of current deficits and on expected future deficits.[17]

TESTING THE EFFECTS OF DEFICITS ON INTEREST RATES: EMPIRICAL ISSUES

The alternative views outlined above have generated many empirical studies that attempt to test the validity of one view or the other. Many of these studies have examined the effect of federal deficits on interest rates; others have considered the effect on variables such as saving, consumption, and investment. Despite many of these studies, several of which are reviewed in the next section, there is still disagreement about the effects of federal deficits. This section considers some of the issues that arise when testing for the interest-rate effects of deficits, especially those involving some type of adjustment to the reported deficit measures.

A regression equation commonly used to relate interest rates to federal deficits has the following general form:

$$i = a_o + a_1 D + AZ + e, \qquad (1)$$

where i is an interest rate, D is a measure of the federal debt or the deficit (here expressed as $G - T$), Z represents other variables that are thought to affect interest rates, a_o and a_1 are coefficients, A is a vector of coefficients, and e is the error term. The conventional view maintains that the coefficient, a_1, is statistically greater than zero, while the Ricardian equivalence proposition maintains that it is not statistically different from zero. The new classical view is that it is statistically greater than zero only when the deficit is unexpected.

Alternative Deficit Measures

Some empirical studies use the NIPA measure of the federal deficit, while others use the unified budget measure. Still others use the changes in the outstanding stock of federal debt. To avoid statistical problems, technically referred to as "non-stationarity" and "heteroskedasticity," these measures sometimes are entered in first difference form and frequently are scaled by population, output, or some other variable.

The NIPA measure is consistent with reported measures of national output and income. Thus, studies that also include NIPA measures of federal taxes or spending in the interest rate equation (as a component of Z) often use the NIPA measure of the deficit for consistency. The unified budget measure of the deficit sometimes is used because it more closely reflects federal credit demands.[18] Finally, changes in the outstanding stock of federal debt are used in studies that stress the importance of stocks rather than flows, or make a distinction between par and market values and between debt purchased by the Federal Reserve and by the private sector.

Inflation and Par-to-Market Adjustments

Many argue that the measure of the federal deficit should reflect an adjustment for changes in the real market value of federal debt due to inflation and movements in interest rates. Such adjustments are prompted by the view that private demands depend upon the real market value of household wealth. When this measure of wealth declines because of inflation or an increase in interest rates, it is argued that households respond by increasing their saving to restore their real wealth positions. Such an increase in private saving tends to offset the credit market impact of a federal deficit, thus reducing the effects of federal deficits on interest rates.

Controlling for Federal Reserve and Foreign Purchases of Federal Debt

In addition to correcting the deficit measure for inflation, many studies also take into account the effects of open-market operations by the Federal Reserve; and some take account of capital inflows from abroad. Both of these factors reduce the amount of government debt that must be absorbed by domestic suppliers of private credit, and thus should reduce the effect of federal deficits on domestic interest rates.

From an econometric standpoint, whether or not one removes from the federal deficit the purchases of federal debt by the Federal Reserve and by foreigners may not matter if these purchases are included as explanatory variables. To illustrate this point, let M and F represent purchases (or holdings) of federal debt by the Federal

Reserve and by foreigners. If D is the deficit (change in total publicly held federal debt, including M and F), then the increase in the debt held by the domestic private sector is $D^* = D - M - F$. When estimating the effect of federal deficits on interest rates, it would not matter whether the explanatory variables were D, M, and F, or D^*, M, and F—that is, the coefficients on D and D^* would be the same, and would have the same standard errors. But the coefficients on M and F would be different in the two cases. When M and F are excluded from the equation, however, the use of D restricts D^*, M, and F to have the same coefficient, while the use of D^* restricts the coefficients of M and F to zero. If these restrictions are invalid, the estimated effect of the federal deficit on interest rates can be biased.

Distinguishing Between Expected and Unexpected Deficits

Some maintain that only the unexpected component of the current federal deficit should have an effect on interest rates. If so, the deficit measure should be $UD = D - ED$, where UD and ED are the unexpected and the expected components of D. From an econometric viewpoint, however, the magnitude and significance of the deficit coefficient should not change if one uses UD instead of D, provided that ED also is included in the equation. In this case, the coefficients on D and ED should be the same but opposite in sign, and the interest rate effect of expected deficits would be the sum of these two coefficients (or zero). Studies that include UD without ED assume the coefficient to be zero rather than estimating the coefficient of ED.

Controlling for Different Tax and Spending Effects

The conventional view distinguishes between the effects of government taxes and spending (purchases). Many studies of the interest rate effects of government deficits, however, do not control for the separate effects of government spending and taxes. Consider the following equations:

$$i = a_o + a_1(G - T) + e_1 \tag{2}$$

$$i = b_o + b_1(G - T) + b_2G + e_2. \tag{3}$$

In equation (2), the coefficient, a_1, measures the net effect of taxes and spending, and restricts both G and T to have the same absolute marginal effect. But according to the Ricardian equivalence proposition, this cannot be the case. Nor is it the case for the conventional view. Thus, it is necessary to use equation (3), in which the effects of an increase in the deficit—holding G constant—is the coefficient b_1. Such an experiment is equivalent to a reduction in taxes. On the other hand, the coefficient, b_2, measures the effect of an increase in government spending, holding the deficit constant, which is equivalent to a tax-financed increase in spending. Finally, the sum of the coefficients, b_1 and b_2, measures the interest rate effect of a debt-financed increase in spending. A similar set of interpretations would apply if T were substituted for G in the last term of equation (3).

Endogeneity Issues

From a statistical viewpoint, problems can arise because both the federal deficit and the interest rate are affected by fluctuations in output. Failure to take this into account can result in biased estimates of the interest rate effect of the federal deficit.

There are alternative ways to deal with this problem. One approach is to use a deficit measure that is purged of cyclical movements, such as the cyclically adjusted deficit. Alternatively, one could use the unadjusted deficit, but with a cyclical variable such as the capacity utilization index or the unemployment rate also included in the regression. (This latter approach removes the same cyclical effects from both the dependent and independent variables.) Both of these approaches, however, involve some arbitrariness with regard to the cyclical adjustment. Moreover, they do not control for the effect of interest rates on the federal deficit. Thus, the use of two-stage least squares may be preferable.[19]

Choosing An Interest Rate

Frequently, a specific view does not dictate the actual choice of the dependent variable. Of course, many alternatives are possible. The interest rate variable can be a short-term, medium-term, or long-term rate or yield on either government or private securities. Moreover, it can be measured either in nominal or real terms, on an expected or realized basis, and can be expressed in before-tax or after-tax terms.

The choice of an interest rate can have a bearing on the choice of explanatory variables. When a long-term rate is used, some model of the term structure often is taken into account by including a short-term rate as an explanatory variable. According to the expectations hypothesis, the long-term rate reflects a weighted average of current and expected future short-term rates. However, empirical tests of this hypothesis have not found much statistical support for it. Indeed, some analysts argue that the best model of long-term interest rates may be a random walk (Pesando 1979).

Other Considerations

An issue that has not received much attention in the debates about the interest rate effects of federal deficits is the power of the statistical tests used for hypothesis testing. If the null hypothesis is that deficits do not affect interest rates, the probability of rejecting this hypothesis when it is true can be set equal to 10 percent, 5 percent, or even lower. However, this does not necessarily produce a very powerful test, because the probability of rejecting the null hypothesis when it is false (that is, when the alternative hypothesis that deficits do affect interest rates is true) may be substantially less then one. Standard statistical tests, such as the t-statistic on a coefficient, may lead to erroneous conclusions if these tests have a low probability of rejecting the null hypothesis when it is false. This is an especially important issue for testing the interest rate effects of deficits or debt, since many of the studies in this area accept the null hypothesis that deficits do not affect interest rates.[20]

A REVIEW OF THE EMPIRICAL EVIDENCE

Not surprisingly, since the emergence of large federal deficits in the 1980s there have been many empirical studies of the economic effects of deficits. Do federal deficits raise interest rates, crowd out investment, and reduce saving? To date, economists seem to be no closer to agreement than was the case six years ago when these basic questions were explored by Barth, Iden, and Russek (1984). There was not then and there is not now a clear consensus on whether there is a statistically and economically significant relationship between government deficits and interest rates, or between deficits and the household saving-consumption decision. Since the available evidence on the effects of deficits is mixed, one cannot say with complete confidence that budget deficits raise interest rates and reduce saving and capital formation. But, equally important, one cannot say that they do not have these effects. The cost of being wrong—believing that there are no costs to deficits when there are—involves a serious risk for future generations (see Penner 1989).

The monetization of deficits is one potentially serious conse-
quence of government deficits that does not currently appear to be
a threat in the United States, although it has occurred in other countries. The evidence relating to whether U.S. deficits in the past have
led to faster money growth and, thus inflation, appears to be somewhat mixed. Recent work suggests that perhaps such a relationship
did exist during some periods, but not others (Miller and Velz 1989).
In any event, regardless of what happened in the past, the Federal
Reserve in the 1980s appears to have strongly resisted any pressures
to monetize federal deficits.

Deficits and Interest Rates

Policymakers would have less reason to be interested in the debate
over whether there is a statistical relationship between deficits and
interest rates if all or most of the studies found that deficits have a
small effect on interest rates. But that is not the case. Some studies,
such as those by de Leeuw and Holloway (1985) and Feldstein (1986),
have found relatively large positive effects, suggesting that an increase in the deficit-to-GNP ratio by one percentage point might raise
interest rates as much as 0.4 to 1.2 percentage points. These studies
indicate that eliminating the deficit could substantially lower interest rates, particularly if expected future deficits are similarly affected.

The main reason that so much attention has focused on the deficit-
interest rate linkage is that most economists believe deficits affect
such variables as investment and economic growth through interest
rates. And Feldstein (1988) has argued that legislation achieving
budget balance over a 5-year period might reduce interest rates as
much as 2 percentage points.

There are a number of important reasons why there is a lack of
consensus on the issue of whether federal deficits significantly affect
interest rates. First, there is relatively little experience with enormously large deficits in the United States. As pointed out earlier,
the large federal deficits of the 1980s are unprecedented in U.S.
peacetime history. Second, there are legitimate differences in opin-
ion among economists about which measure of the federal deficit is
appropriate for analyzing effects, including whether any chosen measure should be adjusted for inflation or changes in the scale of the
economy. Third, there is disagreement concerning the model that
best describes the macroeconomy and the determination of interest
rates. Fourth, the estimating problems encountered when attempting
to resolve the issue empirically are inherently very difficult because

of a number of interactive effects. For instance, deficits are partly endogenous because interest rates affect deficits due to payment of debt service. Furthermore, during some periods monetary policy has sought to stabilize short-term interest rates. As a result of all these factors, existing studies employ a large array of methods and measures, including model of interest rate determination, period of estimation, and statistical estimating technique.

If we cannot settle the issue once and for all, we can at least offer a progress report on the empirical studies and note some interesting patterns that are beginning to emerge.

First, more studies have found a relationship between federal deficits and long-term interest rates, than between federal deficits and short-term interest rates. Second, the choice of which measure of the deficit to use can have important bearing on whether one finds a statistically significant relationship between the deficit and interest rates. In particular, studies that use cyclically adjusted or structural measures of the deficit are more likely to detect a statistical relationship with interest rates. But the use of such adjusted measures of the deficit by no means assures that one will find a statistically significant relationship with either short-term or long-term interest rates. In addition, some studies find more of a positive and statistically significant relationship between federal debt and interest rates than between federal deficits and interest rates.

Third, the time unit of observation or frequency of the data seems to affect the results. Lower frequency data such as annual or moving-averages of annual data are more likely to produce a relationship between deficits and interest rates than higher frequency data, such as quarterly or monthly data.

Fourth, with respect to long-term interest rates, expected or future federal deficits seem to play a greater role than contemporaneous deficits. However, measuring expected deficits is a major problem, and measuring multi-year averages of deficits, as several studies have done, raises questions of interpretation.

Fifth, since a number of factors besides deficits affect interest rates, the findings of studies seem to be sensitive to whether and how they control for these other factors. Among the other factors that could affect interest rates are inflationary expectations, changes in the monetary base (monetary policy) and, in the case of short-term interest rates, a measure of the business cycle.

Finally, while there is substantial controversy over the effects of a change in the tax-borrowing mix of the federal government, there is much less controversy about the effects of government purchases.

The alternative views and the empirical results support the conclusion that an increase in government purchases tends to raise interest rates, especially if the increase in purchases is temporary (Barro 1981b).

Studies that have not found a statistical relationship between federal deficits and interest rates have certain characteristics in common, such as use of high frequency (i.e., monthly or quarterly) data and deficit measures that are not adjusted for cyclical fluctuations. In addition, studies that eschew structural models in favor of a rational expectations approach or vector autoregression (VAR) models usually find no statistical relationship between federal deficits and interest rates.

While the reasons for these patterns in the empirical results are unclear, there are some plausible explanations. First, with respect to the disparity between short-term and long-term interest rates, a number of explanations come to mind. For one thing, during much of the period studied the Federal Reserve followed a policy of stabilizing short-term interest rates, which may have obscured any relationship between federal deficits and short-term rates. Also, the problems in separating out the effects of the business cycle are more severe for short-term interest rates, especially since most studies tend to find a cyclical pattern for short-term interest rates but not for long-term interest rates. Finally, international capital flows may even out inter-country differences more quickly for short-term interest rates than for long-term interest rates.

In general, earlier empirical work on deficits and interest rates shows a lack of robustness. This conclusion applies to both the studies that find a statistical relationship and those that find none. Small changes in model specification, in the way variables are measured, or in the period used for statistical testing can have major implications for the conclusions. Thus, one has to be especially cautious since a simple change such as adding or subtracting a few years of data can undo or seriously weaken any conclusions.[21]

In the remainder of this section, we will discuss selected studies of federal deficits and interest rates. A number of such studies are summarized in table 2.4.

The Conventional View: The Feldstein/Eckstein Approach

The study by Feldstein and Eckstein (1970) was particularly important because it established the framework for a number of studies to follow, and it became the main focus of debate in policy analysis circles in the mid-1980s. This study was based on a conventional

Table 2.4 FEDERAL DEFICITS AND INTEREST RATES: SOME EMPIRICAL FINDINGS

Author (Year of Study)	Interest Rate Variable		Fiscal Variable			Time Period/ Data Frequency	Statistical Technique	Sign/Significance Deficit Variable
	Short-term	Long-term	Federal Deficit	Federal Debt	Other			
I. Studies that found predominantly significant, positive effects:								
Barth and Bradley (1985)		X (Real)			X	1948–76 Annual	OLS	Pos., Yes
Barth, Iden and Russek (1985)	X		(Unanticipated deficit)		X	1955–84 Quarterly	OLS	Pos., Yes
Bovenberg (1988)		X	(Structural deficit)		X	1961–85 A & SA	OLS	Pos., Yes
Carlson (1983)		X		X		1953–83 Quarterly	OLS	Pos., Yes
Cebula (1987)		X	(Structural deficit)		X	1955–79 Quarterly	OLS	Pos., Yes
Cebula (1988)		X	(Structural deficit)		X	1955–84 Quarterly	IV	Pos., Yes
de Leeuw and Holloway (1985)		X (3 yrs.)	(Structural debt)		X	1956–83 Annual	OLS	Pos., Yes
Feldstein and Eckstein (1970)		X		X		1954–69 Quarterly	OLS	Pos., Yes

Study				Period	Method	Results
Feldstein (1986)		X (Expected deficit)	X	1960–84 Annual	OLS & NLS	Pos., Yes
Hoelscher (1986)	X (Differential)	X	X	1953–82 Annual	OLS	Pos., Yes
Hutchison and Pyle (1984)	X (Real)	X		1973–82 Annual	OLS[a]	Pos., Yes
Kudlow (1981)	X	X (Total credit)		1958–80 Annual	OLS	Pos., Yes
Makin and Tanzi (1984)	X (12 mo.)	X (Unanticipated deficit)	X	1960–81 Quarterly	IV	Pos., Yes
Muller and Price (1984)	X	X X (9-Quarter averages)	X[b]	1958–83 Quarterly	OLS	Pos., Yes
Thomas and Abderrezak (1988a)	X (Differential)	X (Expected deficit)	X	1965–86 Quarterly	OLS	Pos., Yes
Thomas and Abderrezak (1988b)	X	X (Expected real deficit)	X	1970–86 Quarterly	OLS	Pos., Yes
Wachtel and Young (1987)	X	X (Deficit announcement)	X	1982–86 Daily	OLS	Pos., Yes

II. Studies that obtained mixed results, some significant but others not:

Study				Period	Method	Results
Dewald (1983)	X (Real)	X (Real deficit)	X	1953–81 Quarterly	OLS	Pos., Yes, Long Neg., No, Short

continued

Table 2.4 FEDERAL DEFICITS AND INTEREST RATES: SOME EMPIRICAL FINDINGS (Continued)

Author (Year of Study)	Interest Rate Variable		Fiscal Variable			Time Period/ Data Frequency	Statistical Technique	Sign/Significance Deficit Variable
	Short-term	Long-term	Federal Deficit	Federal Debt	Other			
Echols and Elliott (1976)	X	X	X			1964–72 Monthly	OLS	Pos., Yes[c] Mixed, No[c]
Kim and Lombra (1989)	X	X	(Unanticipated deficit)		X	1959–85 Quarterly	OLS	Pos., Yes, '59–'80 Mixed, No, '59–'85
Sinai and Rathjens (1983)	X	X	X (Expected deficit)	X	X	1960–82 Quarterly	OLS	Pos., Mixed[d]
Tanzi (1985)	X (12 mo.)		X (Structural deficit)	X	X	1960–84 Annual	OLS	Pos., Yes, Deb Neg., Yes, St. Def.
Zahid (1988)	X (Real, ch.)		X		X (Structural deficit)	1971–82	OLS Quarterly	Mixed, Mixed[e]
III. Studies that found predominantly insignificant or negative effects:								
Bradley (1983)	X	X	(Unanticipated deficit)		X	1966–82 Monthly	IV	Pos., No
Canto and Rapp (1982)	X		X			1929–80 Annual	GS	Zero
Evans (1985)	X	X	X			1979–83[f] Monthly	OLS/IV	Neg., Yes Neg., Yes

Study					Period / Frequency	Method	Result
Evans (1987a)	X	X	X (Expected deficit)	X	1908–84 M & A	OLS/IV	Neg., Mixed
Evans (1987b)	X	X	X	X	1976–85 Quarterly	OLS/IV	Neg., Mixed
Evans (1989)	X		(Real Gross debt)	X	1948–86 Monthly	CI	Neg., No
Feldstein & Chamberlain (1973)	X		X		1954–71 Quarterly	OLS	Neg., No
Frankel (1983)	X		X		1954–80 Annual	TGME	Pos., No
Giannaros and Kolluri (1985)	X	X	X		1966–83 Quarterly	OLS	Pos., No, Long Neg., No, 3 yr
Hoelscher (1983)	X		X (Flow of Funds)	X	1952–76 Quarterly	OLS/IV	Pos., No
Kolluri and Giannaros (1987)	X		X		1977–83 Quarterly	OLS	Neg., mixed
Makin (1983)	X		X	X	1959–81 Quarterly	OLS	Pos., No
Mascaro and Meltzer (1983)	X		X	X	1969–81 Quarterly	OLS	Mixed, No
Motley (1983)	X (Real)		X (Federal borrowing)	X	1958–82 Monthly	OLS	Mixed, No
Plosser (1982)	X		X		1954–78 Quarterly	VAR	Mixed, No

continued

Table 2.4 FEDERAL DEFICITS AND INTEREST RATES: SOME EMPIRICAL FINDINGS (Continued)

Author (Year of Study)	Interest Rate Variable		Fiscal Variable			Time Period/ Data Frequency	Statistical Technique	Sign/Significance Deficit Variable
	Short-term	Long-term	Federal Deficit	Federal Debt	Other			
Plosser (1987)	X	X		X		1967–85 M & Q	VAR	Mixed, No
Swamy, et al. (1988)	X		X (Discretionary)		X	1960–83 Quarterly	VCE[g]	Mixed, No
Tatom (1984)	X	X	X (High-employment deficit)		X	1955–83 Quarterly	OLS	Neg., No
U.S. Treasury (1984)		X	X	X		1965–83 Quarterly	WML	Neg., No

a. Pooled data for 7 major industrial countries.
b. Nine-quarter moving average of the debt scaled relative to private wealth and of deficits scaled relative to total private saving.
c. Positive and significant for maturities of 7 years and under; mixed signs and not significant for maturities 9 years and over.
d. Expected deficits affected the long-term rate, while concurrent deficit affected the short-term rate.
e. In general, the coefficient on the cyclically adjusted deficit measure was positive and statistically significant. The deficit measure was based on flow of funds data.
f. Plus three major war periods.
g. Also used various estimators, including generalized least squares, ridge regression, and Almon polynomial estimates.

KEY

OLS:	ordinary least squares	GS:	Granger-Sims
NLS:	nonlinear least squares	TGME:	Theil-Goldberger mixed estimation
IV:	instrumental variables	VCE:	variable coefficient estimation
M:	monthly	CI:	cointegration
Q:	quarterly	WML:	weighted maximum likelihood estimation
A:	annual	Pos:	positive
SA:	semi-annual	Neg:	negative
VAR:	vector autoregression		

model of income determination and portfolio analysis of the bond market. The interest rate on ten-year government bonds was a function of the log of real per capita government debt, nongovernment GNP, and the monetary base, as well as expected inflation and the lagged change in the dependent variable as a proxy for uncertainty. It was found that the government debt variable had a statistically significant, though small, effect on the interest rate.

The Feldstein/Eckstein paper served as a prototype for several subsequent studies in the 1980s. For instance, Carlson (1983) used a similar model, and reported a statistically significant, though small, effect of the federal debt on interest rates. In replicating the Carlson study, Barth, Iden, and Russek (1984) reported that the coefficient seemed especially sensitive to adding or subtracting a few years of data.

Several other studies emphasized the potential importance of the non-cyclical or structural deficit and debt. A major problem that plagues studies of deficits and interest rates is the fact that both federal deficits and interest rates tend to be affected by the business cycle, but in opposite directions. The business cycle and the federal deficit are inversely related for reasons that are well-known. At the same time, short-term interest rates tend to vary pro-cyclically, rising during booms and falling during slack periods. Thus, there is the potential of spurious correlation between fiscal deficits and short-term interest rates.

De Leeuw and Holloway (1985) developed a portfolio model and reduced-form equation that in several respects resembled the Feldstein/Eckstein equation. In the portfolio model, the interest rate on three-year government securities is a function of federal debt, high-powered money, and inflationary expectations. But instead of using the real federal debt, they used a cyclically adjusted measure of federal debt.

De Leeuw and Holloway found the coefficient on the structural debt variable to be positive and statistically significant, while the change in the structural debt variable was not statistically significant. Moreover, unlike the results of Eckstein and Feldstein, the de Leeuw and Holloway results suggested that changes in federal structural debt relative to trend GNP have a substantial effect on interest rates— a one-percentage point increase in this ratio was associated with an interest rate increase of about 0.4 percentage points. Since the structural debt had already risen almost 3 percentage points as a share of trend GNP from 1980 to 1983, deficits accounted for a roughly one percentage point increase in real interest rates during that period.[22]

Barth, Iden and Russek (1984) found that the de Leeuw/Holloway results were generally robust. For instance, when government spending was added to the regression equation, its coefficient was positive and statistically significant, but the coefficients on structural debt were essentially unaffected.

Tanzi (1987, 1985a) obtained mixed results with respect to the effect of federal deficits and federal debt on one-year Treasury bills. In his regression equation, the interest rate was a function of inflationary expectations (measured by the Livingston Index), the gap between actual and potential GNP, and various deficit and debt measures. When the ratio of federal debt to GNP was used, its coefficient was positive and statistically significant. However, when the structural deficit was used, it had a statistically significant but negative sign.[23]

DISSENTERS: DEFICITS DO NOT RAISE INTEREST RATES

The Feldstein/Eckstein finding is not robust. There should have been some inkling of this when in a later paper Feldstein and Chamberlain (1973) did not find federal debt to be a significant determinant of the interest rate. In addition, researchers at the U.S. Treasury Department (1984) attempted to replicate the results of the original study, but they did not find a positive and statistically significant coefficient on the debt variable. One possible reason, which is mentioned in the Treasury study, is data revisions that occurred since the original study. The Treasury study modified the basic equation in several respects, including the way inflationary expectations were modeled. Several measures of federal debt were tested, but the coefficients were not statistically significant. However, a result not noted in the Treasury study was that an alternative fiscal variable—the NIPA deficit—did have a positive and statistically significant effect on interest rates.

In a study of short-term interest rates, Hoelscher (1983) reported no statistically significant coefficient for federal deficits. In his model, other explanatory variables included inflationary expectations, the monetary base, and the unemployment rate to account for the business cycle. However, Barth, Iden, and Russek (1985, 1984) found that Hoelscher's results were sensitive to whether the deficit measure was adjusted for the business cycle. More specifically, when the structural deficit was substituted for the unadjusted deficit measure, the coefficient was positive and statistically significant.

A study by Tatom (1984), however, illustrated that the mere use of a cyclically adjusted federal deficit measure did not insure that one would find that structural deficits raise interest rates. His results, which included both short-term and long-term interest rates, indicated a negative coefficient on both the actual deficit and the high-employment deficit. These results could be criticized for not taking into account any of the other factors that are believed to influence interest rates, such as inflationary expectations, money growth, and—in the case of short-term interest rates—the unemployment rate.

An early study by Dewald (1983) helped to establish the view that, while deficits may not have been the major explanation for the rise in real interest rates in the 1980s, there seemed to be more evidence for a relationship between deficits and long-term interest rates than between deficits and short-term rates. Dewald analyzed the determinants of real interest rates, and adjusted the federal deficit for the effects of inflation on the real value of the public debt. In addition, he attempted to deal with the business cycle problems by averaging his data over the cycle. The overall conclusion reached by Dewald was that the evidence for a relationship between deficits and interest rates was not strong, and that deficits did not seem to account for much of the rise in real interest rates during the early 1980s. However, his results also suggested that there was more evidence for an effect in the case of long-term interest rates.

Besides the Treasury Department, there were other dissenters from the conventional view that federal deficits affect interest rates, such as Evans (1987a, 1987b, and 1985). In the early study, Evans examined several wartime periods and concluded that there was no evidence that federal deficits were associated with high interest rates. Since conditions are highly unusual during major wars, the most relevant part of his study dealt with the period from October 1979 to December 1983. In particular, Evans analyzed both short- and long-term interest rates, using monthly data and a two-stage least squares estimation technique to take account of the endogeneity between deficits and the business cycle. In addition to federal deficits, explanatory variables included the ratio of "money to GNP" and government spending, since a temporary rise in government spending might well cause an increase in interest rates as long as government spending and private spending are not perfect substitutes. However, Evans did not include an inflationary expectations variable. In any case, the coefficients on the federal deficit variable were *negative* and statistically significant, while the coefficients on government spending were generally positive and statistically significant.

In a more recent paper, which is discussed in greater detail in the following section, Evans (1987a) again analyzed the role of deficits in explaining interest rates. His model was formulated in terms of the change in interest rates being dependent upon changes in deficits, government spending, and the money supply. Monthly and yearly data were used to estimate his model over the period 1908 to 1984, and various sub-periods. For monthly data, the deficit coefficient sums were positive in 11 of 24 cases, but in none of these cases were they statistically significant. On the other hand, in 13 cases the deficit coefficients were negative, and of these, 9 were statistically significant at the 5-percent level. To answer those who have contended that high frequency data have been responsible for finding no relationship, Evans then reestimated his model with annual data. If anything, the results seemed even less favorable for the view that deficits positively affect interest rates.

OTHER APPROACHES

Several other approaches have been used in analyzing the deficit/ interest rate issue, including (a) models of the term structure of interest rates, (b) expected deficits, (c) unanticipated deficits, and (d) variable coefficient models. Studies using these approaches will be discussed in turn.

Term-Structure Models. In a more recent paper, Hoelscher (1986) analyzed the effects of fiscal deficits on the term structure of interest rates and concluded that deficits do have a positive and statistically significant effect on the spread between long- and short-term rates. The long-term interest rate was modeled as a function of the real short-term interest rate, inflationary expectations, and alternative measures of the deficit. His deficit measures, which were all expressed in real per capita terms, included the NIPA federal deficit, the NIPA deficit including the state and local government sector, and a third measure based on the real par value of publicly held federal debt. Hoelscher consistently found the coefficients on the fiscal deficit to be positive and statistically significant—indicating that increases in deficits affect yield spreads. This conclusion was not sensitive to various alternative measures of the deficit. The Hoelscher study will be analyzed further below.

Plosser (1987, 1982) also used a term structure model to test whether fiscal variables affect interest rates. A VAR technique was used to test whether surprises in fiscal policy were associated with deviations from expected holding period returns on financial assets. He concluded that the substitution of debt financing for tax financing had no effect on holding-period yields. Evidence pertaining to the effect of government spending, however, left more room for doubt.

In his earlier paper, government spending did tend to affect holding-period returns; but his later work, which included more data for the 1980s, did not confirm the earlier finding.

Expected Deficits. Several recent papers have investigated whether expected deficits affect long-term interest rates. Financial markets are clearly dominated by forward-looking economic agents. However, the main limitation to studying the effects of expected future deficits is that there are no data to measure exactly what the market expects federal deficits to be in the future. In several studies, such as Muller and Price (1984), Feldstein (1986), Bovenberg (1988), and Thomas and Abderrezak (1988a, 1988b), an attempt has been made to deal with this problem by using actual deficits as proxies for expected deficits and by using DRI deficit projections, CBO's projections, and Gramm-Rudman-Hollings deficit targets as proxies for expected deficits. Such studies report sizable and statistically significant coefficients on the deficit variable. However, since the deficit variable in some of the studies is a moving average of annual deficit data, it is difficult to determine if it is the expectations feature or the moving average feature that is critical to the results. Furthermore, the moving average of actual deficits could be capturing a reverse causation in that a change in interest rates could be affecting the cost of servicing the debt and therefore the deficit.

In a recent study by Feldstein (1986), the interest rate on five-year government bonds is dependent upon the five-year projection of federal deficits, the federal debt (relative to GNP), inflationary expectations, high-powered money, and a variable designed to capture the effects of the tax system on the net interest received by debt holders. For the deficit projection variable, Feldstein used the actual deficit for the years it was available, and then projections by DRI for the years 1985 and beyond. The deficit variable was then adjusted for cyclical fluctuations. He found the coefficient on the deficit variable to be positive and statistically significant. His results indicate that an increase in the projected ratio of the deficit to GNP by one percentage point raises the long-term government bond rate by more than 1 percentage point.

Feldstein also reported some alternative specifications for the deficit variable. When the current value of the structural deficit was employed, its coefficient was small and not statistically significant. In another specification, the use of the actual deficit, unadjusted for the cycle, performed about the same as the cyclically adjusted deficit.[24]

By contrast, Evans (1987a, 1987b), employing a different methodology, also examined the effects of expected federal deficits, but concluded that they do not raise interest rates. In one approach, for example, Evans examined the residuals of interest rate regression equations around the time that policymakers were changing fiscal policy. In another, he used current and past deficits to model expected deficits. In each case, his conclusion was the same: there was no evidence that bigger deficits, expected or otherwise, increase interest rates.

Thomas and Abderrezak (1988a) investigate the determinants of the difference in yield on 20-year U.S. government bonds and 6-month Treasury bills, with emphasis on the role of expected future deficits. They utilize four different measures of the federal deficit, each cyclically adjusted. For each deficit measure they construct "foresight" and "naive" formulations of expected future deficits. The method used to construct their foresight deficit measure is similar to Bovenberg's (1988), although only four quarters of future deficits are used. The naive formulation assumes that expectations are formed on the basis of recent trends. They found that expected deficits, formulated in either manner, exerted a significant and positive influence on yield differentials in the period from 1965-1986.

Unanticipated Deficits. Several studies, such as Barth and Bradley (1989), Makin and Tanzi (1984), and Wachtel and Young (1987), have formulated models based on the notion that only unexpected deficits affect interest rates. Following the lead of Robert Barro, Barth and Bradley found that anticipated bond growth did not significantly raise long-term interest rates, although unanticipated bond growth did have a positive and statistically significant effect. In the Makin and Tanzi analysis, the unanticipated deficit variable (measured as residuals from a univariate time-series model of the government deficit) has a positive and statistically significant relationship on short-term interest rates, although the actual deficit does not.

Wachtel and Young tested whether revisions in the budget projections by the CBO and OMB affect interest rates. They found evidence that "The deficit announcements have a uniform positive effect on interest rates. . . Although the OMB announcements precede the CBO announcements, the coefficients are larger for the CBO announcements. In both cases, the announcement effects are about the same size all along the yield curve and are generally more significant for longer maturities" (Wachtel and Young, 1987, 1010). These effects were quite small—about 3 basis points per $10 billion of announced change in the deficit projection by CBO. However, the authors believed that their results understated the actual effect of new information about deficits because their measures included only revisions in the official deficit projections by CBO and OMB. Much information and speculation in the press and elsewhere typically precede these official projections.

In a very recent study, Kim and Lombra (1989) developed a model of asset price determination, incorporating rational expectations to examine how the effects of deficits on interest rates depend on expectations. Specifically, they examined whether the long-term government bond rate is affected by unexpected values of variables relevant to the pricing of bonds. They generated measures of the expected values by employing a two-step procedure similar to that utilized by Barro (1977). Using quarterly data for the sample period 1959:Q1-1980:Q1, their results provide support for the hypothesis that unanticipated changes in government debt do affect long-term interest rates. However, when they extend the sample period to 1959:Q1-1985:Q4 (a period in which deficits grew very fast), the effect of unanticipated changes in government debt disappears. Their explanation for these differing results is that the stochastic process underlying the evolution of the debt shifted dramatically during the 1980s as taxes were cut and other budgetary changes occurred. They also attribute the difference to the fact that the large deficits of the 1980s were expected by market participants.

Variable Coefficient Models. In a recent study of deficits and short-term interest rates, Swamy et al. (1988) analyzed several interesting variations with respect to measures of the deficit and statistical estimation technique. Using the same basic equation and the same sample period in each experiment, they found that the NIPA deficit seemed to possess more explanatory power than the unified deficit, and that the method of statistical estimation made a difference in terms of the contribution of the deficit variables. However, the deficit variable was usually negative and not statistically significant. Swamy et al. also estimated a stochastic coefficients model, one in which coefficient estimates are allowed to change over time. They found that the estimated coefficient on the deficit varied considerably over time and sometimes changed signs, although it was usually negative.

Deficits, Saving, and Output Composition

Several studies have used regression analysis to investigate whether an increase in the federal deficit relative to GNP was associated with changes in the composition of output and spending (Summers 1986; Eisner 1986; and Boskin 1988). Summers, using ordinary least squares and data for the 1949–1982 period, regressed the net investment share of GNP on a cyclical variable and the federal deficit as a share of GNP—both the nominal and the inflation-adjusted deficits. The coefficient on the federal deficit share was negative and statistically significant, approximately −0.6 for the nominal deficit and −0.4 for the inflation-adjusted deficit. Thus, an increase of one percentage point in the deficit share was associated with a decline in the investment share of 0.4 to 0.6 percentage points. These results also indicate that deficits crowded out net nonresidential investment and net foreign investment. With respect to saving, his analysis indicates that, in response to an increase in the federal deficit share, the net private saving rate and net saving rate by state and local governments both increased, thereby offsetting in part the effect of the rise in the federal deficit on national saving.[25]

In addition, de Leeuw and Holloway (1985) and Makin (1985) investigated the relationship between the federal debt and the capital stock. Consistent with their findings regarding the cyclically adjusted debt and interest rates, de Leeuw and Holloway find evidence of a strong negative relationship between debt and the capital stock.[26] Makin's empirical results also indicate that increases in the ratio of federal debt-to-GNP substantially reduce investment.

In more recent work, Miller and Russek (1989) used data for OECD countries to examine the relationships between government deficits and trade, saving, and investment. They first estimated contemporaneous and distributed lag equations relating the current account surplus, net domestic investment, and net private saving to the general government surplus, using ordinary least squares. The regressions were then reestimated with the data in first difference form, as a check for spurious results. Finally, they examined the data for evidence of non-stationarity, and applied cointegration techniques as a means to test for long-run equilibrium relationships. Although in general their evidence was somewhat mixed, they found in the case of the United States statistically significant and positive relationships between the government surplus and net investment, and between the government surplus and the trade surplus. In addition, their results suggest that changes in the government surplus are not completely offset by changes in private saving.

LARGE-SCALE MODEL SIMULATIONS

Simulations with large-scale macroeconomic models provide another perspective on the question of how deficits may affect the composition of output. Recent work by the CBO (1988) suggests that a decrease in the federal deficit would shift the composition of output toward investment and net exports and away from consumer spending. In this project, undertaken at the request of the National Economic Commission (NEC), three macroeconomic models were used to analyze four different packages of deficit reductions, each package consisting of a multi-year program of reductions totaling $120 billion to $130 billion per year by 1994, or about 2 percent of GNP. (The deficit-reduction packages, which were specified by the NEC staff, emphasized different outlay-reduction and tax-increase approaches.) In one set of simulations, monetary policy was used to offset the declines in output that would otherwise have occurred according to the model results. For two of the models—the Data Resources, Inc. Macro Model and the Washington University Macro Model—the rise in real investment and net exports together averages 7 percent compared with the baseline, after 5 years. The increases in investment came mainly in the residential sector, although there were small increases in business-fixed investment as well. The results for a third model, the Fair Macro Model, suggested similar though smaller effects.

FURTHER EVIDENCE ON BUDGET DEFICITS AND SAVING: TESTING THE RICARDIAN EQUIVALENCE PROPOSITION

Like the empirical evidence on federal deficits and interest rates, the evidence on whether federal deficits affect saving is still inconclusive. Indeed, the number of studies that have found a positive relationship between deficits and personal consumption is roughly matched by the number reporting no relationship. The two controversies tend to be related since one of the principal reasons an increase in the deficit will affect interest rates is because it stimulates consumption and aggregate demand. Those studies not finding a statistical link between deficits and interest rates have frequently cited the Ricardian equivalence proposition as an explanation. However, as Bernheim points out in his recent review (1987), the two issues are not necessarily the same. For instance, if the international capital markets worked perfectly, federal deficits might not have any discernable effect on interest rates, even if the Ricardian equivalence proposition were false.

Our assessment of the empirical evidence in this area is quite similar to our assessment of the evidence on deficits and interest rates. In general, the results of studies in this area are not robust. Conclusions can frequently be overturned or at least substantially weakened by seemingly mild changes in variable definitions or period of estimation. Since literature relating to this issue has been thoroughly reviewed by Bernheim (1987) and Leiderman and Blejer (1988), we will comment only briefly on this area.

It appears that the two sides to the controversy of whether deficits affect overall saving may be coming closer together, at least theoretically. Very few economists subscribe any longer to the rigid conventional view that consumption is primarily a function of current income. At the same time, proponents of the Ricardian equivalence proposition acknowledge that tax discounting may be less than complete. The assumptions that underlie the Ricardian equivalence proposition seem unrealistic to many economists, but that charge is hardly decisive. In any event, the two modern competing theories—the life-cycle hypothesis and the Ricardian equivalence proposition—are not as far apart as the older polar theories. However, one implication is that it may be extremely difficult to formulate tests that are powerful enough to adequately test the competing theories. Bernheim (1987) concludes that it may well be impossible to resolve the issue through the analysis of macroeconomic time series data because of statistical problems associated with such data, and the complexity of the theories that emphasize expectations far into the future.

The results of studies that have examined the effect of government deficits on the household consumption-saving decision are about evenly divided. An early study by Kochin (1974) concluded that government deficits lowered consumption—thus confirming the Ricardian equivalence proposition. However, the coefficient on the deficit variable was substantially smaller than the coefficient on disposable income, suggesting that a cut in taxes would have at least some stimulative effect. Tanner (1979) tested whether government bonds, in addition to the government surplus, had an effect on consumption. He found a positive and significant coefficient for the government surplus variable, and an insignificant coefficient for government bonds. However, research by Yawitz and Meyer (1976), Buiter and Tobin (1979), and Feldstein (1982) took issue with these studies and presented evidence contrary to the Ricardian equivalence proposition. More recent contributions to this debate include studies by Kormendi (1983), Aschauer (1985) and Seater and Mariano (1985), which generally support Ricardian equivalence, and studies by Reid (1985) and Blinder and Deaton (1985), which generally support the conventional or life-cycle model.

Kormendi's (1983) study is an example of the recent literature supporting the Ricardian equivalence proposition, although his results do not appear to be robust. In Kormendi's model, consumption is a function of national income, wealth excluding government bonds, taxes, government transfers, government spending, and government bonds. Using data from the period 1931 to 1976, Kormendi used ordinary least squares to estimate his model. In general, the results were supportive of the Ricardian equivalence proposition. The coefficient on government bonds was *negative* and statistically significant, contrary to the conventional view. In addition, the coefficient on personal taxes was insignificant. However, subsequent work by Barth, Iden and Russek (1986) found that Kormendi's results were sensitive to the period used for estimation and to seemingly minor changes in the definitions of several of the variables. In particular, when more recent data was substituted for data for the World War II and pre-World War II period, the coefficient on government debt became positive, although still not statistically significant. Seemingly minor changes in the definition of some of the variables, for example, use of par versus market value of the government debt, and including state and local government with the federal government, reversed the major conclusions. Kormendi and Meguire (1986) present additional results of interest in their reply.

Deficits and Aggregate Demand

We will briefly mention the results of three recent studies that bear on this issue. First, Eisner (1986) found a positive and statistically significant relationship between his measure of the federal deficit, adjusted for inflation and the level of employment, and real GNP. In his model, the only other determinant of real GNP growth that was included was the monetary base. This paper will be discussed in more detail in the next section. Second, de Leeuw and Holloway (1985) also found evidence of a positive and statistically significant relationship between their measure of the structural debt, scaled by trend GNP, and the level of GNP. Last, Cohen (1989) tested whether the change in the high-employment surplus and his model-based measure of changes in fiscal policy, respectively, were related to changes in real GNP. He found that with quarterly data the sum of the fiscal policy coefficients was always significant and positive. With annual data, the results were more ambiguous for a high employment measure of the deficit.

DETAILED ANALYSIS OF SELECTED EMPIRICAL STUDIES

Several years ago, Barth, Iden, and Russek (1984, 1985) examined the robustness of various empirical studies that tested whether federal deficits affect interest rates (and other economic variables). Their conclusion was that the results in most of the studies examined were sensitive to changes in the sample period, the definition of the deficit measure, or the statistical technique employed.

This section undertakes a similar task, based on a selection of recent studies of whether government deficits affect interest rates and whether deficits alter the composition of output. As it turns out, the task is more difficult than it was several years ago. With the passage of time, researchers have become more aware of the potential for a lack of robustness in their results, and seem to have designed their studies accordingly. Thus, we find that more recent studies are more robust. Nevertheless, the results are sensitive to some changes, and there are differences among conclusions that deserve examination and discussion.

Interest Rate Studies

The first interest rate study we consider is by Hoelscher (1986). He estimates the effect of government deficits on the nominal 10-year government bond rate for the 1953-1984 period. The specific equation estimated by Hoelscher has the form:

$$RL = a_0 + a_1 P^e + a_2(RS - Pe) + a_3 \Delta Y + a_4 D + e, \qquad (4)$$

where RL is the interest rate on 10-year government bonds, P^e is expected inflation as measured by the June estimate of 12-month-ahead inflation reported in the Livingston survey, RS is the 1-year Treasury bond rate, ΔY is the change in real GNP, and D is the federal deficit measured in various ways: on the NIPA basis, change in the par value of government debt, cyclically adjusted NIPA basis, and NIPA basis including the state and local sector.[27] Most of the regressions are reported with a correction for first-order serial correlation, although Hoelscher also reports some results for first-differenced data.

As shown in the first regression reported in table 2.5, Hoelscher finds that the deficit has a positive and significant effect on the long-term interest rate: an increase in the deficit-GNP ratio of one percentage point raises the long-term interest rate by 41 basis points. Our effort to duplicate his results is reported as the second regression in table 2.5, and is quite close to the regression reported by Hoelscher, despite subsequent revisions in the NIPA data.

Our first change was to extend the sample period through 1988. The third regression in table 2.5 reveals that this lengthening of the

Table 2.5 ORIGINAL, REPLICATION, AND ADDITIONAL RESULTS FOR HOELSCHER'S REGRESSION (Dependent Variable: Interest Rate on 10-year Government Securities)

	Constant	P^e	RS – P^e	ΔY	D/Y	NFI	$\bar{R}^2$/SE	DW	RHO
Original (1953–1984)	1.14 (6.14)	0.777 (24.6)	0.780 (17.3)	.0041 (2.03)	0.414 (9.52)		.999 .332	2.52	.292 (2.96)
Replication (1953–1984)	1.228 (4.37)	0.740 (17.42)	0.679 (13.11)	0.002 (1.96)	0.370 (7.58)		.984 .340	1.703	0.620 (4.473)
Sample Period (1953–1988)	1.395 (3.79)	0.752 (14.04)	0.651 (9.99)	.002 (1.62)	0.354 (6.29)		.979 .388	2.030	.702 (5.914)
Foreign Capital (1953–1988)	1.245 (5.78)	0.737 (23.14)	0.716 (14.51)	0.001 (0.89)	0.362 (7.14)	0.631 (8.77)	.983 .351	1.813	.339 (2.159)
Nominal RS (1953–1988)	1.042 (4.14)		0.735 (21.86)	.002 (2.23)	0.425 (8.33)		.980 .396	2.004	0.460 (3.115)
Change in RL (1953–1988)	–0.417 (1.68)		0.179 (4.81)	.001 (0.44)	–.348 (5.26)		2.037		
Change in RL (1953–1988)	0.421 (1.84)			0.001 (0.41)	–.191 (2.58)		.117 .798	1.526	

Note: The dependent variable is the rate on 10-year government securities; P^e = Livingston survey measure of expected inflation; RS = rate on 1-year government securities; NFI = net foreign investment; ΔY = change in real GNP; and D/Y = NIPA measure of the federal deficit relative to GNP. T-statistics are in parentheses.

sample period does not alter the finding that the federal deficit positively affects long-term interest rates. Moreover, substituting the cyclically adjusted deficit (that is, the middle-expansion measure estimated by BEA) for the actual deficit does not alter this result (not shown), nor does the addition of net foreign investment. Also, as Hoelscher reports, the coefficient on the deficit remains significantly positive when the nominal short-term interest rate is substituted for the terms P^e and $(RS - P^e)$; in our regression this occurs even when we extend the sample period through 1988.

Some economists argue that the federal deficit affects the change rather than the level of interest rates.[29] When the first difference of the long-term rate is regressed on the other variables, the coefficient on the deficit variable no longer is significantly positive. In fact, it becomes significantly negative. This result also holds when the short-term rate is excluded.[30]

The second study we examine is by Evans (1987a). He estimates the interest rate effects of past, current, and expected future deficits, using a conventional IS-LM model with rational expectations imposed. With rational expectations and a stable autoregressive structure, he argues that the sign on future expected deficits would be the same as the sign on the sum of current and past deficits.

The equation estimated by Evans has the form:

$$RL = a_0 + a_1 RL_{-1} + a_2 M + a_3 \Delta D + a_4 G + e, \qquad (5)$$

where RL is the rate on Moody's AAA bonds, M is the real money supply, G is real federal government purchases, and ΔD is the change in the real market value of privately held federal debt. All the explanatory variables are measured relative to real potential GNP, and the regression is estimated in first differences with current and one-period lagged values of the variables. Evans finds that the sum of the coefficients on the deficit measure is significant but negative, and thus concludes that there is no positive connection between deficits and interest rates, regardless of whether the deficit is past, current, or expected in the future.

Our empirical examination of the Evans results are presented in table 2.6. The replication is quite close to the original results, as shown in the first and second regressions. In particular, the sum of the coefficients on the current and lagged deficit measures is significant and negative.

One difference between the regression estimated by Evans and the one estimated by Hoelscher is that Evans does not include a short-term interest rate. Bernheim (1987) questions the validity of this type

Table 2.6 ORIGINAL, REPLICATION, AND ADDITIONAL RESULTS FOR EVANS' REGRESSION (Dependent variable: AAA Bond Rate, Nominal. Estimates are the sums of the coefficients on current and one-period lagged values of variables.)

	Constant	Δ(D/Y)	ΔRL_{-1}	Δ(G/Y)	Δ(M/Y)	ΔRS	R^2/SE	DW
Original (1956–1979)		−.254 (0.11)	.427 (0.16)	.138 (0.10)	−.136 (0.21)			
Replication (1956–1979)	.199 (1.71)	−.219 (2.21)	.426 (2.31)	.098 (1.10)	−.030 (0.20)		.446 .353	2.27
Sample Period (1956–1988)	−.117 (0.66)	−.374 (2.79)	.372 (1.65)	.335 (1.74)	−.683 (3.02)		.403 .712	2.04
One-year Bill Rate Added	.022 (0.14)	.127 (0.96)	.130 (0.70)	.089 (0.61)	−.151 (0.73)	.570 (3.03)	.687 .515	2.40
Par Value of Debt (Change in real)	.071 (0.60)	.400 (3.82)	.030 (0.29)	−.300 (0.28)	.057 (0.34)	.702 (4.27)	.793 .419	2.20
Par Value with M Omitted	.032 (0.40)	.335 (3.70)	−.055 (0.29)	−.055 (0.49)		.795 (6.86)	.787 .426	2.011

Note: The dependent variable, RL, is the nominal AAA bond rate; D = change in real market value of privately held federal debt (except in the last two regressions, which use the change in the real par value); G = real federal government purchases; M = real money supply (M1); RS = rate on 1-year government securities; Y = real potential GNP (from Appendix A in Gordon 1987). The sample period for equations (4) through (6) is 1956–1988. All coefficients (except that on the lagged value of RL) are the sum of the coefficients on the current period and one-period lagged values of the explanatory variables. T-statistics are in parentheses.

of omission, and argues that it dramatically alters the interpretation of all the coefficients. When we add the current and past changes in the short-term interest rate to Evans' equation, the coefficient on the deficit term is positive, but remains insignificant.

As noted by de Leeuw and Holloway (1985), the coefficient on the change in the market value of government debt in an interest rate equation is likely to have simultaneous-equation bias problems, because the market value of federal debt is influenced by interest rate movements. When we used instead the change in the par value of government debt, the sum of the coefficients on the deficit variables in fact was positive and significant. This last finding is not altered when the money supply variable is dropped from the equation.[31]

The third interest rate study we examine is by Barro (1981a). Even though he does not explicitly consider the interest rate effects of deficits, this study combined with others by him provides us with the chance to examine the link between unanticipated deficits and interest rates, with data produced by Barro himself.

Barro examines the hypothesis that the interest rate (measured as the realized real rate of return on a composite holding of stocks) is negatively related to current and lagged unexpected movements in the money stock, and positively related to the temporary component of government purchases. His empirical results confirm a (marginally) significant coefficient on the temporary component of government purchases. The lagged but not the contemporaneous measure of unexpected money growth also was significant.

Our examination of Barro's results involves two parts. First, we used his data on the unexpected components of bond and money growth and on the temporary component of government purchases to determine whether all these variables affect the realized real rate of return. The second part attempts to reconstruct Barro's data and extend it through 1988 to determine if the findings are similar when the sample period is extended.

The results for the first part are shown in table 2.7. The first column shows Barro's regression with his data, and the results are very close although not identical. The second column is simply a transition to the third column, and reflects a slight change in time period. That is, the sample period is 1948–1976 instead of 1949–1977. The reason for this slight change in sample period is that Barro's data on the unexpected growth in the federal debt is not available after 1976.

The third column shows that when actual growth in government debt is included along with the unexpected growth in money and the temporary component of government purchases, its coefficient is positive but not significant.[32] In contrast, the fourth column shows that the unexpected component of federal debt has a significantly positive coefficient. The next two columns, respectively, show that the significance of the unexpected debt variable increases when the lag on the money variable is increased, but that its significance vanishes when the contemporaneous monetary variable is excluded along with the second lag of the money variable.

The next-to-last column shows the results when expected inflation is included in the regression, and when the dependent variable is the nominal rate of return instead of the realized real rate. The coefficient of unexpected bond growth is significantly positive, but the coefficents on the other variables are no longer statistically significant at the 5-percent level.

The final column differs only in that the dependent variable is the nominal rate on 10-year government bonds instead of the stock market yield. This change provides a common basis for comparison with the other long-term interest rate studies. All of the variables except expected inflation are insignificant.[33]

Our efforts to update these regressions through 1988 required us to construct estimates of unexpected money growth, unexpected bond growth, and the temporary component of federal purchases, based on Barro's methodology. Although we were able to approximate these variables using Barro's methodology, there were differences in the estimated time series that probably explain why we could not duplicate his results with our updated estimates, even for the original 1949–1977 period. That is, with our data we found no evidence that unexpected borrowing affects the realized real rate of return on stocks, when the latter is an updated series obtained from the same source used by Barro (the Center for Research in Securities Markets at the University of Chicago).

The last interest rate study we examine is by Bovenberg (1988). He focuses on the long-term interest rate effects of expected future deficits, measured by the average value of the current plus the next four years of the cyclically adjusted federal deficit.[34] The only other variable he includes in his regression is a measure of expected inflation. His findings are reported as the first regression in table 2.8.

To reestimate Bovenberg's equation, we used the five-year forward average of the middle-expansion deficit, including the current year. In place of his measure of expected inflation for the period 1979–1985, we used the same measure he used for the years 1961–1978—the 12-month forecast from the Livingston survey. Our replication and update of the Bovenberg regression yielded a positive and sig-

Table 2.7 REPLICATION AND ADDITIONAL RESULTS FOR BARRO'S REGRESSION (Dependent Variable: realized real rate of return on composite holding of stocks.)

Dependent Variables	RRS	RRS	RRS	RRS	RRS	RRS	NRS	NRL
Constant	0.1197 (0.04)	.1251 (0.04)	.1097 (0.04)	.1280 (.04)	.1418 (0.04)	0.1197 (0.04)	0.1832 (0.053)	.0231 (.0021)
$(G-G^*)$	5.6342 (2.89)	5.2886 (2.68)	5.2963 (2.77)	5.7456 (2.84)	7.3695 (2.77)	4.4370 (2.43)	4.8498 (2.705)	-.1263 (.108)
UM	-1.3720 (2.66)	-0.7313 (2.58)	-0.3300 (2.59)	-2.7576 (3.05)	-3.4598 (2.87)		-1.6596 (.1317)	-.0279 (.107)
UM_{-1}	-8.3201 (2.75)	-8.8349 (2.65)	-8.2136 (2.69)	-6.9319 (2.99)	-6.6022 (2.80)	-6.5128 (2.94)	-6.1852 (3.703)	.0074 (.109)
UM_{-2}					-4.8403 (2.33)		-2.7935 (2.725)	.1658 (.091)
UB				3.4030 (1.71)	3.9499 (1.62)	2.6612 (1.51)	3.1663 (2.288)	.0651 (.061)

UB_{-1}			-1.6526 (1.79)	-2.1797 (1.69)	-2.1389 (1.71)	-0.0834 (1.536)	$.1117$ (.064)
B		0.6479 (0.56)					
P^e						-1.2128 (1.872)	$.7881$ (.075)
$\bar{R}^2$	.1885	.2283	.2381	.3018	.3897	.3043	.2858	.8582
DW	2.113	2.296	2.068	2.165	2.292	2.247	2.494	1.223
SSR	.7708	.7084	.6715	.5840	.4875	.6087	.4116	.001

Note: RRS = realized real rate of return on composite holding of stocks; NRS = nominal return on composite holding of stocks; NRL = nominal rate on 10-year government securities; G = government purchases as a share of GNP; G* = permanent component of G; UM = unexpected money growth; B = growth in privately held, marketable government securities; UB = unexpected component of B; P^e = expected component of B; P^e = expected inflation. Sample period is 1949–1977 for the first regression, and 1948–1976 for all the rest. T-statistics are in parentheses.

nificant coefficient on the deficit variable. Similar findings (not shown in table 2.8) were obtained when a five-year forward average of the unadjusted NIPA deficit was used. Also, it turns out that the current value of the deficit is sufficient to obtain a positive and significant coefficient in this regression, and that the coefficient on expected future federal purchases (calculated the same way as expected future deficits) was positive but not significant. However, as shown in the fourth regression, when the years 1980–1988 are removed from the sample period, Bovenberg's measure of expected future deficits becomes insignificant. Also, when the equation is estimated for the entire updated 1955–1988 period, but in first differences, the deficit variable is not significant at the 5-percent level. Finally, when the lagged long-term interest rate is added, the coefficient on the deficit variable is insignificant at the 10-percent level.[35]

SUMMARY

As a group, these four studies of the interest rate effects of federal deficits provide mixed evidence. However, the results of each study

Table 2.8 ORIGINAL, REPLICATION, AND ADDITIONAL RESULTS FOR BOVENBERG'S REGRESSION (Dependent Variable: interest rate on 10-year government securities.)

	Constant	P^e	D	RL_{-1}	$\overline{R}^2$	DW	RHO
Original (1961–1985)	1.17 (1.37)	0.51 (5.33)	1.59 (3.37)		0.87	1.94	0.32
Republican (1961–1985)	1.729 (2.78)	0.472 (4.71)	1.582 (6.59)		0.939	1.616	0.560 (3.38)
Update (1955–1988)	2.612 (4.85)	0.486 (4.75)	1.200 (5.29)		0.943	1.609	0.670 (5.26)
Sample Period (1955–1979)	3.156 (20.40)	0.584 (11.44)	0.243 (1.60)		0.952	1.892	0.250 (1.29)
First Difference (1955–1988)	0.025 (0.18)	0.459 (3.41)	0.937 (1.95)		0.260	1.847	
Lagged RL* (1955–1988)	1.010 (2.52)	0.375 (5.39)	0.286 (1.12)	0.571 (4.61)	0.950	1.876	0.270 (1.61)

*This regression is estimated with first-differenced data.
Note: The dependent variable, RL, is the 10-year government bond rate; pe = 12-month expected inflation as repeated in the June Livingston survey; D = 5-year forward average of the ratio of middle-expansion deficit to middle-expansion GNP; and RL_{-1} = RL lagged one-period. T-statistics are in parentheses.

appear to hold for to many common types of changes. Thus, the differences in conclusions appear to be due more to differences in the underlying models than to differences in the sample period, the way the deficit is measured, or the statistical technique employed.

Of course, differences in underlying models may sometimes result in what might appear to be inconsequential differences in the specification of the regression equation. For example, Evans includes the lagged value of the dependent variable as a regressor, while Hoelscher includes an unlagged short-term interest rate, and neither Barro nor Bovenberg include an interest rate. Both Evans and Barro include money growth as a regressor, while Hoelscher and Bovenberg both include expected inflation. Nevertheless, the differences in conclusions about the interest-rate effect of federal deficits can depend on what other variables are included in the regressions.

To illustrate this point, table 2.9 presents four sets of interest rate regressions. In each regression, the long-term interest rate is regressed on some combination of the short-term (1-year) interest rate, the lagged value of the short-term interest rate, the lagged value of the long-term interest rate, and the NIPA federal deficit measured relative to GNP. In the first set of regressions, all the variables are in levels. In the second set, the regressions are in levels, but with a correction for first-order autocorrelation. In the third set, the regressions are estimated with first differences. Finally, in the last set of regressions, the change in the long-term interest rate is regressed on the levels of the explanatory variables. Plus and minus signs indicate significantly positive and negative coefficients, while NS and EX, respectively, indicate that the coefficient is not significant and that the variable was excluded from the regression.

According to these results, the coefficient on the deficit is generally positive and significant when the current value of the short-term interest rate is included in the regression. In contrast, this coefficient is generally insignificant or significantly negative when the current value of the short-term interest rate is replaced by its lagged value or by the lagged value of the dependent variable.[36] (The major exception to this generalization is in the last set of regressions, in which the deficit is significantly positive only in the first row.[37] Other exceptions are the sixth and eighth rows of the first set, and the sixth row of the fourth set.) When no interest rate is used as an explanatory variable, the deficit has a significantly positive coefficient only in the first set of regressions.

This pattern of coefficients may help to explain why Hoelscher finds a significant and positive coefficient for the federal deficit,

Table 2.9 ILLUSTRATIVE INTEREST RATE REGRESSIONS

			Sample Period — 1953–1988				
RL	RS	RS_{-1}	RL_{-1}	D/Y	$\bar{R}^2$	DW	RHO
(Levels)	+	−	+	+	.9877	2.3	
	+	EX	EX	+	.9723	1.2	
	EX	+	EX	NS	.8849	1.7	
	EX	EX	+	NS	.9307	1.9	
	+	NS	EX	+	.9715	1.3	
	+	EX	+	NS	.9842	1.9	
	EX	NS	+	−	.9339	2.1	
	EX	EX	EX	+	.5116	0.9	
RL	RS	RS_{-1}	RL_{-1}	D/Y	$\bar{R}^2$	DW	RHO
(Levels with	+	−	+	+	.9880	2.1	−0.16
autocorrelat-	+	EX	EX	+	.9800	2.1	0.84
ion correction)		+		−	.8867	1.8	0.17
	EX	EX	+	−	.9310	1.9	0.07
	+	NS	EX	+	.9800	2.0	0.85
	+	EX	+	NS	.9842	1.9	0.04
	EX	NS	NS	NS	.9361	2.0	−0.06
	EX	EX	EX	NS	.9086	1.2	0.96
ΔRL	ΔRS	$ΔRS_{-1}$	$ΔRL_{-1}$	Δ(D/Y)	$\bar{R}^2$	DW	RHO
(First	+	NS	NS	+	.7587	2.3	
differences)	+	EX	EX	+	.7669	2.3	
	EX	+	EX	−	.1794	2.1	
	EX	EX	NS	NS	.0668	2.0	
	+	NS	EX	+	.7663	2.2	
	+	EX	NS	+	.7655	2.4	
	EX	+	NS	−	.1582	2.1	
	EX	EX	EX	NS	.0052	1.5	
ΔRL	RS	RS_{-1}	RL_{-1}	D/Y	$\bar{R}^2$	DW	RHO
(First dif-	+	−	−	+	.8585	2.3	
ferences of	+	EX	EX	−	.5210	2.2	
dependent	EX	+	EX	−	.2707	2.1	
variable)	EX	EX	NS	−	.2013	1.9	
	+	−	EX	NS	.6985	2.2	
	+	EX	−	NS	.8174	1.9	
	EX	NS	NS	−	.2612	2.1	
	EX	EX	EX	−	.1380	1.6	

Note: RL = rate on 10-year government securities; RS = rate on 1-year government securities; D = NIA deficit; Y = GNP. The autocorrelation coefficient is a maximum likelihood estimate. Plus and minus signs indicate statistically significant positive and negative coefficients. NS indicates that the estimated coefficient is not statistically significant, and EX indicates that the variable is excluded from the regression.

while Evans does not. That is, it appears that whether or not one finds that deficits affect long-term interest rates can depend on what, if any, interest rate is included as an explanatory variable. This is not a distinguishing feature of the competing views about the interest rate effects of federal deficits.

More generally, the opposing views of whether deficits affect interest rates say little if anything about whether the interest rate regression should include an interest rate as a regressor. Long-term and short-term interest rates, current and lagged, could appear in competing model frameworks. So, if the empirical tests of whether deficits do or do not matter depend on which interest rates are included, such interest rate studies may not be an adequate testing ground for the alternative views.[38]

Studies of Government Deficits and the Composition of Output

In addition to the interest rate studies, we considered two studies that estimate the effects of deficits on the composition of output and reach different conclusions despite similar methodologies. In fact, most of the concern about the economic effects of deficits is about their effect on the division of output between investment and consumption. The interest rate studies focus on what many believe to be the main channel of this effect.

The first of these studies is by Eisner (1986), who estimates the effects of price-adjusted and cyclically adjusted federal deficits on subsequent changes in consumption, investment, and GNP.[39] His regressions have the form:

$$\Delta X/Y = a_0 + a_1(D/Y)_{-1} + a_2(\Delta M/Y)_{-1} + e, \qquad (6)$$

where Δ indicates first differences, X is either personal consumption or gross domestic investment, D is the price and cyclically adjusted deficit, M is the monetary base, and Y is GNP. The explanatory variables are lagged one period. His findings, reported in table 2.10, are that deficits crowd in both consumption and investment. In other words, the coefficient on the lagged deficit variable is significantly positive.

Our findings show that, although we are able to replicate his results for the original sample period, these results are changed when the sample is extended through 1988. The deficit measure no longer is significant in either the consumption or investment equations. In the analysis shown in table 2.10, we used a cyclically adjusted measure of the deficit, whereas Eisner's deficit measure was both cycli-

Table 2.10 ORIGINAL, REPLICATION, AND ADDITIONAL RESULTS FOR
EISNER'S REGRESSIONS

	C_1	C_2	$(D/Y)_{-1}$	$(\Delta M/Y)_{-1}$	RHO	R^2/SE	DW
GROSS INVESTMENT							
Original	2.613	1.135	1.383	3.587	.282	.570	1.99
(1962–1984)	(2.22)	(2.10)	(3.34)	(1.49)			
Replication	1.386	−1.010	1.636	3.088	.314	.331	1.90
(1962–1984)	(1.80)	(1.47)	(3.91)	(1.15)	(1.59)	1.205	
Update	1.498	.715	.283	.238	−.020	−.080	2.00
(1962–1988)	(1.98)	(1.08)	(0.69)	(0.08)	(0.11)	1.489	
CONSUMPTION							
Original	3.401	2.339	.642	2.393	.092	.580	1.91
(1962–1984)	(5.04)	(7.72)	(2.44)	(1.50)			
Replication	5.365	3.816	.433	1.366	.873	.524	2.05
(1962–1984)	(5.59)	(4.23)	(2.40)	(1.06)	(8.57)	.650	
Update	5.174	3.714	.317	1.542	.873	.471	2.04
(1962–1988)	(5.42)	(4.19)	(1.87)	(1.21)	(9.30)	.662	

Note: Dependent variables are $\Delta I/Y$ or $\Delta C/Y$, where I = gross private domestic investment; C = personal consumption expenditures; and Y = GNP. C_1 = intercept for period 1962–1966; C_2 = intercept for period after 1966; D = high employment surplus, except for equations designated "original" in which Eisner also adjusted for changes in the real value of federal debt; Y = high employment GNP; and ΔM = change in real monetary base. T statistics are in parentheses.

cally adjusted and inflation-adjusted. But we found that a similar result is obtained when the federal deficit is adjusted for the decline in the real value of federal debt, and when this adjustment is entered as an explanatory variable (not shown).

The last study we examine is by Summers (1985). He estimated the effects of current government deficits on net personal saving and net domestic investment, both expressed as a share of GNP.[40] His regressions have the general form:

$$X/Y = a_0 + a_1(D/Y) + a_2(\text{cyclical variable}) + e, \qquad (7)$$

where X is either net private investment or net private saving, Y is GNP, D is the current-period NIPA measure of the federal deficit, and the cyclical variable is the current and lagged values of the percent change in real GNP or the current and lagged values of capacity utilization. Summers finds that the federal deficit in the current period has a significantly negative impact on the investment share, and a significantly positive impact on the saving share.

Our replication and update of Summers' regressions yielded the same results (table 2.11). The results are unchanged when the cyclically adjusted deficit is used instead of the unadjusted deficit (not shown).[41] However, the results for net private saving do change when the regressions are estimated in first-difference form. In this case, the coefficient of the actual deficit is not significant. When the lagged value of the deficit is used instead of the current value in the first-

Table 2.11 REPLICATION AND ADDITIONAL RESULTS FOR SUMMERS' REGRESSIONS (Dependent Variables: Net Investment and Net Private Saving as Shares of GNP.)

	Constant	D/Y	$\dot{Y}$	$\dot{Y}_{-1}$	RHO	$\bar{R}^2$/SE	D–W
Net Investment							
Replication	6.366	−.660	.265	.038	.70	.910	1.62
(1949–1982)	(18.30)	(8.67)	(7.04)	(1.26)	(5.74)	.485	
Update	6.089	−.601	−.300	.072	.62	.898	1.70
(1949–1988)	(18.23)	(8.20)	(8.20)	(2.31)	(4.99)	.541	
First differences	−.041	−.670	.288	.054		.892	1.95
(1949–1988)	(0.39)	(8.54)	(7.31)	(1.75)		.651	
Deficit lagged	4.313	.065	.460	.157	.74	.732	1.65
(1949–1988)	(7.43)	(0.56)	(8.92)	(2.96)	(7.01)	.876	
Deficit lagged	−.144	−.037	.498	.010		.675	2.17
First differences	(0.79)	(0.29)	(8.58)	(1.76)		1.132	
Net Private Saving							
Replication	6.898	.177	.134	.028	.70	.459	1.69
(1949–1982)	(16.36)	(1.91)	(2.93)	(0.75)	(5.71)	.590	
Update	5.906	.204	.138	.039	.92	.713	2.14
(1949–1988)	(5.69)	(2.38)	(3.45)	(1.19)	(14.92)	.628	
First difference	−.117	.128	.124	.012		.136	2.24
(1949–1988)	(1.02)	(1.47)	(2.86)	(0.36)		.718	
Deficit lagged	6.944	−.164	.108	−.021	.83	.697	2.19
(1949–1988)	(11.99)	(1.91)	(2.93)	(0.54)	(9.46)	.645	
Deficit lagged	−.053	−.166	.111	−.025		.182	2.48
First differences	(0.47)	(2.08)	(3.11)	(0.73)		.699	

Note: Dependent variables are I/Y or S/Y, where I = net investment; S = net private saving; and Y = GNP. The explanatory variables are $\dot{Y}$ = percentage change in real GNP, and D/Y, where D = NIPA measure of the federal deficit. T-statistics are in parentheses.

difference regression, the coefficient is significantly negative. In the case of investment, the results remain unchanged in the first-difference regression, but the coefficient on the deficit becomes insignificant when the lagged instead of the current value of the deficit measure is used.

SUMMARY

As in the case of the interest rate studies, the studies by Eisner and by Summers reach different conclusions despite what might appear to be minor differences in the specification of the regression equations. Some illustrative sets of regressions may help to explain why.

Table 2.12 presents five sets of investment-share regressions. The dependent variable takes three forms: I/Y, Δ(I/Y), and (ΔI)/Y, where

Table 2.12 ILLUSTRATIVE INVESTMENT SHARE REGRESSIONS

I/Y	(D/Y)	$(D/Y)_{-1}$	$\bar{R}^2$	DW	RHO
(Levels)	−	+	0.43	0.856	
	−	EX	0.162	1.154	
	EX	NS	−.013	1.471	

I/Y	(D/Y)	$(D/Y)_{-1}$	$\bar{R}^2$	DW	RHO
(Levels with	−	+	0.665		.778
autocorrelation	−	EX	0.569		.844
correction)	EX	NS	0.040		.320

Δ(I/Y)	Δ(D/Y)	$\Delta(D/Y)_{-1}$	$\bar{R}^2$	DW	RHO
(First differences)	−	+	0.792	1.890	
	−	EX	0.758	1.858	
	EX	NS	0.065	2.072	

(ΔI/Y)	(ΔD/Y)	$(\Delta D/Y)_{-1}$	$\bar{R}^2$	DW	RHO
(Scaled changes)	−	−	0.712	1.680	
	NS	EX	0.051	2.093	
	EX	+	0.160	2.006	

(ΔI/Y)	(ΔD/Y)	$(\Delta D/Y)_{-1}$	$\bar{R}^2$	DW	RHO
(Scaled changes	−	+	0.711		0.157
with autocorre-	NS	EX	0.060		−.187
lation correction)	EX	+	0.143		−.107

Note: I = gross domestic investment; Y = nominal GNP; and D = NIPA measure of the deficit (with reversed sign). T-statistics are in parentheses. The autocorrelation coefficients are maximum likelihood estimates. Plus and minus signs indicate statistically significant positive or negative coefficients. NS indicates that the estimated coefficient is not statistically significant, and EX indicates that the variable is excluded from the regression.

Δ is the first difference operator, I is gross investment, and Y is GNP. The explanatory variables are combinations of current and lagged federal deficit in forms corresponding to the form of the dependent variable.

Table 2.12 reveals the following patterns. The coefficient on the contemporaneous deficit is never positive and significant, while the coefficient of the lagged deficit is never negative and significant. With the exception of the last two sets of regressions (the ones corresponding to the Eisner regressions), the current value of the deficit is always negative and significant when it is included by itself in the regression. On the other hand, the last two sets of regressions are the only ones in which the lagged value of the deficit is positive and significant when it is included without the contemporaneous value. In all cases, when both the contemporaneous and lagged values of the deficit are included, the coefficient on the current value is significantly negative, while the coefficient on the lagged value is significantly positive.[42] The sum of these coefficients, however, generally is not significantly different from zero. (The exception is in the first-difference regressions, where the sum is significant and negative at the 5-percent level.)

These illustrative regressions suggest that the difference between the findings reported by Summers and those reported by Eisner largely reflects whether the contemporaneous or lagged value of the deficit is included in the regression, and whether the variables are entered in the form (I/Y) or (ΔI/Y). It also appears that when the contemporaneous and lagged values are entered together, the sum of the two coefficients generally is not statistically different from zero. This finding appears to contradict the findings of both Eisner and Summers.

CONCLUSION

The relatively high level of real interest rates and the low share of output in net investment are features of the 1980s that are consistent with the conventional view that large federal deficits matter. In addition, national saving has been low and the trade deficit very large, compared with the earlier post-World War II period. Nevertheless, the debate continues about whether or not federal deficits have adverse economic consequences.

A survey of the empirical literature illustrates that the evidence is still mixed. Some patterns, however, do emerge. In particular, there appears to be more evidence that federal deficits raise long-term rather than short-term interest rates, and some evidence that federal debt (rather than federal deficits) matters. Also, expected future deficits and unexpected current deficits seem to show a more consistent effect on interest rates. A more detailed analysis of several empirical studies suggests that the empirical results are somewhat more robust than several years ago. In particular, more recent results seem less sensitive to the period of estimation, the choice of the deficit measure, and the application of alternative statistical methods. Nevertheless, the results are sensitive to specification changes that do not necessarily distinguish the conventional view from the alternative.

Policymakers are now engaged in a difficult and continuing effort to reduce (and possibly eliminate) the federal budget deficit. The general belief is that a successful completion of this task will raise future living standards by lowering interest rates and thus creating a more favorable climate for capital formation. Also, reducing the federal deficit is viewed as the most effective way to increase the national rate of saving and to reduce the persistently large trade deficit.

These popular perceptions, which reflect the conventional view among economists, are not shared by economists who believe in the validity of the Ricardian equivalence proposition. This proposition maintains that government deficits do not affect interest rates. Empirical research over many years has not settled this issue. This lack of agreement means that policymakers must decide on other grounds whether or not to pursue substantially smaller federal deficits. Faced with uncertain outcomes, many would argue that it is too risky to adopt the view that deficits do not matter when, in fact, this view may be incorrect.

Notes

The authors wish to thank John R. Sturrock and Thomas Lutton for many helpful discussions, Mark Decker for excellent research assistance, and Dorothy J. Kornegay and L. Rae Roy for their skillful word processing. The views expressed in this paper are the authors' and do not necessarily reflect those of the Office of Thrift Supervision, the Congessional Budget Office, or their staffs.

1. In the recent "bailout" of the thrift industry, part of the cost appears on-budget and part is financed off-budget.

2. A distinction also can be made between marketable and nonmarketable federal debt, and between interest-bearing and non-interest-bearing federal debt.

3. The Congressional Budget Office (CBO) estimates that under current policies, the debt-to-GNP ratio has essentially stabilized.

4. For recent analyses of trends in national saving, see de Leeuw (1984), Holloway (1989), and Wilson et al. (1989).

5. See de Leeuw (1989), Council of Economic Advisers (1989), and Tatom (1989) for detailed analyses of gross versus net and nominal versus real investment issues.

6. Some analysts have attributed part of the early burst of strength to the investment tax incentives that were introduced by the Economic Recovery Tax Act of 1981. See Feldstein and Elmendorf (1989).

7. One of the main strands of the conventional view focuses on the development of portfolio models in which government securities constitute one type of asset among others, including equities and money. Portfolio models focus on investor's decisions about the allocation of their wealth among alternative assets. For a pioneering article on portfolio models, see Brainard and Tobin (1968).

8. The reason that a tax deduction is temporary is that a permanent increase in federal debt is explosive when interest rates are assumed to exceed the growth of output. The budget is therefore assumed to be balanced in a present value sense.

9. There are several important assumptions that are required for the Ricardian equivalence proposition to hold, and the relaxation of these assumptions can result in federal deficits having a positive effect on interest rates. See Leiderman and Blejer (1988).

10. Bailey (1972) stressed the possibility that government purchases are to some extent direct substitutes for private purchases. The conventional model implicitly considers direct substitution between government and private spending to be zero.

11. Cox (1985) argues that to the extent that deficits are perceived to be permanent, Ricardian equivalence does not apply. In this respect, Cox argues that if interest payments on government bonds are bond-financed, as opposed to being backed by taxes, then government bonds are net nominal wealth. An increase in government debt will in these circumstances have the same effect on the price level as an increase in the money supply. For additional issues, see Buiter and Tobin (1979, 1980) and Brunner (1986).

12. The debt-neutrality view also makes other assumptions, such as assuming perfect captial markets. Our purpose, however, is not to discuss all these assumptions but to indicate aspects of this view that suggest a particular empirical specification or interpretation of empirical results. Many economists question these assumptions.

13. Shaw (1987), for example, has shown theoretically that a tax-induced fiscal deficit has a zero effect on economic variables, whereas an expenditure-induced deficit has a positive effect on output, employment, interest rates, and tax receipts. In addition, Hall (1980) has also noted that an increase in government expenditures can increase interest rates as well as income within a rational expectations framework.

14. Empirical evidence of a positive linkage between government purchases and interest rates has been found in some of the results by Barro (1987a, 1985), and Plosser (1987, 1982), discussed below.

15. We are referring here to primary deficits and a situation in which the rate of interest exceeds the growth rate in output. See McCallum (1984) and Sargent and Wallace (1981) for a more detailed discussion of these issues. It is important to note in this regard that if the rate of interest is less than the growth rate in output (a situation that Barrow admits he "cannot rigorously rule out"), then "debt issue would be regarded as net wealth and would therefore raise aggregate demand." (Barro 1976,

344–345). See Darby (1984) and Barth, Iden and Russek (1986a) for a discussion of this entire issue.

16. The new classical view emphasizes the distinction between anticipated and unanticipated budget deficits. However, the new classical view, unlike the Ricardian equivalence proposition, does not assume that households in their saving decisions offset budget deficits.

17. A number of authors have attempted to test this proposition, and some of these studies will be discussed in a later section. For now, it should simply be noted that Kim and Lombra (1989) have developed a model of asset price determination, assuming rational expectations, in an effort to examine how the effects of deficits on interest rates depend on expectations. More specifically, they examine the effects of unanticipated effects on current interest rates.

18. Empirically, it usually does not seem to make much difference which of these two deficit measures is employed.

19. Cebula (1988) uses two-stage least squares, and finds a significantly positive interest rate effect for the structural and cyclical components of the federal deficit. Darrat (1989), however, argues that "correlation-based analysis . . . cannot differentiate between cause and effects," and finds that multivariate Granger causality tests indicate only one-way causality from long-term interest rates to federal deficits. In contrast, Kim and Lombra (1989) imply that such causality tests, which include lagged values of the deficit, are inappropriate if the true relationship is between interest rates and unexpected deficits.

20. Swamy et al. (1984) discuss this and related issues.

21. For other surveys of the effects of deficits on interest rates, see McMillin (1986), Seater (1985), Dwyer (1985), U.S. Treasury (1984), Bernheim (1987), and Congressional Budget Office (1989a, 1989b, and 1984a).

22. In a later paper, de Leeuw (1986) expanded the model to include net international assets.

23. Spiro (1987) corrected an initial misinterpretation of the sign on the deficit variable in Tanzi's study.

24. Bovenberg's approach and results were similar to Feldstein's, including the finding that expected deficits have a large positive effect on long-term interest rates. His study will be discussed below.

25. Although Boskin (1988) made several refinements in analyzing the effects of the federal budget, the results of his crowding out analysis were similar to Summers' results. Eisner's work will be discussed in the next section.

26. Barth, Russek, and Wang (1986), using a number of tests for non-stationarity, concluded that these findings could be spurious.

27. Although Hoelscher enters most of his deficit measures in real per capita terms, he finds that scaling by GNP instead of by population does not change his results. To facilitate comparison with other studies, we use his déficit measured relative to GNP.

28. Hoelscher found the net foreign investment had a positive but insignificant coefficent. In contrast, our coefficient estimate is significantly positive, even when the federal deficit is the measured net of these flows. The conventional view suggests that the coefficient on net foreign investment should be significantly negative.

29. For example, de Leeuw and Holloway (1985) report that the stock of federal debt (but not the deficit, which is the change in the stock), has a significantly positive effect on the interest rate level. This finding implies that deficits affect the change in interest rates.

30. The use of two-stage least squares does not alter the findings about the sign and significance of the deficit variable in any of the regressions reported in table 2.5.

31. Similar results are obtained when the level rather than the change in the real market value of the federal debt is used. Also, the use of two-stage least squares does not alter the findings about the sign and significance of the deficit coefficients in any of the regressions reported in table 2.6.

32. Barro uses the privately held, interest-bearing, marketable federal debt.

33. The expected inflation measure was computed according to a methodology suggested by de Leeuw and McKelvey (1984).

34. Miller and Roberds (1989) imply that measures of expected deficits such as the one used by Bovenberg are model-inconsistent.

35. The coefficient on the deficit is significantly negative when the dependent variable is the change in the interest rate and the explanatory variables are entered in undifferenced form.

36. This general pattern is not altered when the change in the money stock is added, or when the Livingston measure of expected inflation is added.

37. Kim and Lombra argue that efficient capital markets imply that the change in interest rates depends on the unexpected component of the deficit. Thus, the general lack of a positive relationship in this last set of regressions could be the result of expectations of the deficit that proved to be overly pessimistic.

38. Bernheim (1987) makes the point that interest rate studies may not be able to test the validity of the Ricardian equivalence proposition because they cannot distinguish between this proposition and the hypothesis of perfect capital markets.

39. Eisner also examined the effect of these deficits on the trade balance, an issue we did not examine because it is the topic of another paper here (see the Helliwell paper).

40. Summers also considered the effect of deficits on net foreign investment and state and local government saving.

41. To facilitate comparison with the study by Eisner and Peiper, we used the standardized-employment deficit estimated by the CBO instead of the middle-expansion deficit. The findings, however, do not depend on which of these two cyclically adjusted measures of the deficit is used.

42. These results are changed somewhat when the current and lagged growth rate of GNP are added to the regression. In particular, the positive sign on the lagged deficit becomes insignificant in the first rows of the second and third sets of regressions and in the last row of the fourth regression. On the other hand, the coefficient on the unlagged deficit becomes significantly negative in the second row of the last set of regressions.

References

Aschauer, David A. 1985. "Fiscal Policy and Aggregate Demand." *American Economic Review* 75, no. 1 (March): 117–127.

Bailey, Martin, J. 1972. "The Optimal Full-Employment Surplus." *Journal of Political Economy* 80 (July/August): 649–661.

Barro, Robert J. 1989. "The Ricardian Approach to Budget Deficits." *Journal of Economic Perspectives* 3, no. 2 (Spring): 37–54.

———. 1987. "Government Spending, Interest Rates, Prices, and Budget Deficits in the United Kingdom, 1701–1918." *Journal of Monetary Economics* 20, (September): 221–247.

———. 1981a. "Intertemporal Substitution and the Business Cycle." In *Carnegie-Rochester Conference Series on Public Policy* 14, edited by Karl Brunner and Allan H. Meltzer, 237–268. Amsterdam: North-Holland.)

———. 1981b. "Output Effects of Government Purchases." *Journal of Political Economy* 89, no. 6 (December): 1086–1121.

———. 1980. "Federal Deficit Policy and the Effects of Public Debt Shocks." *Journal of Money, Credit and Banking* 12, no. 4 (Nov., part 2): 747–762.

———. 1979. "On the Determination of Public Debt." *Journal of Political Economy* 87, no. 5, part 1 (October): 940–971.

———. 1977. "Unanticipated Money Growth and Unemployment in the United States." *American Economic Review* 67, no. 2 (March): 101–115.

———. 1976. "Reply to Feldstein and Buchanan." *Journal of Political Economy* 84, no. 2 (April): 343–349.

———. 1974. "Are Government Bonds Net Wealth?" *Journal of Political Economy* 82, no. 6 (November/December): 1095–1117.

Barth, James R. and Michael D. Bradley. 1989. "Evidence on Real Interest Rate Effects of Money, Debt, and Government Spending." *Quarterly Review of Economics and Business* 29, no. 1 (Spring): 49–57.

Barth, James R., George Iden, and Frank S. Russek. 1986a. "The Economic Consequences of Federal Deficits: An Examination of the Net Wealth and Instability Issues." *Southern Economic Journal* 53, no. 1 (July): 27–50.

———. 1986b. "Government Debt, Government Spending, and Private Sector Behavior: Comment." *American Economic Review* 76, no. 5 (December): 1158–67.

———. 1985. "Federal Borrowing and Short Term Interest Rates: Comment." *Southern Economic Journal* 52, no. 2 (October): 554–559.

———. 1984–85. "Do Federal Deficits Really Matter?" *Contemporary Policy Issues* 3, no. 1 (Fall): 79–95. A more technical version is printed in *Interest Rates*, Hearings before the Subcommittee on Economic Goals and Intergovernmental Policy of the Joint Economic Committee, U.S. Congress, 98:2 (September 13, 1984): 22–56.

Barth, James R., Frank S. Russek, and George H. Wang. 1986. "A Time Series Analysis of the Relationship between the Capital Stock and Federal Debt: A Comment." *Journal of Money, Credit and Banking* 18, no. 4 (November): 527–538.

Bernheim, B. Douglas. 1987. "Ricardian Equivalence: An Evaluation of Theory and Evidence." In *Macroeconomics Annual* 1987, edited by Stanley Fischer, 263–304. Cambridge, Mass.: MIT Press.

Blinder, Alan S. and Angus Deaton. 1985. "The Time Series Consumption Function Revisited." *Brookings Papers on Economic Activity*, no. 2: 465–511.

Blinder, Alan and Robert Solow. 1973. "Does Fiscal Policy Matter?" *Journal of Public Economics* 2. (November): 319–337.

Boskin, Michael J. 1988. "Concepts and Measures of Federal Deficits and Debt and Their Impact on Economic Activity." In *Economics of Public Debt*, edited by K. J. Arrow and M. J. Boskin, 77–112. New York: St. Martin's Press.

Bovenberg, A. Lans. 1988. "Long-term Interest Rates in the United States." *IMF Staff Papers* 35, no. 2 (June): 382–390.

————. 1987. "Long-Term and Short-Term Interest Rates in the United States: An Empirical Analysis." International Monetary Fund, Fiscal Affairs Department, IMF Working Paper, WP/87/84, December 10.

Bradley, Michael D. 1986. "Government Spending or Deficit Financing: Which Causes Crowding Out?" *Journal of Economics and Business* 38, no. 3 (August): 203–214.

Brainard, William and James Tobin. 1968. "Pitfalls in Financial Model Building." *American Economic Review* 58 (May): 99–122.

Brunner, Karl. 1986. "Fiscal Policy in Macro Theory: A Survey and Evaluation." In *The Monetary Versus Fiscal Policy Debate: Lessons From Two Decades*, edited by R. W. Hafer, 33–116. Totowa, New Jersey: Rowman and Allanheld.

Buiter, Willem and James Tobin. 1980. "Fiscal and Monetary Policies, Capital Formation and Economic Activity." In *The Government and Capital Formation*, edited by G. M. von Furstenberg, 73–151. Cambridge: Ballinger.

————. 1979. "Debt Neutrality: A Brief Review of Doctrine and Evidence." In *Social Security versus Private Saving*, edited by G. M. von Furstenberg, 39–63. Cambridge, Mass: Ballinger.

Canto, Victor A. and Donald Rapp. 1982. "The 'Crowding Out' Controversy: Arguments and Evidence." Federal Reserve Bank of Atlanta, *Economic Review* (August): 33–37.

Carlson, Jack. 1983. "The Relationship Between Federal Deficits and Interest Rates." Statement before the Joint Economic Committee, October 21.

Cebula, Richard J. 1988. "Federal Government Budget Deficits and Interest Rates: A Brief Note." *Southern Economic Journal* 55, no. 1 (July): 206–210.

————. 1987. *The Deficit Problem in Perspective*. Lexington, Massachusetts: D.C. Heath & Co.

Cohen, Darrel. 1989. "A Comparison of Fiscal Measures Using Reduced-

Form Techniques", Division of Research and Statistics, Board of Governors of the Federal Reserve System. Washington, D.C.

Congressional Budget Office. 1989a. "Deficits and Interest Rates: Theoretical Issues and Empirical Evidence." Staff Working Paper (January). Washington, D.C.

————. 1989b. "Deficits and Interest Rates: Theoretical Issues and Simulation Results." Staff Working Paper (January). Washington, D.C.

————. 1988. "Economic Effects of Deficit Reduction in Commercial Econometric Models." A Report to the National Economic Commission (December 7). Washington, D.C.

————. 1985a. *The Economic and Budget Outlook: Fiscal Years 1986–1990* (February). Washington, D.C.

————. 1985b. *The Economic and Budget Outlook: An Update.* (August). Washington, D.C.

————. 1985c. "The Dollar in Foreign Exchange and U.S. Industrial Production." Staff Working Paper (December). Washington, D.C.

————. 1984a. "Deficits and Interest Rates: Empirical Findings and Selected Bibliography, Appendix A." *The Economic Outlook* (February): Washington, D.C. 99–102.

————. 1984b. *Federal Debt and Interest Costs*, Special Study (September). Washington, D.C.

Council of Economic Advisors. 1989. *Economic Report of the President 1989.* Washington: U.S. Govt. Printing Office.

Cox, Michael W. 1985. "Inflation and Permanent Government Debt." Federal Reserve Bank of Dallas, *Economic Review* (May): 25–31.

Darby, Michael. 1984. "Some Pleasant Monetarist Arithmetic." Federal Reserve Bank of Minneapolis, *Quarterly Review* 8 (Spring): 15–20.

Darrat, Ali F. 1989. "Fiscal Deficits and Long-Term Interest Rates: Further Evidence from Annual Data." *Southern Economic Journal* 56, no. 2 (October): 363–374.

de Leeuw, Frank and Thomas M. Holloway. 1985. "The Measurement and Significance of the Cyclically Adjusted Federal Budget and Debt." *Journal of Money, Credit and Banking* 17, no. 2 (May): 232–242.

de Leeuw, Frank and Michael J. McKelvey. 1984. "Price Expectations of Business Firms: Bias in the Short and Long Run." *American Economic Review* 74, no. 1 (March): 99–110.

de Leeuw, Frank. 1989. "Interpreting Investment-To-Output Ratios: Nominal/Real, Net/Gross, Stock/Flow, Narrow/Broad." Bureau of Economic Analysis, Discussion Paper 39 (June).

————. 1986. "The Cyclically Adjusted Federal Debt and the Economy." Paper presented at the meetings of the Western Economic Association, San Francisco, July.

————. 1984. "Conflicting Measures of Private Saving." *Survey of Current Business* 64, no. 11 (November): 17–23.

Dewald, William G. 1983. "Federal Deficits and Real Interest Rates: Theory and Evidence." Federal Reserve Bank of Atlanta, *Economic Review* (January): 20–29.

Dwyer, Gerald P. 1985. "Federal Deficits, Interest Rates, and Monetary Policy." *Journal of Money, Credit and Banking* 17, no. 4, part 2 (Nov.): 655–681.

———. 1982. "Inflation and Government Deficits." *Economic Inquiry* 20, no. 3 (July): 315–29.

Echols, Michael E. and Jan Walter Elliott. 1976. "Rational Expectations in a Disequilibrium Model of the Term Structure." *American Economic Review* 66, no. 1 (March): 28–44.

Eisner, Robert. 1986. *How Real Is the Federal Deficit?* New York: The Free Press.

Evans, Paul. 1989. "A Test of Steady-State Government-Debt Neutrality." *Economic Inquiry* 27 (January): 39–55.

———. 1988. "Are Consumers Ricardian? Evidence for the United States." *Journal of Political Economy* 96, no. 5 (October): 983–1004.

———. 1987a. "Interest Rates and Expected Future Budget Deficits in the United States." *Journal of Political Economy* 95, no. 1 (February): 34–58.

———. 1987b. "Do Budget Deficits Raise Nominal Interest Rates? Evidence From Six Countries." *Journal of Monetary Economics* 20, no. 2 (September): 281–300.

———. 1986. "Is the Dollar High Because of Large Budget Deficits?" *Journal of Monetary Economics* 18, no. 3 (November): 227–249.

———. 1985. "Do Large Deficits Produce High Interest Rates?" *American Economic Review* 75, no. 1 (March): 68–87.

Fackler, James S. and W. Douglas McMillin. 1983. "Government Debt and Macroeconomic Activity." Paper presented at the meetings of the Southern Economic Association, Washington, D.C., November.

Federal Reserve Bank of Boston. 1983. *The Economics of Large Government Deficits.* Conference Series no. 27.

Feldstein, Martin S. and Otto Eckstein. 1970. "The Fundamental Determinants of the Interest Rate." *Review of Economics and Statistics* 52, no. 4 (November): 363–375.

Feldstein, Martin S. and Gary Chamberlain. 1973. "Multimarket Expectations and the Rate of Interest." *Journal of Money, Credit and Banking* 4, no. 4 (November): 873–902.

Feldstein, Martin S. and Douglas W. Elmendorf. 1989. "Budget Deficits, Tax Incentives, and Inflation: A Surprising Lesson From the 1983–84 Recovery." Working Paper no. 2819, National Bureau of Economic Research.

Feldstein, Martin S. 1988. "Halving the Pain of Budget Balance." *Wall Street Journal*, 25 May.

———. 1986. "Budget Deficits, Tax Rules, and Real Interest Rates." NBER Working Paper no. 1970.

_____ . 1982. "Government Deficits and Aggregate Demand." *Journal of Monetary Economics* 9, no. 1 (January): 1–20.

Frankel, Jeffrey A. 1983. "A Test of Portfolio Crowding-Out and Related Issues of Finance." National Bureau of Economic Research. Working Paper no. 1205 (September).

Frenkel, Jacob A., and Assaf Razin. 1986. "Fiscal Policies in the World Economy." *Journal of Political Economy* 94, no. 3, part 1 (June): 564–594.

Giannaros, Demetrios S. and Bharat R. Kolluri. 1988. "The Budget Deficit Debate: A Review of the Recent Empirical Studies." *Journal of Applied Business Research* 4, no. 2 (Spring): 86–97.

Girola, James A. 1984. "Federal Deficits and Interest Rates." Paper presented at the annual meeting of the Society of Government Economists, Washington, D.C., March.

Gordon, Robert J. 1987. *Macroeconomics.* Fourth edition. Boston: Little, Brown & Co.

Hall, Robert E. 1980. "Labor Supply and Aggregate Fluctuations." *Carnegie-Rochester Conference Series on Public Policy* 12 (Spring): 7–33.

Hoelscher, Gregory P. 1986. "New Evidence on Deficits and Interest Rates." *Journal of Money, Credit and Banking* 18, no. 1 (February): 1–17.

_____ . 1983. "Federal Borrowing and Short Term Interest Rates." *Southern Economic Journal* 50 (October): 319–333.

Holloway, Thomas M. 1989. "Present NIPA Saving Measures: Their Characteristics and Limitations." In *The Measurement of Saving, Investment, and Wealth,* edited by Robert E. Lipsey and Helen Stone Tice, 21–93. Chicago: University of Chicago Press.

Hutchison, Michael and David H. Pyle. 1984. "The Real Interest Rate/Budget Deficit Link: International Evidence, 1973–1982." Federal Reserve Bank of San Francisco, *Economic Review.* (Fall): 26–35.

Kim, Sun-Young, and Raymond E. Lombra. 1989. "Why the Empirical Relationship Between Deficits and Interest Rates Appears So Fragile." *Journal of Economics and Business* 41, no. 3 (August): 241–251.

Kochin, Levis, A. 1974. "Are Future Taxes Anticipated by Consumers?" *Journal of Money, Credit and Banking* 6, no. 3 (August): 385–394.

Kolluri, Bharat R. and Demetrios S. Giannaros. 1987. "Budget Deficits and Short-Term Real Interest Rate Forecasting." *Journal of Macroeconomics* 9, no. 1 (Winter): 109–125.

Kormendi, Roger C. 1983. "Government Debt, Government Spending and Private Sector Behavior." *American Economic Review* 73, no. 5 (December): 994–1010.

Kormendi, Roger C. and Phillip Meguire. 1986. "Government Debt, Government Spending, and Private Sector Behavior: Reply." *American Economic Review* 76, no. 5 (December): 1180–1187.

Kudlow, Lawrence. 1981. Statement before the Senate Budget Committee (statistical appendix), October 20.

Leiderman, Leonardo and Mario Blejer. 1988. "Modeling and Testing Ricardian Equivalence: A Survey." *IMF Staff Papers* 35, no. 1 (March): 1–35.

Lucas, Robert E., Jr. 1976. "Economic Policy Evaluation: A Critique." In *The Phillips Curve and Labor Markets*, edited by Karl Brunner and Allen H. Meltzer, 19–46. Amsterdam: North-Holland.

Makin, John H. 1985. "The Effects of Government Deficits on Capital Formation." In *Essays in Contemporary Economic Problems: The Economy in Deficit*, edited by Phillip Cagan, 163–194. Washington: American Enterprise Institute.

―――――. 1983. "Real Interest, Money Surprises, Anticipated Inflation and Fiscal Deficits." *Review of Economics and Statistics* 65, no. 3 (August): 374–384.

Makin, John H. and Vito Tanzi. 1984. "Level and Volatility of U.S. Interest Rates: Roles of Expected Inflation, Real Rates and Taxes." In *Taxation, Inflation, and Interest Rates*, edited by Vito Tanzi, 110–142. Washington: International Monetary Fund.

Mascaro, Angelo and Allan H. Meltzer. 1983. "Long- and Short-Term Interest Rates in a Risky World." *Journal of Monetary Economics* 12, no. 4 (November): 485–518.

McCallum, Bennett T. 1984. "Are Bond-financed Deficits Inflationary? A Ricardian Analysis." *Journal of Political Economy* 92, no. 1 (February): 123–135.

McMillin, W. Douglas. 1986. "Federal Deficits and Short-term Interest Rates." *Journal of Macroeconomics* 8, no. 4 (Fall): 403–422.

Miller, Preston J. and William Roberds. 1989. "How Little We Know About Budget Policy Effects." Federal Reserve Bank of Atlanta. Working Paper no. 4 (May).

Miller, Preston J. 1983. "Examining the Proposition That Federal Budget Deficits Matter." In *The Economic Consequences of Government Deficits*, edited by Lawrence H. Meyer, 3–24. Boston: Kluwer-Nijhoff.

Miller, Stephen M., and Frank S. Russek. 1989. "International Evidence on the Trade, Saving, and Investment Effects of Government Deficits." Paper presented at the annual meetings of the Western Economic Association (June), Lake Tahoe, Nevada.

Miller, Stephen M. and Orawin T. Velz. 1989. "The Influence of Presidential Administrations on Monetary Policy." Department of Economics, University of Connecticut.

Mishel, Lawrence R. 1989. "The Late Great Debate on Deindustrialization." *Challenge* 31, (January/February): 35–43.

Motley, Brian. 1983. "Real Interest Rates, Money and Government Deficits." Federal Reserve Bank of San Francisco, *Economic Review* (Summer): 31–45.

Muller, Patrice and Robert Price. 1984. "Public Sector Indebtedness and Long-Term Interest Rates." Paper presented at the World Bank/

Brookings Institution Workshop on the International Consequences of Budgetary Deficits in the OECD, Washington, D.C., September.

Penner, Rudolph G. 1989. *Dealing with the Budget Deficit*. Washington, D.C.: National Planning Association.

Pesando, James E. 1979. "On the Random Walk Characteristics of Short- and Long-Term Interest Rates In an Efficient Market." *Journal of Money, Credit and Banking* 11, no. 4 (November): 457–466.

Plosser, Charles I. 1987. "Fiscal Policy and the Term Structure." *Journal of Monetary Economics* 20, no. 6 (September): 343–367.

————. 1982. "Government Financing Decisions and Asset Returns." *Journal of Monetary Economics* 9, no. 3 (May): 325–352.

Poterba, James M. and Lawrence H. Summers. 1987. "Recent U.S. Evidence on Budget Deficits and National Savings." Working Paper no. 2144, National Bureau of Economic Research (February).

Reid, Bradford G. 1985. "Aggregate Consumption and Deficit Financing: An Attempt to Separate Permanent From Transitory Effects." *Economic Inquiry* 23 (July): 475–487.

Roley, V. Vance. 1983. "Asset Substitutability and the Impact of Federal Deficits." In *The Economic Consequences of Government Deficits*, edited by Laurence H. Meyer, 85–115. Boston: Kluwer-Nijhoff.

Sargent, Thomas J. and Neil Wallace. 1981. "Some Unpleasant Monetarist Arithmetic." *Federal Reserve Bank of Minneapolis Quarterly Review* 5 (Fall): 1–17.

Shaw, G. K. 1987. "Macroeconomic Implications of Fiscal Deficits: An Expository Note." *Scottish Journal of Political Economy* 34, no. 2 (May): 192–198.

Seater, John J. and Roberto S. Mariano. 1985. "New Tests of the Life Cycle and Tax Discounting Hypotheses. *Journal of Monetary Economics* 15 (March): 195–215.

Seater, John J. 1985. "Does Government Debt Matter? A Review." *Journal of Monetary Economics* 16, no. 1 (July): 121–131.

Sinai, Allen and Peter Rathjens. 1983. "Deficits, Interest Rates, and the Economy." *Data Resources U.S. Review* (June): 1.27–1.41.

Spiro, Peter S. 1987. "The Elusive Effect of Fiscal Deficits on Interest Rates: Comment on Tanzi." *IMF Staff Papers* 34 (June): 400–403.

Stone, Charles F. and Isabel V. Sawhill. 1986. "Labor Market Implications of the Growing Internationalization of the U.S. Economy." National Commission for Employment Policy, Research Report Series no. RR-86-20 (June).

Summers, Lawrence H. 1986. "Issues in National Savings Policy." In *Savings and Captial Formation*, edited by F. Gerard Adams and Susan M. Wachter, 65–88. Lexington, Mass.: Lexington Books, D.C. Heath & Co.

Swamy, P.A.V.B., Bharat R. Kolluri and Rao N. Singamsetti. 1988. "What Do Regressions of Interest Rates on Deficits Imply?" Division of Research and Statistics, Board of Governors of the Federal Reserve System. Finance and Economics Discussion Series no. 3 (January).

Swamy, P.A.V.B., Roger K. Conway and Peter von zur Muehlen. 1984. "The Foundations of Econometrics—Are There Any?" Federal Reserve Board, Studies Paper no. 182 (February).

Tanner, Ernest J. 1979. "An Empirical Investigation of Tax Discounting." *Journal of Money, Credit and Banking* 11, no. 2 (May): 214–218.

Tanzi, Vito. 1987. "The Effect of Fiscal Deficits on Interest Rates: Reply to Spiro." *IMF Staff Papers* 34, no. 2 (June): 404–407.

——— . 1985a. "Fiscal Deficits and Interest Rates in the United States, an Empirical Analysis, 1960–1984." *IMF Staff Papers* 32, no. 4 (December): 551–576.

——— . 1985b. "The Deficit Experience in Industrial Countries." In *Essays in Contemporary Economic Problems: The Economy in Deficit*, edited by Phillip Cagan, 81–119. Washington, D.C.: American Enterprise Institute.

Tatom, John A. 1989. "U.S. Investment in the 1980s: The Real Story." Federal Reserve Bank of St. Louis. *Review* 71, no. 2 (March/April): 3–15.

——— . 1984. "A Perspective on the Federal Deficit Problem." Federal Reserve Bank of St. Louis. *Review* 66, no. 6 (June/July): 5–17.

Thomas, Lloyd B. Jr., and Ali Abderrezak. 1988a. "Anticipated Budget Deficits and the Term Structure of Interest Rates." *Southern Economic Journal* 55, no. 1 (July): 150–161.

——— . 1988b. "Long-Term Interest Rates: The Role of Expected Budget Deficits." *Public Finance Quarterly* 16, no. 3 (July): 341–356.

U.S. Treasury Department. 1984. *The Efffects of Deficits on Prices of Financial Assets: Theory and Evidence* (March). Washington, D.C.

Wachtel, Paul and John Young. 1987. "Deficit Announcements and Interest Rates." *American Economic Review* 77, no. 5 (December): 1007–1012.

Wilson, John F., James L. Freund, Frederick O. Yohn, Jr., and Walther Lederer. 1989. "Measuring Household Saving: Recent Experience from the Flow-of-Funds Perspective." In *The Measurement of Saving, Investment and Wealth*, edited by Robert E. Lipsey and Helen Stone Tice, 101–145. Chicago: University of Chicago Press.

Yawitz, Jess B., and Laurence H. Meyer. 1976. "An Empirical Investigation of the Extent of Tax Discounting." *Journal of Money, Credit and Banking* 8, no. 2 (May): 247–254.

Young, Allan H. 1989. "BEA's Measurement of Computer Output." *Survey of Current Business* (July): 108–115.

Zahid, Khan H. 1988. "Government Budget Deficits and Interest Rates: The Evidence Since 1971, Using Alternative Deficit Measures." *Southern Economic Journal* 54, no. 3 (January): 725–731.

COMMENTS ON "THE EFFECTS OF FEDERAL BUDGET DEFICITS ON INTEREST RATES AND THE COMPOSITION OF DOMESTIC OUTPUT"

John H. Makin

Barth et al. have taken on the daunting task of reviewing the literature on effects of federal budget deficits on interest rates, capital formation and the mix between traded and non-traded goods production. They have done an admirable job in assembling the relevant historical data and in providing us with a complete and evenhanded treatment of a large and growing body of literature on this topic.

For their considerable trouble, the authors are rewarded with the usual outcome that befalls an evenhanded effort to examine a controversial issue where measurement is difficult. They conclude that the hypothesis that deficits affect real interest rates cannot decisively be rejected. They add that in the absence of clear statistical results we should be cautious about the level of deficits.

I shall try to provide a few general perspectives to help the reader of Barth et al.'s excellent paper discern some threads from among the myriad of reported results. My emphasis is not inconsistent with that of the authors, but I shall be a little more opinionated. The authors would be well-served by selecting what they view as a "best" model, both to narrow the field of contenders and to suggest which investigations ought, a priori, to yield the most satisfactory empirical results.

A great deal of the literature on the effect of deficits on interest rates and other variables follows a conventional flow of funds framework that suggests a relationship between deficits that measure an addition to government debt and interest rates. The conventional view suggests that since the deficit adds to debt, a rise in real interest rates is required to clear the flow debt market, provided that some other variable does not shift the demand for debt.

In my view this paradigm is incorrect. Interest rates are determined by a stock equilibrium whereby the stock of debt in existence is willingly held at some equilibrium real interest rate. The desire to hold the stock of debt is conditional on the real interest rate plus some scale variable such as gross income, which in turn may or may not serve as a proxy for aggregate wealth, the true scale variable determining the desire to hold debt. Deficits may, under this view, be related to changes in interest rates, but not to the level of interest rates.

The inconsistency across numerous empirical investigations of the relationship between deficits measured in many ways and real interest rates is due to the unreliability of deficits as a proxy for debt or debt relative to GNP.

Another factor widely ignored, and likely to have been most significant during the 1980s, is the distribution of global wealth and changes in regulations governing capital flows among nations. The 1980s saw both a relaxation of controls on capital outflows, especially in Japan, and a remarkable increase in the total wealth of investors outside of the United States. By 1988 gross saving flows in industrial countries outside of the United States had reached approximately $1.5 trillion, or triple the same gross flows inside the United States. It has become clear during 1989, that such large wealth outside of the United States means that the dollar can appreciate substantially in the presence of a current account deficit. The reason is that the supply of dollars generated by the current account deficit is less than the demand for dollars generated by portfolio managers adding to or maintaining their dollar positions.

Based on my own research on deficits and interest rates, in which I committed many of the errors of omission and commission elucidated by Barth et al., I concluded that if deficits were large enough to cause an *acceleration* in the rise of the debt to GNP ratio, real interest rates would be positively affected. The rise would be due to the anticipation of higher real yields necessary to induce investors to hold a larger share of dollar denominated debt in their portfolios.

What now seems clear is that this notion needs to be modified for factors that include the increased integration of global capital markets, and the absolute size of wealth outside of the United States. While it may be true that an acceleration in the debt to GNP rise may be a necessary condition for higher real interest rates in the U.S., it may not be sufficient if the absolute growth of wealth outside of the U.S. is large enough and/or if the U.S. central bank is acting to restrain inflation as aggressively or more aggressively than other central banks.

Accurately defined, unexpected deficits proxy for unanticipated additions to debt, and may thereby produce transitional effects on real yields. Here again, the mixture of results concerning the effect of unanticipated deficits or unanticipated debt changes may be due to the many pitfalls involved in actually estimating "surprise" changes in deficits or debt.

The contradictory results of studies of deficits and debt and their impact on real interest rates notwithstanding, some policy conclusions may still be discerned from our unusual experience during the 1980s. First, during the 1984–85 period, when deficits were large and prospectively rising, and the private saving rate was on a negative trend, the prospective net addition to debt relative to the domestic capacity to absorb it probably did put upward pressure on real interest rates and, simultaneously, on the real dollar exchange rate. Since 1985, a sharp deceleration in the growth of federal spending and an attendant drop in the growth of debt relative to GNP probably has accounted for some reduction in real interest rates and an attendant fall in the real dollar exchange rate.

In 1989, with nominal deficits hovering around $150 billion or slightly below 3 percent of GNP, there is a tendency to forget the role of international factors. Even if the deficit as currently measured remained at $150 billion into the indefinite future, the debt to GNP ratio would gradually fall, suggesting that its effect on real interest rates would be absent or even negative. The actual path of real interest rates in the future depends on the growth of global wealth and on a comparison of risk-adjusted U.S. real interest rates with returns available elsewhere. So far in 1989, even with a current account deficit of $120–$130 billion, annually central banks have had to sell $50 billion worth of dollar reserves in order to contain the appreciation of the U.S. dollar to the 10 to 15 percent range on a trade-weighted basis. This reality has forced even the most skeptical analysts to conclude that the current budget and trade deficits are "sustainable." Those who continue to criticize budget deficits have been forced to question their "desirability" or to raise questions about the intergenerational effects of such deficits.

Against the background of this debate, it is probably worth noting that along with the federal budget deficit, the American current account deficit is falling steadily, from 3.7 percent in 1987 to around 2.0 percent in 1989. In this sense, the debate about budget deficits and external deficits has become one about the pace of adjustment, with critics suggesting that the pace is too slow while non-critics suggest that in the face of evidence given by real interest rates and exchange rates, the pace is adequate.

Whatever the outcome of the great deficit debate, it can surely be said that the events of the 1980s, unusual as they were by peacetime standards, have generated enough theoretical and empirical research to have added to our knowledge about the effect of accumulation of government debt in a world of integrated capital markets. Future researchers who wish to review the evidence will be well-served by the efforts of Messrs. Barth et al.

COMMENTS ON "THE EFFECTS OF FEDERAL BUDGET DEFICITS ON INTEREST RATES AND THE COMPOSITION OF DOMESTIC OUTPUT"

Frank de Leeuw

Back when the Congressional Budget Office was about two years old, an enterprising staffer designed a CBO T-shirt. It had a picture of two hands, one with the thumb pointing up and the other with the thumb pointing down. Above the picture appeared the words, "On the one hand . . . "; below, " . . . on the other." The staff loved it, and bought up the initial supply right away. Perhaps it is still in production.

Whether or not the T-shirt still exists, its message lives on in this paper. A tabulation of 42 studies that bear on the deficit-interest rate link classifies 17 as finding "significant, positive effects," 19 as finding "predominantly insignificant or negative effects," and 6 as obtaining "mixed results." The authors conclude that "one cannot say with complete confidence that budget deficits raise interest rates and reduce saving and capital formation; but—equally important—one cannot say that they do not have these effects."

I hasten to add that I do not criticize the authors for these "on-the-one and-on-the-other" statements. This able study simply reflects a stubborn deadlock among economists on these important issues. The deadlock persists, as the authors note, even though policymakers now seem to agree that reducing the deficit is an important goal.

What I will try to do in these comments is to ask, *are there any promising leads that might loosen the deadlock?* The first section of the comments looks at the results reported in the paper from this perspective, finding some useful contributions. The second section argues that one promising way to help break the deadlock is to recognize that the competing theories are not as rigid, and therefore not as incompatible, as many seem to believe. Both the "conventional view" and the "Ricardian equivalence view" (to use the terms adopted by the authors) have already undergone important changes. The changes so far have not brought the two views closer together, but a further change, proposed at the end of the comments, would do so.

The Paper's Contributions

The authors of this paper review dozens of studies containing literally hundreds of individual findings, and add to these a battery of their own tests. It is useful to try to single out ways in which all this material may contribute to breaking the deadlock between opposing views about federal deficits.

One of the most valuable contributions of the paper is its challenging of two extreme findings. The first is Paul Evans' finding that in time series for the United States there is a significant *negative* relation between deficits and long-term interest rates, rather than the positive relation that advocates of the conventional view expect. The paper shows that this result is highly sensitive to the measure of the deficit that Evans uses. His measure—the change in the market value of federal debt—rises when interest rates fall and falls when interest rates rise, because of the automatic link between interest rates and bond prices. But this built-in negative relation has no bearing on how a legislated change in federal spending or taxes affects interest rates.

The authors show that measuring the deficit as the change in par value rather than of market value, in order to eliminate the automatic bond-price effect, transforms Evans' results. In fact, that change, plus the addition of a short-term rate to the list of explanatory variables, produces a significant positive relation between deficits and long-term rates, contrary to Evans' negative one. The rationale for adding a short-term rate, however, is less clear to me than the rationale for avoiding the use of market values.

The second finding that the paper challenges is Eisner's finding, based on annual U.S. time series from 1961 through 1984, that the price-adjusted, cycle-adjusted federal deficit has a significant positive effect on the change in investment (both the deficit and investment change are measured as a percentage of GNP). Since this result is not confined to periods of depression (where many economists—myself included—would expect to find it), the finding runs counter to a central conclusion of the "conventional view." The authors of the paper show that simply adding the four years 1985 through 1988 to the sample period reduces Eisner's coefficient to less than one-fifth of the value he reported, and eliminates its statistical significance.

In addition to challenging extreme findings, the authors contribute to loosening the deadlock by discovering patterns in the choice of variables, methodology, and other aspects of various studies that are related to differences in results. They report that a positive deficit-interest rate link is more likely in studies that:

☐ Use a structural or cyclically adjusted measure of the deficit;
☐ Use a measure of federal debt rather than a measure of the deficit;
☐ Attempt to measure expected future deficits rather than actual current deficits;
☐ Attempt to measure unexpected current deficits rather than actual current deficits; and
☐ Use a long-term rather than a short-term interest rate as the dependent variable.

The findings about expected future and unexpected current deficits suggest to me that the *permanence* of a deficit has an important bearing on its impacts. I will return to this possibility at the end of these comments. For now, I will simply point out that the very fact that the choice of variables and methodology ranges so widely among the studies suggests that the two views are flexible rather than unalterable visions—the theme of the next section of these comments.

Theories in Motion

Contrary to the impression that many authors—including, in places, the authors of this study—convey, both the conventional view and the Ricardian equivalence view have been evolving in response to the analysis of past data and the unfolding events of the last decade. The fact that both views are evolving offers at least the possibility that they may move closer together.

The conventional view has undergone at least three major modifications. In the early versions of that view, growing actual federal deficits crowd out investment. In more recent statements:

☐ *Expected* federal deficits are important, perhaps more important than actual deficits;
☐ *Net exports* as well as investment are crowded out, and a growing fraction of the returns to investment go to foreign residents; and
☐ In at least some versions of the conventional view, it is *federal debt* rather than federal deficits that affect future levels of income.

A representative "conventional view" now, in contrast to a decade ago, might be that expectations of a rising ratio of federal debt to GNP in a large economy raise interest rates, and reduce some combination of domestic capital and net international assets. These changes in the conventional view are a response—a sensible response, it seems to me—to events after 1981 and to a sifting of the evidence both before and after 1981.

For the Ricardian equivalence view, the behavior of interest rates when federal deficits rise is not a very powerful test. A finding that interest rates do *not* change can be explained by theories other than Ricardian equivalence—for example, as the paper points out, by highly mobile international capital markets. A more powerful test of the Ricardian equivalence view is the behavior of private saving in response to a fall in public saving.

The fact that U.S. private saving as a percent of GNP, according to current estimates, fell rather than rose in the 1980s thus presents a challenge to advocates of the Ricardian equivalence view. Not surprisingly, advocates of that view have responded by adding a new element to the view—capital gains—that improves its explanatory power. The amended view is that rising stock prices and real estate prices limit the amounts that households feel they need to save out of current income, and therefore may interfere with the offset between public saving and private saving. Alternatively, private saving can be redefined to include capital gains, but then national saving is no longer equal to the investment that adds to the future flow of capital services.

The evolution of the two theories has not yet brought them much closer, but is a hopeful sign because it indicates they are not as rigid as we have been led to believe.

There is a modification of the Ricardian equivalence view that would bring the two views closer together and *would* make the Ricardian view much more plausible to me. I am not aware that this modification has been proposed or tested, so let me conclude these comments by proposing it.

The modification I propose is that the *more temporary* a change in public saving is perceived to be, the more likely it is that a change in private saving will offset it. A clearly temporary change, such as postponing for one month the date a tax payment is due, will have minimal effects on household consumption plans or business investment plans, and hence will be almost totally offset by changes in private saving. Wartime deficits, when the war and the economic conditions that accompany it (including public borrowing) are expected to end in a few years, might similarly lead to relatively mino changes in consumption plans and hence might fit the Ricardian equivalent model reasonably well.

In contrast, a succession of deficits of long and uncertain duration—the situation in the 1980s—is much more puzzling to interpret. There is no expected future day of reckoning to make households cautious about their consumption plans. It is therefore less likely that private saving will offset changes in public saving in this case.

A reinterpretation of the Ricardian equivalence view incorporating this feature would bring it closer to the conventional view and would, in my view, also make it more plausible.

Part Three

TAXES: A LICENSE TO SPEND OR A LATE CHARGE?

TAXES: A LICENSE TO SPEND OR A LATE CHARGE?

George M. von Furstenberg

Writings like this in political economy are not value-neutral. For this reason the reader should be forewarned about how the author approaches the subject and what concerns he would like to share.

The writer views himself as a fiscal conservative, one who believes that the struggle against overextension of government spending and of its regulations, obligations, and promises should continue. Because collective decisionmaking and bureaucratic implementation do not have efficiency at heart, and because the government tends to save at the wrong place, it is difficult to isolate waste for surgical removal. Inefficiency in government can only be fought indirectly and across a broad spectrum, by putting intense pressure on all types of spending and turning up the searchlights in hopes of increasing the political sense of shame.

Moreover, the incentives to overspend, implied by the easy recourse to debt financing, must be eliminated. The healthy discipline that requires the demonstration of political ability and willingness to pay before approving any government spending project has been undermined by the experience of public debt piling up without apparent economic strain or political backlash.

Although both major political parties continue to borrow the rhetoric of fiscal conservatism, their actions belie their words. Cast out into the political wilderness, fiscal conservatives have to talk softly and appear conciliatory. To convince their fellows, they have to rely on arguments based more on reason than ideology. If pressed, they are willing to admit that the greater the government's efficiency for the public, the larger it should be from the demand side; the more valued its services at the margin, the more it should give. On the other hand, in securing these services, the larger government's size in the economy and the more distortive its taxes, the less efficient government tends to be. Since from the supply side the location of these upwards-sloping "demand" and downward-sloping "supply" schedules is uncertain, so is the point at which the two schedules intersect. Thus, the optimal size of government is always debatable, and is dependent on anything affecting the public's valuation of its services or the costs of securing them.

Fiscal conservatives are prepared to admit the above in principle, though not in politics. They presume, correctly I think, that the current actual and planned levels of government spending are too high in the aggregate. These levels would appear excessive to them even if the efficiency of government-organized supply were not artificially depressed through government-sector wage freezes at below-market levels and by the costly erosion of prudential and fiduciary standards. The question this paper addresses is whether and how a reduction in the relative size of public spending could be assisted by restoring the principle of "pay as you go," used in a particular sense that is defined later.

The paper is organized as follows: after discussing the harmful attractions of spending without taxes, we take up the intertemporal government budget constraint, whose harsh reality implies that current deficits inevitably raise future taxes. The paper points out that present tax cuts not earned or validated by spending cuts not only force a tax rise later on, they also raise the average level of taxation that must be imposed on any tax-sensitive base over the long term. The paper discusses Italy as a country that so far has failed to face up to the fiscal realities closing in on it, while it cites the United Kingdom as a country that reformed its budget practices in good time, and describes how this was accomplished. Whether our federal government will be continuously mired in budget crises or whether it can make a more prudent contribution to national priorities is now being decided.

THE POLITICS OF SPENDING WITHOUT TAXES

How could any politician justify the pain of higher taxes except by pointing to the potential benefits of increased government spending? Yet tax hikes strike a terror all their own, as if they had nothing or nothing good to do with the other side of the budget.

Disjuncture between the two sides makes tax increases a frightening story that keeps being retold in more or less entertaining ways. In the 1911 play *Kismet*, whose later musical version, *Kismet: A Musical Arabian Night*, has been especially popular, an innovative but starving poet, begging outside the main mosque of Baghdad, tries

out new fund-raising techniques by threatening to lay curses on those
who refuse to give. At first nothing seems to work. Curses like "May
your wives sleep with every chimney sweep in Baghdad" produce
incredulous laughter but no offerings. Then the clever beggar-poet
hits upon a curse, the faintest hint of which brings on a propitiatory
shower of coins. It is: "May your taxes be raised."

Perhaps such popular disjuncture between the two sides of the
budget is understandable in despotic societies where the rulers'
spending is financed by the taxes of the oppressed without much
common good. However, our own officials occasionally have used
the same ploy as the Syrian beggar-poet. President Bush, for instance,
keeps trying to seed the clouds and make them rain Republican votes
when he invokes the spectre of "those liberal Democrats who cherish
new taxes, like moths drawn to some kind of candle" (Hoffman 1989).

While one gets burned for raising taxes, cutting taxes is always
sweet, though perhaps bad for the teeth. If deficits are to be left
unchanged, tax cuts for "us" must mean tax increases or spending
cuts for "them." Politically, redirecting spending priorities and
increasing deficits, but only for "us," has proved much easier to
do. Then "we" can have lower taxes *and* increase "our" type of
spending, while "they" have lower taxes and less of "their" type
of spending, or no change in either present taxes or spending if
they prefer. Either way the outcome seems to be politically great
for "us" here and now and tolerable for "them"—a winning combination.

So who in government could possibly find profit in threatening
to impose higher taxes unless, like President Bush and the beggar-
poet in the story, they are trying to sell *stays* for this curse? Yet
the thesis of this paper is that, for safe passage of the ship of state,
the threat of higher taxes should be hung not just on others, like
tar and feather, but be resurrected by those in a position to carry
it out. Through a compact between the parties and a common
commitment of will that no legislation can coerce, this threat must
be made credible. An end must be put to the belief that higher
taxes are always avoidable, rather than the price that must eventually be paid for higher government expenditures, and to the
belief that taxes can be reduced without ever cutting public spending. Once voters become convinced that not only their children,
but they themselves (if they expect to live a good while longer)
are being had, they may yet get nasty with the purveyors of habitual
outsized deficit spending.

THE GOVERNMENT BUDGET CONSTRAINT,
NOW AND FOREVER

The decade of the 1980s will be noted in economic history for its concerted efforts to curtail the growth of government and to lower tax rates in several major countries (Pechman 1988; Lee and McKenzie 1989). In the United States this effort experienced more success with lowering taxes than with restraining government spending, with the difference put on the cuff. Carlson (1989) has calculated that relative to the 1981 Reagan budget plan, which called for a budget very close to balance by 1986, in 1986 total receipts were overestimated by about $170 billion, while total outlays were underestimated by about $30 billion. Carlson's further examination of outlays revealed a roughly $70 billion error in the projection of net interest paid on the public debt. The error was largely offset, however, because the actual defense buildup fell below projections by 1986. Other sympathetic observers, like Boskin (1987, 264), have reached the comparable conclusion that "*relative to the level of government spending and tax revenue projected prior to the Reagan program,* tax cuts were the major source of the deficit."[1] Figure 3.1 summarizes the fiscal outcomes for the past decade.

For perspective, the average aggregate tax rate (defined as the total receipts of the federal government on a national-income-and-product-accounts basis divided by GNP) fell from a peak of 20.9 percent in 1981 to a low of 19.2 percent in 1984 before starting to creep up again. This rate had been 19.6 percent in 1978, before the surge of inflation around the start of the 1980s. Hence the initial rate reductions enacted in 1981 (Stockman 1986, 268), which were partly offset by subsequent rate increases (Stein 1989b), on balance can be viewed as having provided little more than inflation adjustment before indexation took over.

Even so, the good economic growth and contentment of 1983–89 helped sell the notion that you can both lower taxes and maintain levels of government spending forever. As a result, deficit financing has become respectable for all seasons, not just when resources are substantially underutilized because the economy is in a slump.

Stretching yourself *ad infinitum* into the future you would find that in the end you always have to pay for what you get. In that remote land, which economists treat under the code name "Ricardian equivalence," deficit financing would have the same economic effects as tax financing, since private saving would immediately offset

Figure 3.1. FISCAL HISTORY OF THE UNITED STATES FEDERAL GOVERNMENT, 1979–1989

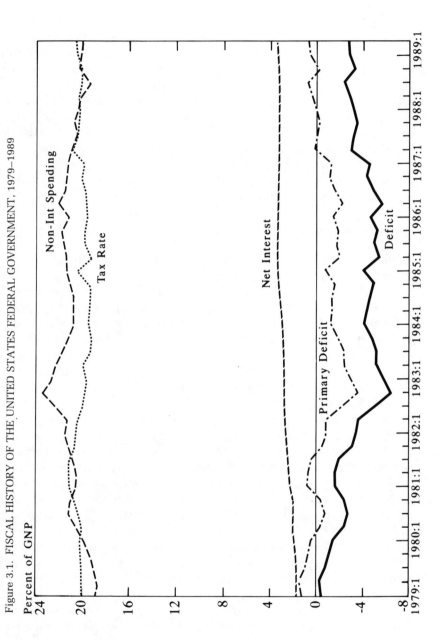

any change in public (dis)saving. With transfer payments treated as negative taxes, and with important but second-order microeconomic incentive effects of the fiscal system[2] set aside, the size of government purchases alone would matter for the allocation of output to its different uses. As one form of financing would be known to lead to the other, the distribution of economic effects over time would be the same either way. Leiderman and Blejer (1988) and Barro (1989) have provided alternative surveys of "Ricardian equivalence" and two different readings of the evidence for it.

Rather than incant code words and leave it at that, sadly, like accountants, we must at this point try to be precise.

Present-Value Reckoning

Doing present-value calculations with, say, annual flows over an infinite horizon, there simply is no way to avoid paying a sum of discounted taxes that is equal to the national debt plus the sum of discounted annual flows of government spending on everything other than interest on the national debt, if that debt is not to be abrogated. Hence, the infinite time machine that spins out the intertemporal government budget constraint makes it impossible to cut the present value of taxes, or to raise it, without doing likewise to noninterest government expenditures.[3] The reason, however, is not that tax changes prompt such expenditures to move in the same direction, but rather the reverse. It is that the expected present-value sum of taxes, from here to infinity, regardless of what is done to taxes now, is tied to the present-value sum of government noninterest spending and cannot change without it if the government's credit is to be preserved.

A little bit of algebra is useful to demonstrate the point. This will first be done without taking account of economic growth, although the point applies quite generally. During the 1980s, U.S. government debt held by the public, expressed in percent of annualized third-quarter GNP, increased by two-thirds from 25 percent at the end of FY 1979 to 42 percent 10 years later. Exaggerating a bit, let us assume that the ratio of such debt to GNP doubled, to show in the simplest way possible that any such event could not have affected the present value of future taxes, as long as government noninterest spending was not expected to change. Consider, therefore, two fiscal programs, one in which government debt is kept at its starting level of D (the *base* program) and one in which it is allowed to double to $2D$ in the first period and is then maintained at that level forever after (the *alternative* program). Compared with the base program, taxes are at first reduced by the amount D in the alternative program. But once the deficit and hence government debt have increased by that amount, from the end of the first period on, more interest must be paid in the alternative program. That then requires higher taxes if the debt is to be kept at $2D$. The present value of those added taxes, equal to rD per period starting in the second period, all discounted to the first period, is exactly equal to D if the real interest rate on government debt, r, is also used as the discount rate. Hence there is no net change in the present value of expected future tax liabilities altogether: D less in the first period is matched by D more in present value from higher taxes spread out over all time beyond.

It appears, therefore, that as long as government noninterest spending is not changed, taxes can only be redistributed over time. Their present value cannot possibly be changed under the previous assumptions if the government debt is to be stabilized at any level. Hence, as long as the "no default" requirement is met, government noninterest spending would seem to be the only side of the budget that matters. From the point of view of the intertemporal government budget constraint with infinite horizon, there simply is no other independent macroeconomic fiscal variable that can be manipulated. In particular, whether current government spending is financed by borrowing or taxes is a distinction without a difference: in the end without end, it all gets paid in full. Knowing that, everybody enters in his or her memory bank a liability for future taxes that is just as large and burdensome as any taxes would be that need not currently be paid. Or do they?

Charge It to Posterity

If things were just as described, nobody could seriously believe that borrowing, rather than paying cash, could make you richer. However, if someone else may have to repay or will no longer stand to inherit what you borrow, and you do not mind passing the tab, having such borrowing opportunities more widely available is leading you into temptation. One should not blind oneself to the fact that such borrowing opportunities can damage efficiency. As James Buchanan and Richard Wagner (1978) and William Niskanen (1978) have warned for some time, deficit financing can reduce voters' perceptions of the cost of government programs and thereby puff up government spending.

The Buchanan/Wagner hypothesis, that deficit financing can abet government noninterest spending, is based on an "honest" misperception among citizens. Voters confuse the present tax price with the actual resource cost of government spending, and demand more spending when the tax price is set below the economic cost of providing government services. Because of this error of inference, government spending will be bloated and additional taxes[4] will be laid in store for the future, as deficits balloon until political and capital-market revulsion sets in. But all these troubles for the future are made unintentionally.

Such innocence does not characterize all of those who seek to profit from below-cost financing of government spending in their time. Over short horizons, there are ways to profit from fiscal deficits other than through increased government spending. For some, lower taxes will raise *private* spending, leaving a worse balance sheet for posterity than if the full tax price had currently been exacted.

To keep from insulting anyone else, let me tell a story about the typical present day middle-aged American male, a fellow very much like myself except that, of course, no one is typical. This fellow, who is partial to bad puns, thinks that infinity is not all there is. He is divorced, with three more-or-less grown children (he has forgotten their birth dates) from two previous marriages. He has a well-paying but not really engaging job, and an empty social life. He is "rationally mean" so to speak, first cousin of *homo oeconomicus*. He welcomes any reasonable opportunity to exploit any mark he can find, preferably members of some younger generation or generations to come who tend to be quite defenseless. In the language of Cukierman and Meltzer (1989), he is (negative) bequest-constrained—legally prevented from obliging future generations to pay his debts or to pay him back. In fact, however, he would welcome a chance to get his alimony back from his children if a way could be found.

Just such an opportunity may present itself when the government cuts individual income taxes. A reduction by one-quarter would be worth around $100 billion at the present time. For the typical American male who is one of about 100 million units currently filing income taxes, the saving would be $1,000. That is also what, on his behalf so to speak, would be added to the national debt.[5]

Let's now assume two things: 1. the man of sour disposition rationally expects to live another 30 years; 2. fiscal policy was arranged prior to the tax cut so as to keep the ratio of government debt to GNP unchanged. If the government then forces the man to do his bit to get the ratio back down to where it would have remained otherwise during his lifetime, and the real interest rate is 4 percent, he would be paying $57.83 "real" dollars for 30 years—the level inflation-adjusted payment that would be necessary to retire a debt of $1,000 at the assumed real interest rate. To determine how many nominal dollars of the kind one can actually touch that would come to be in any future year, he would multiply $57.83 by a cost of living index that starts out at 1 in the year of the tax cut ($t = 0$). If inflation is 6 percent the next year, the value of the index would be 1.06 and the next annual payment would be $61.30, and so on. Our mean fellow would still have to be required to buy life insurance that would pay off the balance of the $1,000 should he die before 30 years are up. Assuming the actuarial facts of life and death are such that a 12 percent surcharge would cover the mortality risk, he would therefore be paying $64.77 per year, multiplied by the appropriate index value, for at most 30 years.[6] If he knows nothing more about his mortality risk than his insurance company, letting him borrow at 4 percent real interest plus insurance cover would be doing him no favor at all, unless, of course, he would have to pay more than 4 percent real interest if he borrowed privately, or if he is such a poor credit risk that he could not borrow at all but would like to do so.

Now consider how much less he would have to pay if the government were more indulgent. Assume that the government wanted to commit its citizens to keep the debt-to-GNP ratio stable at the level reached just after adding $100 billion to the debt, and not to return to the status quo ante in their lifetime. This (one-time?) self-indulgence would follow the pattern of the *alternative* program described earlier. In the absence of any growth in real GNP, 40.00 rather than 57.83 "real" dollars would have to be paid for 30 years, now that the doubling of the debt no longer needs to be reversed during the individual's expected lifetime. This implies a saving of almost one-third.

Twice as much can realistically be saved under the *alternative* program if economic growth is also taken into account, and even more of the interest on the debt increment can be shifted to future generations by letting it grow. If real GNP is expected to increase at an average annual rate of 2.5 percent, the same rate as actually observed over the 10 years ending with the latest quarter (the third quarter of 1989), then all the sour fellow would have to pay is the difference between 4 percent and 2.5 percent on the growing debt. Since the debt starts at $1,000, that comes to $15.00, but this amount must grow each year with the real growth rate of 2.5 percent.[7] Even so, the present real (i.e., constant-dollar) value of this stream of payments is just $353 in relation to the current addition to the debt of $1,000. Since the life insurance premium added to the annual charges only insures that a sum actuarially valued at $353 does, in fact, get paid on average, this is the amount now typically collected from the selfish individual on $1,000. Thus, during his lifetime he can keep almost two-thirds of the initial tax reduction, if he is so disposed.

You and I know that this fellow will vote for a tax cut anytime, and if his vote carries, raise his lifetime income, and increase his personal consumption, which is the point of it all. So who says you cannot cut taxes without curbing government spending? Here is a case of a present tax cut increasing (private) spending and reducing national saving. So, for the common class of selfish brutes, the fact that there is no such thing as a truly *permanent* tax cut without cutting government spending may be beside the point.

DEFICITS AND TAXES

So far we have had to acknowledge that tax cuts without spending cuts cannot last forever, and that increases in the present-value sum of noninterest spending must eventually be covered by matching tax hikes. Hence, anything that raises fiscal deficits now—be it a tax cut or increase in government expenditures—will force up taxes tomorrow or the day after.

A little elaboration is needed to clarify this assertion. We assume that the tax bases now in use are not so sensitive to taxes, and marginal tax rates have not been kept so high that lowering tax rates would stand a good chance of increasing the present value of future tax revenues. Rather, we take it for granted that if such attractive possibilities ever existed, they were fully exploited.[8] Thus no easy choices remain.

Turning to the hard choices, we have already seen that credible constraints against recurring growth of government debt in relation to GNP are what rein in a government budget. These constraints will be viewed as softer the longer they are violated overtly or through "off-budget" devices that pretend that the taxpayers' obligation to service all public and publicly guaranteed debt can somehow be augmented without first recognizing the deficits that make net debt grow. Hence, if government noninterest spending proves politically impossible to constrain, tax increases are the only resort left to ensure the soundness of the government's credit. Deficits that lead to seemingly unstoppable increases in the ratio of government debt to GNP under current tax policies will then force a change in those policies.

The result, in short, is that deficits raise (future) taxes, with the above conditions in mind.

The Intertemporal Federal Budget Constraint

In its simplest form, the government budget constraint is:

$$T(t) = G(t) + rD(t-1) - [D(t) - D(t-1)], \qquad (1)$$

where tax (and nontax) receipts, T, in period t are linked to noninterest government spending, $G(t)$, and interest. In the formula above, interest paid in period t is taken to be paid at the annual rate r on the stock of debt outstanding at the end of the previous year, $D(t-1)$. To the extent that the sum of the two spending components exceeds the receipts total, there will be a deficit signed by the change it produces in the course of the current year in the face value of government debt outstanding, $D(t) - D(t-1)$.

A caution must be added here about the need to be consistent in the definition of the interest rate and the deficit. If r is defined as the (ex post) real interest rate, $D(t-1)$, would have to be expressed in current, i.e., t-period prices above. In that case, an amount equal to the product of the inflation rate in year t and the nominal debt outstanding at the end of the previous year $t-1$ would be eliminated from the deficit. The remaining deficit would then relate to the change not in the nominal, but in the real value of government debt measured in current dollars (for more complete discussions see Tanzi et al. 1987; Dewald 1988). Either way, one could require identity (1) to be satisfied with the last, bracketed term set to zero if constraints are in place that keep the real or nominal value of the national debt from rising absolutely, as a balanced-budget amendment might seek to do.

If, instead, the debt is to be kept equal to a fixed percentage of cycle-average GNP, and real GNP grows at n percent a year on average, then the identity can more suitably be written:

$$z = g + (r-n)k(-1) - dk, \qquad (2)$$

where z = T/GNP, g = G/GNP, k = D/GNP, $k(-1)$ = k one period earlier, and dk = (d/dt)k = the change in k over one period. The formula appears to have the beguiling implication that, as long as the real interest rate on government debt (r) is below the growth rate of the economy (n) so that $r-n$ is negative as it was for much of the 1970s, the tax rate, z, can be lower the higher the preceding ratio of government debt to GNP, $k(-1)$, given g. However, if politicians try to capitalize on this "debt dividend" by temporarily cutting taxes or raising spending so that k rises, they will soon find that their plans to lower z by raising k are frustrated because r is driven up and n falls until increased taxes are required to stabilize k at the higher level.[9]

In the 1980s, r generally exceeded n, frequently by 1 percentage point or more, so that $(r-n)$ is now clearly positive. Holding the ratio of national debt to GNP constant at its end of FY 1989 value of 0.42, so that k is 0.42 and dk is 0, we can determine the value of the average aggregate federal tax share, z, that would satisfy the equation above for a government noninterest spending share, g, of 0.1988, r of 0.04 and n of 0.025. The answer is 0.2051, which compares with an actual first quarter 1989 tax share, z, of 0.2027 on the national income accounts basis. Given a GNP of around $5 trillion, it appears that at the time of writing we were a mere $12 billion away from stabilizing the ratio of government debt to GNP. Two or three thousandths of GNP would not seem to be worth getting excited about among grown boys.

Unfortunately, if this is the best that can be done at a time of peace and prosperity, it is unlikely to be the happy end of the matter. If a seasonal laborer in his peak earnings season comes within striking distance of not having his debts grow faster than his income, he is still in trouble. His banker in Alaska, who is used to looking beyond one happy season, would shudder. There is a lesson here. A recession like that of 1982 would raise government spending by an amount probably no greater than 1 percent of cycle-average GNP, but it would reduce the tax percentage by at least 2 percentage points from its 1989 level, assuming 1989 is cyclically comparable to the peak year 1979. Instead of having a $12 billion problem, there would be an additional $150 to $160 billion of expected fiscal deficit[10] over the amount currently compatible with keeping k unchanged. The latter amount is equal to the growth rate of cycle-average nominal GNP (2.5 percent plus the rate of inflation) multiplied by federal debt held by the public that recently stood officially at $2.2 trillion. With inflation of 3.5 percent, for instance, a deficit of up to $134 billion would be sustainable by this standard, compared with the nearly $300 billion to which the federal deficit might rise in 1989 magnitudes if there is a recurrence of anything like the recession of 1982. Therefore, balancing the budget in any conventional sense is not what this conjecture is about.[11]

Of course, neither the best nor the worst of times should underlie policy planning for the intermediate run. Furthermore, it can be argued that the ratio of federal government debt to GNP is still so low in the United States that the 1990s could be fiscally as unbalanced as the 1980s and still not raise a formidable threat to the government's credit. Others might trust the temporarily hyperventilating social security tax pump to absorb the red ink in the rest of the federal budget. This could help mask the growing problem of fiscal sustainability[12] for at least another generation. Surely people like me, who do not remember the ages of their children, care less about their grandchildren. The worries of their political representatives, who would not dare shame them, are even more confined to the here and now. So who is to worry?

A Lesson from Rome

Perhaps the Italians will worry. After all, it is easier to see the speck in the eye of another if it is a thorn. In Italy, at over a quadrillion lire, the stock of government debt is now about flush with the Gross National Product (Banca d'Italia 1989). Italians, like most foreigners, prefer to refer to the Gross Domestic Product, GDP, rather than GNP, but we will not bother with the difference. Hence k would be measured as 1 for our purposes at yearend 1988. Italy's fiscal deficit since then has been running at about 11 percent of GNP. Nominal interest payments on the debt of the Italian state sector are only 8 percent of GNP even though the inflation rate was close to 7 percent until recently.

However, the very low ex post average real interest rate, that is still depressed by some of the low-rate issues placed with banks or pension funds once subject to secondary reserve requirements, is bound to go up. Interest rates on new (mostly variable-rate) issues have ceased to be supported by such requirements, and the central bank has been relieved from the statutory requirement to act as residual buyer of public debt since its 1981 "divorce" from the Treasury. Furthermore, Italian economists have raised the possibility that the risk premium, which appears to have materialized on Italian government debt since the removal of most capital controls in 1988, could rise further after the liberalization of financial markets in much of Western Europe by the middle of 1990.

Since most of the Italian government's debt is very short-term, it may be appropriate to look at the three-month Eurolire deposit interest rate to gauge the prospective free-market cost of funds. On August 1, 1989, that rate was 12.25 percent. Hence, assuming that interest on a public debt equal to GNP before long will amount to about 12 percent of GNP, rather than the 8 percent mentioned before, the added interest payments would boost the ratio of the fiscal deficit to GNP from 11 percent to 15 percent, ceteris paribus. With an average annual growth rate of real GNP of just under 3 percent and with 7 percent prospective inflation, two-thirds of this 15 percent deficit could be financed by increased borrowing without raising k.

The remainder, a deficit equal to about 5 percent of GNP, would have to be eliminated right away if the ratio of government debt to GNP should be kept from rising any further. However, it is difficult to see how any country could muster the political will to make such an enormous adjustment in one step, Italy being no exception. In addition, within any political system there is strong resistance to raising tax rates beyond some level purely for the sake of reining in an unsustainable deficit without providing any other benefits. Although the precise level at which voters will balk cannot be known beforehand, an average fiscal tax rate of 35 percent may represent an illustratively useful limit on what Italians will tolerate under the existing system before resorting to increased monetization and inflation. We here ignore any commitments to greater price stability that may arise from Italy's accession to the tight exchange rate mechanism of the European Monetary System.

Assume, therefore, that the most that can be achieved in any year is a partial fiscal correction equal to 0.5 percent of GNP. For comparison, that would be about $26 billion in the United States, which is far more than the average annual correction in the cyclically adjusted budget deficit so far achieved under Gramm-Rudman.[13] Hence holding the share of noninterest Italian government (current and capital) spending, g, at 0.315 of GNP and the real interest rate ($r = 5\%$) net of the real economic growth rate ($n = 3\%$) at 0.02, the aggregate tax share, z, can rise from its current level of 0.285 to 0.290, 0.295, etc. in successive years. This process can go on until z reaches (i), the maximum politically tolerable level assumed to be 35 percent, or (ii), the value compatible with no further growth in the ratio of government debt to GNP ($dk = 0$), whichever is smaller. Unfortunately, that second value, which would be 0.335 (i.e., 0.315 + 0.02) if z could be raised to that level immediately, keeps sliding up as k keeps growing during the phase of adjustment.

Details can readily be calculated using identity (2) to solve for dk. The entire adjustment process is laid out in table 3.1. It will take until the year 2000 or 2001 to stabilize k under the assumed conditions. By that time, k will have risen from its yearend 1988 value of 1 by almost one-third. As a result, z comes perilously close to its assumed political maximum of 35 percent before the fiscal correction is completed. Indeed, should the debt to GNP ratio, k, ever exceed a certain trajectory, which with maximum feasible growth in z leads k to 1.75 at the time the cap on z has been reached, the government's

Table 3.1. A FISCAL CORRECTION PROCESS OF ITALIAN MAGNITUDE

Year	z	g	k(−1)	(r−n)k(−1)	dk
1989	0.285	0.315	1.0	0.02	0.05
1990	0.290	0.315	1.05	0.021	0.046
1991	0.295	0.315	1.096	0.0219	0.0419
1992	0.300	0.315	1.1379	0.0228	0.0378
1993	0.305	0.315	1.1757	0.0235	0.0335
1994	0.310	0.315	1.2092	0.0242	0.0292
1995	0.315	0.315	1.2384	0.0248	0.0248
1996	0.320	0.315	1.2632	0.0253	0.0203
1997	0.325	0.315	1.2835	0.0257	0.0157
1998	0.330	0.315	1.2992	0.0260	0.0110
1999	0.335	0.315	1.3102	0.0262	0.0062
2000	0.340	0.315	1.3164	0.0263	0.0013
2001	0.345	0.315	1.3177	0.0264	−0.0036

financial condition would become unsustainable. In that event, the budget situation would have entered the region where k could no longer be stabilized with the means assumed.

Confronted with such a cliffhanger, according to this illustration financial markets could well become nervous in the course of the present decade and demand an even higher real interest rate than the 5 percent assumed here. This would make the achievement of fiscal stability even more difficult in Italy.[14]

Are there any lessons here for the United States? In my view, one should take care never to get close to such a situation and the onerous conditions for adjustment it imposes. In the process just portrayed, the effect of past and present deficits has been to raise the aggregate tax rate from 28.5 percent to between 34 percent and 34.5 percent of GNP permanently, even though government noninterest spending commands only 31.5 percent of GNP. This truly has been a case of deficits raising taxes. In addition, tax rates have been made uneven over time, and we will show below that this implies welfare costs over and above those associated with permanently higher future tax rates.

WHY RAISE TAXES?

The normal motivation and political incentive for tax increases is to finance a rise in government spending currently contemplated, and not to pay for prior spending or to reduce government debt or deficits. If anything resembling a rule of balancing the budget under assumed conditions of high employment is respected, as it was in the United States even at the federal level until about eight years ago (von Furstenberg 1983), there is rarely a reason to raise taxes except to increase government spending. This section deals with those exceptional circumstances under which such a link may not prevail because policymakers wish to change the relation between the two sides of the budget or reduce the size of government by pulling taxes down first.

In the discussions so far we have mainly dealt with the eventual consequences of tax cuts.[15] The reason for this was perhaps that, unlike in investments where costs of plant and equipment must usually be incurred before benefits can be reaped, in politics the easy and pleasant things tend to get done first. As House Speaker Thomas Foley has observed, "Any proposal for cutting taxes, even one [that is] ill-timed and inequitable . . . has the prospect of succeeding. . . . A proposal to reduce taxes is extremely popular" (Broder 1989). Tax increases may be presumed to be correspondingly unpopular. Yet one needs to consider their logical possibilities and likely consequences, as I will attempt to do here.

In spite of their unquestioned popularity, broad tax cuts that are not matched or preceded by expenditure cuts may impede attempts to curb the size of government measured by its spending in percent of GNP. Indeed, we already have identified two ways in which present tax cuts may *increase* government expenditures in the near or longer terms. First, by reducing current voters' perceived cost of government programs, higher government noninterest spending may be induced through the political process directly. Second, by increasing budget deficits, present tax cuts will raise government interest payments on the national debt in the future. If either of these reasons applied symmetrically to tax increases, a present tax hike would tend to *reduce* prospective government spending.

Traditional Views of Fiscal Incontinence

The opposite effect, however, is frequently attributed to tax increases. In 1982 and in years before and after, Milton Friedman made the same point, which President Reagan was fond of making more concisely:

> You cannot reduce the deficit by raising taxes. Increasing taxes only results in more spending, leaving the deficit at the highest level conceivably accepted by the public. Political Rule Number One is government spends what government receives plus as much more as it can get away with. (Friedman quoted in Anderson et al. 1986, 631)

Like it or not, the political process is said to work in such a way that tax actions that are meant to reduce fiscal deficits end up doing nothing of the kind. The argument here is not that contractionary effects on aggregate demand of raising average tax rates and the disincentive effects to supply from increased marginal tax rates would combine to frustrate the objective of garnering additional revenues from higher tax rates from the start. Rather, the assumption is that before long any additional revenue will be diverted from deficit reduction to additional spending. This assertion, which Stein (1988) has identified as one of Parkinson's Laws, and which development economists know as the [Stanley] Please effect, means that government expenditure rises to meet the available revenue.

In recent years, federal spending has shown no tendency to keep to the limit set by tax availability, as tax reductions have proved incapable of compressing spending by the amount required to maintain respect for the tax constraint. Because this "balance" constraint has become soft even under conditions of high employment, a more restricted formulation of the "Law," which Stein found ill-supported, would seem to be necessary if it is to have any chance at all. According to this restricted and asymmetric formulation, *tax increases are held capable only of leading to marginally-balanced budget expansion, thereby raising the size of the public sector.* Proponents treat this assertion as fact that should be used as the working assumption by all, and they shame the intelligence or forthrightness of those who would deny it. The implication is that tax increases can be wanted only for prospective expenditure increases and not for such "Keynesian" reasons as cooling an overheated economy or for such "classical" reasons as putting the public finances back on a sound footing.

Some industrial countries, such as West Germany from 1969 through 1973, managed budget surpluses for several years in a row. Since that time, fast-growing Singapore has had fiscal surpluses consistently at least through 1986, to supplement the pool of saving available for private investment. The United States itself had a recurring fiscal *surplus* problem in much of its pre-World War I history. Nevertheless, the view that you cannot actively seek to raise taxes to generate fiscal surpluses, and succeed as planned, is very old and generally correct. As discussed elsewhere (von Furstenberg et al. 1985, 323), President Calvin Coolidge articulated this traditional appraisal when he remarked, "Nothing is easier than spending public money. It does not appear to belong to anybody. The temptation is overwhelming to bestow it on somebody" (Larkey et al. 1984, 65). It is true that in the nineteenth century aversion to having credit employed unproductively and to burdening the working classes with regressive taxes to pay interest on the public debt at times led to strenuous efforts to reduce or eliminate such debt. Efforts to do so succeeded repeatedly in the United States. For instance, debt mostly contracted during the War of 1812 was retired by 1835. In 1836, President Jackson's last year in office, he therefore inveighed against surpluses (mostly from burgeoning customs duties) beyond those required to retire the national debt:

> The experience of other nations admonished us to hasten the extinguishment of the public debt; but it will be in vain if we have congratulated each other upon the disappearance of this evil if we do not guard against the equally great one of promoting the unnecessary accumulation of public revenue. (Kimmel 1959, 20–21)

However, if high tax elasticities or discretionary tax actions that lead to actual surpluses invite increases in government spending to fritter away these surpluses, the reverse does not seem to hold for tax cuts. Indeed, in 1960 Senator Barry Goldwater had already articulated those lessons, which in recent years have often been repeated (Weidenbaum 1983, 11). Goldwater had said:

> While there is something to be said for the proposition that spending will never be reduced as long as there is money in the federal treasury, I believe as a practical matter spending cuts must come before tax cuts. If we reduce taxes before firm, principled decisions are made about expenditures, we court deficit spending . . . . (Stein 1984, 255)

What should one conclude from the historical account given thus far? If tax increases initially lead to an actual budget surplus, increased spending will soon follow and prevent these surpluses from continuing. This is to be expected, except when the public debt is viewed as such a burden that reducing or eliminating it becomes a viable political objective. Kimmel (1959, 68–69) explains that reduction and eventual extinguishment of the public debt has not been such an objective in the United States since about 1870, although reducing the ratio of government debt in relation to the tax base or to the collective "ability to pay" in peacetime has continued to be a popular concern. On the other hand, if taxes are cut and this tax cut creates a deficit, reduced spending will fail to follow nearly as predictably to keep the deficits from continuing.

In neither case does it matter very much whether the tax change is discretionary or whether it is due to economic growth and inflation interacting with the existing tax structure in such a way as to change the average aggregate tax rate. These economic forces can yield a "fiscal dividend," as was common under the largely unindexed tax and budgeting systems of the United States that prevailed until the mid-1970s, and to a diminishing extent until the mid-1980s.[16] They can also yield the opposite, a fiscal "gap" that arises from tax bases being inelastic with respect to output or income, or from lags in tax collection lowering their real value, as is common with inflation in developing countries (Tanzi 1977).

For decades, tax reform in such countries has involved attempts to broaden the tax base and to improve tax administration so as to reduce both taxation through inflation and reliance on official external borrowing in favor of strengthening fiscal revenues. Comprehensive accounts of this appear in Gandhi (1987) and Gillis (1989), while the reverse direction of effect, from macroeconomic policies to the level of taxation, is discussed in an important essay by Tanzi (1989). In the United States, however, conventional wisdom now questions whether tax increases can be lastingly effective in reducing fiscal deficits or can help lead back to a fiscally sustainable position.

The history of fiscal crises and how they have been resolved sheds little light on the current situation in this regard. There are no very telling episodes to be culled from U.S. fiscal affairs in the nineteenth or twentieth century, although econometric evidence obtained from the entire post-Korean period (and even longer periods) will be summarized briefly at the end of this section. For instance, President Buchanan, in the panic and recession of 1857–58, was convinced that economies alone would not solve the budget deficit problem and that additional revenue would be needed, but Congress failed to pass the tax legislation he had proposed (Kimmel 1959, 26–27). Had those tax increases been enacted, they would undoubtedly have been overtaken soon afterwards by a previously still unintended and unanticipated event, the outbreak of the Civil War in 1861, without anyone rightly thinking that prior taxes would have "caused" this surge of spending, which ultimately got started without them (Kimmel 1959, 62–63).

Counterfactuals of this sort may contain a useful caution against careless attribution of causation, but they are best used for refutation or sowing doubt, and not for supporting an established position. President Johnson's income tax surcharges, finally adopted in 1968, also did not provide a clear test of the ability of tax hikes to reduce deficits without inviting equal increases in spending. However, there is a striking recent example of just such a capability from the United Kingdom.

The Example Set by Prime Minister Thatcher

Meeting the public sector borrowing requirement (PSBR), which had grown rapidly through the 1970s, had put strong pressure on the U.K. monetary authorities to condone rising rates of inflation. Thus, in its second budget of March 1980, to change this the Thatcher administration adopted a medium-term financial strategy (MTFS), embracing both fiscal and monetary policy. According to the accounts of Walters (1986), Maynard (1988), Peele (1989), and Byatt (1989), particularly Maynard, this policy had a comprehensive program. As promulgated in 1980, it involved reducing the PSBR linearly from 3.75 percent of GDP in 1980–81 to 1.5 percent in 1983–84, while the annual rate of increase in the money supply (sterling M3) would be cut from a range of 7 to 11 percent to a range of 4 to 8 percent over the same period. The immediate coupling of disinflation with the planned reduction of fiscal deficits was based not on the "Keynesian" belief that lower fiscal deficits were needed to reduce aggregate demand and *thereby* cut inflation. Rather, the assumption was that monetary targeting for disinflation would appear more credible and have a greater immediate effect in dampening inflationary expectations if the government were seen to be reducing its own demand for credit. Thus, disinflation would not only be more assured in the end but also less costly in terms of lost output and employment.

When the PSBR turned out to exceed the government's target by almost 2 percentage points in 1980–81, the entire strategy was in jeopardy and the government set out to raise taxes by what it hoped would turn out to be just such an amount for 1981–82. The main proposals were the non-indexation of tax thresholds and most allowances, so that the reduction in their real value raised direct taxes, and an increase in indirect taxes (largely excise taxes but not the value added tax, VAT, which had been raised from rates ranging from 8.5 to 12 percent to a uniform 15 percent already in 1979).

To appreciate the size of this sudden tax change, it is worth noting that a tax change equal to almost 2 percent of GDP that was wrought in a single year in the United Kingdom would in 1989 amount to about $100 billion in the United States. Predictably, against a background of recession, such a large tax increase provoked intense criticism from mainstream economists, not just those in the United Kingdom. Nevertheless, the U.K. economy had already bottomed out in the fourth quarter of 1980, some months before this criticism reached a crescendo.

Because of the tax increases and because the United Kingdom nevertheless did not share the relapse into recession that engulfed much of the rest of the world in late 1981 and much of 1982, the realized PSBR for 1981–82 turned out to be more than 2 percentage points below that of 1980–81 and close to the 3 percent of GDP originally targeted for 1981–82 in the MTFS. Thus in Maynard's (1988, 69) judgment, the 1981 budget was crucial for the MTFS as it seemed to establish beyond doubt the government's determination to reduce inflation. Tax hikes coupled with tighter controls on government spending formed an essential element of this strategy. The strategy worked first of all to cut the fiscal imposition on the monetary authorities to condone inflation. It then supplied room for fiscal authorities to turn to the determined pursuit of supply-side restructuring. By 1986, that pursuit had led to successive reductions in the top individual and corporate income tax rates and to measures that dramatically reduced tax and benefit disincentives to employment nearer to the bottom of the income scale. All of these actions subsequently contributed to strong gains in output and employment, with overheating not becoming evident until 1989.

Regarding the use of raising taxes, U.K. public expenditures fell from 45.75 percent of GDP in 1980–81 to 42.75 percent in 1986–87. The PSBR declined from over 5 percent to less than 1 percent over the same period. Although the expenditure share did not start to fall below its 1980–1981 level until 1983–84, tax increases clearly were dedicated to deficit reduction and were kept from raising government expenditures. Indeed, a *negative* relation between tax increases and changes in government spending may have proved feasible politically, as both sides of the budget appear to have contributed to deficit reduction.

Tax Increases and Spending Cuts: U.S. Precedents

A weak but negative relation between at least one major federal expenditure component, defense, and tax innovations has also been reported for the United States in at least one econometric study. In that study (von Furstenberg et al. 1986), raising taxes and then reducing defense spending and, at other times, cutting taxes before defense spending was raised, appeared to be a pattern emerging with quarterly data for 1954–82, just as lowering taxes and then increasing defense expenditures was the pattern in the early 1980s. Hence it is quite possible that if there is political pressure to raise defense expenditures during peacetime without a dire military threat looming ahead, the "butter" of tax cuts must grease the additional "guns." By the same token, tax increases and cuts in the area of defense are enlisted to fight jointly against deficits, once deficit reduction has become the principal political objective. This combination has clearly gained in relevance recently as defense spending as a share of GNP has declined since the mid-1980s while some taxes have been nudged up.

In other areas of spending, however, and for government spending as a whole, the null hypothesis that tax innovations have no effect on expenditures, either up or down, after allowing for any temporary fiscal cross-effects of business cycles and inflation, cannot be rejected with U.S. data for the post-Korean period (von Furstenberg et al. 1985; 1986) or for the entire period after World War II (Anderson et al. 1986). The evidence from annual data going back to 1929 is more equivocal (Manage and Marlow 1986) but also historically less relevant to current relations. It suggests that taxes may have a unidirectional link with spending in a substantial minority of cases. Cases are distinguished by the maximum length of lags allowed and by the construction of the variables used to represent government spending and receipts. However, the link from taxes to spending, if significant, is not necessarily positive (see the results reported in Manage and Marlow's appendix, 626–628).

If there was any recurring hint in all but the last of these studies, it was that at the federal level positive spending innovations tended to be followed by higher taxes and not the other way around. Holtz-Eakin et al. (1986) have found that at lower levels of government the situation may, of course, be different. Particularly if legislative sessions are few and short and restrictions on debt financing tight, tax initiatives may have to be voted before any expenditure initiatives, which are used to justify the tax initiatives with the voters, can start to be implemented.

TAX SMOOTHING

Outside mechanical systems, time sequences and causation can be related quite variably and must be interpreted with caution. In an honest boxing ring, the punch comes before the knockout, and the time count follows the punch that caused the knockout. Outside physical systems, however, consciousness and preparedness enter, which can scramble how time sequences relate to causation and suspend the mechanical logic of *ex post ergo propter hoc*. It therefore becomes a matter of prior judgment to decide what is reasonable to assert about the workings of the existing political system.

For instance, there is a good theoretical argument, usually credited to Barro (1979), that the aggregate tax rate (which can be visualized as a VAT without exemptions) should always be set in such a way as to preclude the need for further change given what we know now. That is, if government expenditures were to adhere exactly to the future path currently expected, no further rate change would ever be necessary to keep the ratio of government debt to GNP from diverging permanently from its current level. Hence, as soon as the prospect arises that government expenditures will be higher at any time in the future than previously thought, tax rates will have to be raised immediately so that they will not have to be changed again when the expected deviation occurs. Of course the permanent, or at least indefinite, tax rate change that balances the upward revision in current estimates of future government spending on a present-value basis is higher if the increase in government spending is expected to be permanent rather than transitory, or sets in sooner rather than later. But if anticipations are keen and Barro's guidelines are followed, whatever is enacted on the tax front would likely be done *before* any of the newly expected future spending innovations have a chance to materialize. A mechanical application of *ex post ergo propter hoc* would therefore blame higher taxes for having caused higher government expenditures.

The Efficiency of Keeping Tax Rates Steady

The truth, of course, would have been the reverse of the above logic if policymakers had gone by Barro's laudable principle of tax smoothing. It is designed to minimize the excess burden of taxation over time, given that this burden rises at an increasing rate with the rate of taxation. To make calculations easy, assume that, in the neighborhood of a particular tax rate, the real rate of economic growth, and hence the growth of the real value of the tax base, happens to be equal to the real interest rate on government debt. In this neighborhood, tax rates could then be substituted at a 1:1 rate across time between different periods of the same length, if the growth of the base were not disturbed by tax-rate variation.

Barro's principle now states that having an aggregate tax rate of 28 percent one year and 38 percent in another, instead of having 33 percent in each, involves needless economic waste. In fact, presenting the argument by means of an increasingly upward sloping (though still positively sloped) Laffer-curve segment, figure 3.2 shows that the steady rate would not need to be 33 percent. Rather, it could be as low as 30 percent to yield the same sum total of revenue over 2 years: 1050 and 1050 rather than 1000 and 1100. The reason is that distortions induced by a tax rate 5 percentage points higher than average are considerably more costly to the economy and its tax base than the (economic) "welfare" benefits derived from keeping the marginal tax rate below average by the same amount for the same length of time. The fact that the temptation to create loopholes rises with the size of marginal tax rates lends additional, political substance to this point. Hence, 28 percent alternating with 38 percent tax rates produces less revenue than holding the tax rate steady at 33 percent. Conversely, tax rate disturbances of the kind that come from cutting taxes now and raising them later push up the average rate of taxation for the period as a whole. This rise would be from 30 percent to 33 percent in the example just given.

Although there are no complete estimates of how much would be added to the excess burden of taxation through rate variability, the size of such estimates would be proportional to the change in the slope of the Laffer curve in the relevant range. Estimates such as those of Browning (1989) suggest that changes in this slope can already be substantial at tax rates of around 20 percent, since the revenue-maximizing marginal tax-rate on labor income may be only about twice as high. Assuming, therefore, that tax-rate smoothing is highly desirable on efficiency grounds, any change in the outlook for government expenditures should be translated into tax action as soon as it possibly can.

Anticipatory Taxation?

To see whether anticipatory taxation has, in fact, been practiced in the United States, or is likely to be practiced in the future, one must first attempt to isolate situations in which increases in future levels of government spending must clearly have come to be expected. One can then see whether tax action was taken promptly as this realization dawned. Since the United States did not enter either of the two world wars until they had been under way for more than two years, while the probability of U.S. entry mounted, there was considerable time for acting on anticipations of increased future spending. Yet during World War I, what advance provision for vastly increased future defense spending was made, mainly through in-

Figure 3.2. THE EXCESS BURDEN OF TAX RATE VARIATION

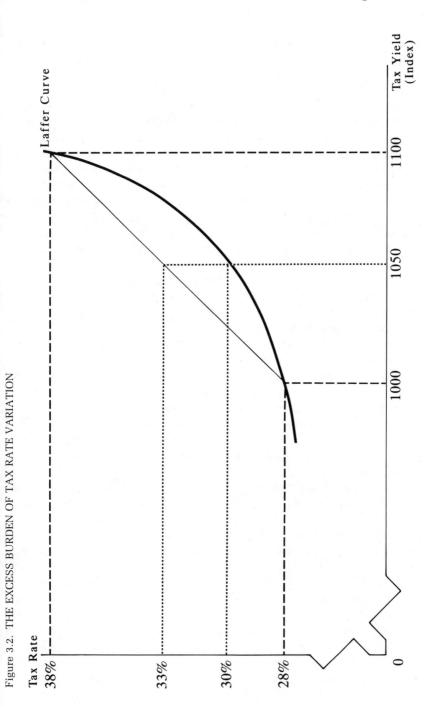

creasing income tax rates in September 1916 (Noyes 1926, 194) was little and late. The first war finance bill of April 1917 concerned authority to borrow, not to tax. Indeed it was not until October 1917, half a year after U.S. entry into the war, that a war revenue act could be passed (Noyes 1926, 172–75).

There is just as little evidence that expenditures associated with U.S. entry into World War II cast a long shadow forward even if it is granted that, absent the surprise attack on Pearl Harbor in December 1941, the United States might not have become a combatant until some time in 1942. Indeed, from FY 1940 to FY 1941, total government expenditures increased twice as much as receipts, and the deficit rose from over $3 billion to over $5 billion (U.S. Office of Management and Budget 1989, Table 1.4). Hence, debt financing of the military buildup already started before the United States entered World War II, when defense expenditures had risen to barely 6 percent of GNP compared with 39 percent three years later, in FY 1944.

Anticipatory tax financing certainly did not characterize the early period of the Vietnam War either. The escalation of U.S. participation extended over a number of years, with the first major announcement of troop withdrawals in June 1969 coming four years after the first commitment of combat troops, which itself evolved gradually. None of this lead time appears to have been used. Rather, when Congress and President Johnson finally reached a compromise permitting passage of the tax surcharge in 1968 (Pierce 1971, 7–8), the economy had already experienced two-and-a-half years of excess demand and rising inflation, and Vietnam War expenditures were about to crest. Countercyclical Keynesian, not tax smoothing, considerations belatedly won out.

Moving up to the present, there is no need to belabor the fact that the desire for tax-rate smoothing did not accompany the defense buildup planned for the 1980s and then largely executed during President Reagan's first term. Of course it can be argued that had there been sufficient reason to expect nondefense expenditures to fall a little more in percent of GNP than defense expenditures were scheduled to increase, it would have been correct to cut tax rates right away according to Barro's principle, and not to wait for a net decline in government expenditures in relation to trend GNP to materialize first. Debating points aside, however, except perhaps for the social security program, tax-rate smoothing does not command much heed in the fiscal politics of the United States. Indeed, even this instance of tax-rate smoothing is being sabotaged by tax rate disturbances laid in store by the rest of the budget, as large temporary surpluses in the social insurance funds—that in FY 1989 had already risen to over $100 billion a year—are used to reduce pressures for deficit reduction elsewhere. This will add to the upward pressure on general tax rates once the surpluses in the social insurance funds, which have started to absorb mountains of federal debt and reduced net interest paid as accounted for to the public, cease to grow within one generation and then start being disgorged in the next.

A lack of concern with tax-rate smoothing is evident, with tax preparations ignored even when future increases in government expenditures are planned or anticipated quite openly and argued to be imperative. Such a lack of concern must then apply *a fortiori* to the hidden and conflicting expenditure agendas inevitably attributed to "tax raisers" by those who hold with Milton Friedman's dictum quoted earlier. How could those with unannounced spending intentions possibly persuade their colleagues and the body politic to raise tax rates in advance of revelation or any semblance of agreement on the nature of future spending initiatives? Surely, even granting that some politicians must want pork for their constituents, they would not agree to buying, let alone prepaying for, a pig in a poke through the politically costly expenditure of taxes.

KEEPING UP THE BAD WORK?

By disparaging tax increases for being associated with undesirable increases in public spending, the Bush Administration has succeeded only too well. Tax increases are now avoided even if Congress decides that it desires to increase spending after all. Indeed, spending may have become easier and cutting spending less rewarding since from the tax side there is no penalty for the former or reward for the latter. Instead, large budget deficits have become the norm, and closing them anytime soon under conditions of high employment has become a paper goal that can be circumvented, redefined, or officially deferred. Furthermore, some have found it politically tempting to conclude that if tax increases are always wrong, as the Bush Administration has taught so far with single-minded devotion, then even revenue-losing tax-rate reductions (with gain or loss measured in terms of the present value of future tax receipts) must be right, regardless of what happens to government spending.

By contrast, raising tax rates in anticipation of previously unplanned increases in government expenditures could be the responsible thing to do if there is a political consensus that such increases are imperative and are not self-reversing in short order. Milton Friedman has argued that tax rises, even those ostensibly adopted for deficit reduction, always make government expenditure increases politically imperative no matter how undeserving they may be. Prime Minister Thatcher has given a splendid demonstration to the contrary when she managed to raise taxes in her 1981 budget and then within a few years succeeded in greatly reducing both the deficit and the relative size of government. By initially setting out in the opposite direction and cutting taxes "before firm, principled decisions [were] made about expenditures," (Goldwater's 1960 words, as quoted above) the Reagan Administration failed to achieve either of these goals to a comparable degree. In particular, lowering income tax rates and overall tax collections proved incapable of pulling government spending down as much as hoped, though early on some inroads were made into nondefense spending, except for interest.

Such incapacity should not have come as much of a surprise. Interpreters of the public choice processes of Western-type societies, like Peacock (1985), have long concluded that tax limitation, used on its own, is not effective as a control over government expenditure. Hence, if limiting government spending, and the resource drafts and distortions of command economy that tend to go with it, is what ultimately matters, taxes must be restored immediately as the *sine qua non* for spending initiatives. Cash in advance or pay-as-you-go is a way of chilling the ardor for increased spending that the habitual use of debt-financing has abetted. There is no sense in which the two forms of financing are equivalent in their effects on public spending. As Benjamin Friedman (1988, 109–133) has characterized the matter, spend and borrow, and raise taxes only after all my possible terms are over, is an easy and attractive principle for politicians to survive by.

Prime Minister Thatcher showed some years ago that where there is more regard for the long-term future of the nation, and where there is strong resolve and motivation for better budget balance, there is a way to manage tax policy to help achieve it.[17] In the United Kingdom, at least, fiscal discipline came to mean once again holding the line against government spending and retrenching it when and wherever possible. Holding that line just against taxes while letting borrowing flood in is a failed policy. Those who are not made to pay full price for their spending excesses will indulge in many more.

Mrs. Thatcher thus proved that in the parliamentary system of the United Kingdom, where there is a will there is a way. Even though proceeds from the sale of government industry assets, in a series of major efficiency-enhancing privatizations (Walters 1989), were counted the same as tax receipts "above" the line (rather than being treated as a financing item like government debt "below the line"), the over-all sweep of deficit reduction in the United Kingdom rested on solid achievement. More importantly, it had a deeper purpose: the curbing of inflation and then structural reforms to reinstate and invigorate free-market principles and practices. These were meant to strengthen Britain's economic foundations and to reignite the spark of positive freedom and individual opportunity that the welfare state had squelched.

By comparison, the endless diddling to meet Gramm-Rudman tar-gets in the United States, aptly characterized by West (1988), Miller (1989), and Brinner (1989), appears puny and indecisive. In the scur-rilous juggling of numbers that these targets have produced, there has been no guiding purpose (other than deficit reduction) to mo-tivate an investment in credibility through close adherence. A rep-etition of the "options" for reducing the deficit found year after year in the reports of the U. S. Congressional Budget Office (e.g., 1989) only adds to the sense of aimlessness. As already documented for other major countries (Roubini and Sachs 1989), this stalemate in budget policies may be due as much to interparty strife within gov-erning coalitions or between branches of government as to a general lack of will and vision.

A succession of stopgap measures to deal with recurring fiscal crisis, whether inherent in the imbalance of accounts or the rules they are supposed to fit, hardly contributes to making well-consid-ered allocative choices. As Stein (1989a) has emphasized, these al-locative choices should regard the nation's entire product and its public use. Threats of sequestration, like driving in a rainstorm, are hardly conducive to scanning the broad horizon. Indeed, some have argued that the United States now has a "peso" problem (Daniel 1989), waiting to mend its public finances heaven knows when. In the meantime the U.S. government would maintain uncertainty about the impending policy change and impose costly forecast errors not just on its own officials, but also on the private sector and on other countries.

Stein (1989b) has recently concluded that "a tax increase of $50 billion to $100 billion is not large relative to the size of our debt and deficit problem, relative to the amount that can easily be raised without adverse economic effects and relative to the amount that Mr. Reagan showed was politically acceptable" when he started raising some taxes soon after the Tax Reduction Act of 1981. Should the present Administration learn as quickly as its predecessor that the political bias is on the side of cutting taxes and raising spending, it would have to start promoting the opposite combination very soon.

SUMMARY AND CONCLUSION

Normally, taxes are to government spending what cash-in-advance is to private purchase: a needed reminder of the opportunity cost of things. Recently, however, the tax constraint has become soft without any cyclical excuse, and spending has cut loose. Unless taxes can be made to catch up with, and be put in charge of, the government spending train, structural budget deficits—deficits larger than compatible with constancy of the ratio of government debt to GNP from cycle to cycle—cannot be eliminated. As long as the current disregard for the principle of payment continues, there is no obvious defense against tax cuts and spending increases that would raise deficits further.

Some have argued that you can never catch up with spending by raising taxes because doing so will just make the rate of spending that much larger. Unfortunately, the corollary of this view, that you should reduce taxes to get spending down, has not been confirmed by events. Since the tax constraint implied by a (marginally-balanced-budget) financing requirement for spending initiatives has gone soft, cutting present taxes has led mainly to larger deficits. With real interest rates on government debt exceeding the growth rate of real GNP, larger structural deficits now mean higher taxes in the future.

Some economists have tried to convince us that we should not worry about the income effects of intertemporal tax substitutions because they may be negligible. Instead, we should rely on the truism that in a present-value calculation set up for the representative agent and stretched to infinity, in an accounting sense, the time shape of future taxes is immaterial for household balance sheets. As long as the government's primary spending, its interest rate, and the economy's growth rate remain the same, some taxes now versus more taxes later, discounted at the government's borrowing rate, inevitably must come to the same amount as long as the government honors its debt.

There is a salutary lesson in that, taken to infinity, taxes can neither ɔe cut nor raised, without doing likewise to noninterest government spending. Yet few of us selfish individuals care to discount the income effects of present tax cuts quite this way, and none of our political representatives acts as if such cuts did not matter to their (and our) well-being.

Even if the income effects were totally discounted, we would still have to worry about substitution effects. Since the excess burden of taxation rises at an increasing rate with the (marginal) rate of taxation, low tax rates now for high tax rates later is a bad trade. Yet that is the losing game we are currently playing. We are told to go on playing it by "never" raising taxes even though the late charges for the undiminished rate of government spending are bound to come after us very soon.

It is easy to summarize the reasons for this appraisal. First of all, as others have emphasized for over a decade, cutting present tax rates payable on any given amount of spending may lead the myopic political process to demand more government expenditures because the political cost per unit of such spending has been lowered. Secondly, presently low taxes and a higher debt-to-GNP ratio mean that spending for interest on the national debt, net of the amount by which the nominal amount of such debt can be scaled up on account of economic growth and inflation, must rise. This will necessitate higher tax rates in the future if the debt ratio is to be stabilized. Furthermore, that ratio must be stabilized at a level low enough not to exceed society's political willingness to generate primary surpluses, an ability that is being strained not only in many developing countries, but also in some European countries such as Italy. A final point is that because the inefficiency of the tax system rises at an increasing rate with the marginal rate of taxation, tax rate disturbances raise the *average* level of taxation. This adds to the inevitability of higher future tax rates that is already built into the growth of the debt-to-GNP ratio per se in a manner that is most unfortunate.

What does all this add up to? The policy of cutting taxes to lower government spending is literally bankrupt. The failure to keep spending under tax constraints has instead laid in store increased future spending, not just for interest on the public debt. It took the Reagan Administration about one year into office to realize that lower taxes and increased spending are both more popular than is good for the future of the nation. This is why it began to understand the need to ward off spending pressures with the threat of higher taxes. Indeed, it carried out that threat on several occasions, starting in 1982. One can only hope that the Bush Administration will recognize that pledging no new taxes no matter what, amounts to a promise not to punish big spenders in their time. In a present-value sense, which politicians seek to deny, taxes are being raised every day for which outsized deficits have persisted.

Notes

The author wishes to thank William G. Dewald of the Department of State's Planning and Economic Analysis Staff, and Michele Fratianni of Indiana University for their valuable comments. The views expressed here are the sole responsibility of the author.

1. George Plesko (1988, 499) has found that "on the whole, estimates made of the revenue consequences of proposed tax law changes accurately anticipated the realized effects." Hence, errors in receipts forecasts were due not to incorrect quantification of the consequences of tax law changes per se, but to forecasts of real and nominal GNP from 1980 on that greatly exceeded the levels eventually realized.

2. These effects are considered further below.

3. Noninterest government spending is often referred to as primary spending in other studies.

4. These may include inflation taxes on money balances buttressed by capital controls, as monetary policy is commandeered to finance larger additions to the government's debt than can be placed at affordable real interest rates with private investors in free markets. For an analysis of how this and related pathologies have recently been played out in a number of countries, see Montiel (1989).

5. If earlier generations had been as eager to collect from posterity as the typical American male of this parable, government debt would already have been sky high and might be difficult to increase further in relation to GNP. We assume, therefore, that the decline in public finance "morality" and intergenerational benevolence is a fairly recent phenomenon that has arisen with the growing breakdown of families.

6. Since the annual payment of real value $64.77 would stop if the person died before 30 years had passed from the time of the tax cut, the actuarial value of this stream of payments would be the same as $57.83 paid for the full 30 years.

7. Assuming real GNP increases by 2.5 percent per annum without benefit of population and labor force growth, government debt per head also grows at that rate. To translate the real value of interest obligations on the growing debt per head into current-dollar terms, real values must again be multiplied by a price index, in this case the GNP deflator set to 1 in the starting year, as explained earlier.

8. If taxes are imposed to raise revenue rather than discourage a particular activity, as some sumptuary taxes may be intended to do, no government will knowingly have raised a marginal tax rate to a level where its marginal contribution to the revenue goal is negative. However, even if lowering any tax rate in isolation would raise the deficit, there may be beneficial trade-offs that allow some high tax rates to be cut much more than low tax rates are raised, and still yield the same revenue. Indeed, the argument for tax-rate smoothing over time, taken up later in this paper, is based on this premise. Income tax rate cuts, coupled with a reduction in deductibles and other legislated increases in the tax base which were the centerpiece of the 1986 tax reform legislation, also provide opportunities for revenue-neutral changes enhancing the efficiency of taxation in a manner not further considered here.

9. If r, n, and g are constant over time and k is kept unchanged, the present value (at time $t = 0$) of all future tax receipts is equal to $[(1+r) gGNP (0)]/(r-n) + (1+r)k(-1)$ GNP (0). In this, real GNP at time 0, GNP (0), grows at the rate n. Provided that $r-n$, which is taken to be positive, is invariant to policy change, the discounted present value of all future taxes does not change if k is stabilized at any level other than $k(-1)$ as long as it is stablized at some level.

Below we will argue in connection with the example from Italy that this level of k may not only have to be finite but in fact quite low, given the practical limits on z. Formula (2), of course, says nothing about such limits even though the share of taxes in GNP can only be driven so far in any actual economy.

10. This estimate can be supported further. In 1982, real GNP was 8 percent below the level at which it would have been if it had grown at the average annual rate of 2.5 percent from the peak year 1979 on. DRI (1989, 21) has a "late recession" simulation in which real GNP, by 1992, is 9.7 percent below what it would be in their optimistic comparison path. DRI estimates that the federal deficit would be $205 billion higher under the late-recession simulation in 1992. Adjusting for growth and inflation in the optimistic scenario, this figure for 1992 is compatible with an estimate of about $170 billion with 1989 magnitudes. Adjusting further for the difference in severity of the actual 1982 and DRI's 1992 recessions could scale this estimate back to $140 billion.

11. Although I would not agree with Eisner's (1986, 179) judgment that "a budget balanced by current federal rules of accounting is an invitation to economic disaster," there is no prospect of such a policy being followed. Rather, the risks are all on the other side. On inflation-adjustment of Fiscal deficits, see also Tanzi et al. (1987) and Dewald (1988).

12. Wilcox (1989) has found the 1975–84 U.S. fiscal stance to be unsustainable if continued unchanged. In the subsequent discussion of Italy, we will use a somewhat more dynamic criterion of sustainability. A fiscal stance will be viewed as unsustainable if a country cannot succeed in stabilizing the ratio of government debt to GNP without possibly runaway inflation or system change. Then even the maximum tax (or expenditure) adjustments that are taken to be politically feasible under the existing system each year would not be sufficient to stabilize the fiscal situation. Hence, political dimensions will enter.

13. The cyclically-adjusted federal deficit on the national income and product accounts basis (NIPA) increased by $5 billion from calendar year 1987 to 1988 after declining by about $30 billion from 1986 to 1987. So far in 1989, the NIPA deficit has shown little change from its 1988 level of $146 billion. For the three years from 1986 to 1989, the average annual reduction in the cyclically-adjusted fiscal deficit thus was a paltry $8 billion on the NIPA basis. See Wakefield (1988, 24; 1989, 33).

14. This discussion is inspired by Blanchard's (1984) derivation—using Belgian data—of analogous limits under a proportional rather than fixed-increment adjustment scheme. The original Gramm-Rudman target limits for the federal deficit were set to fall in fixed decrements of $36 billion per fiscal year from $108 in 1988 to zero in 1991. Under the first revision of these targets, the fixed decrement was maintained, with the decline scheduled to go from a greatly raised level of $136 bilion in 1989 to $28 billion in 1992. Although Congress has made a mockery of these targets, they may reveal a political preference for targeting in fixed increments or decrements that actually get you to the goal in relatively short order, at least on paper.

15. Economic consequences of a cut in government spending that is not reversed or accompanied by tax cuts for at least 10 years have been estimated by Herd (1989) for major industrial countries.

16. Now that the fiscal dividends have vanished, Congress goes on declaring them as if they existed and spending may be increased or taxes cut whenever the annual

deficit falls below, say, $150 billion. Obviously, there is no binding procedural constraint on the size of the fiscal balance if deficit targets are so stretchable over the years. If these targets instead were binding and treated as fixed for any year, marginally-balanced budget change would be all that is allowed once the fiscal stance has been put on target.

17. An impressive demonstration has also been given by the government of Prime Minister Hawke in Australia. For a description of the process that began with the 1986–87 budget, see Keating and Dixon (1989, 9–20).

References

Anderson, William, Myles S. Wallace, and John T. Warner. 1986. "Government Spending and Taxation: What Causes What?" *Southern Economic Journal* 52, no. 3 (January): 630–639.

Banca D'Italia. 1989. *Economic Bulletin* 8 (February).

Barro, Robert J. 1989. "The Ricardian Approach to Budget Deficits." *Journal of Economic Perspectives* 3, 2 (Spring): 37–54.

————. 1979. "On the Determination of the Public Debt." *Journal of Political Economy* 87 (October): 940–71.

Blanchard, Olivier J. 1984. "Current and Anticipated Deficits, Interest Rates and Economic Activity." *European Economic Review* 25, no. 3 (June): 7–27.

Boskin, Michael J. 1987. *Reagan and the Economy: The Successes, Failures and Unfinished Agenda*. Institute for Contemporary Studies. San Francisco: ICS Press.

Brinner, Roger E. 1989. "Fiscal Policy Planning: Assessing the Mid-Session Review of the Budget." DRI/McGraw-Hill *Review of the U.S. Economy* (August): 13–18.

Broder, David S. 1989. "Capital Gains Tax Might be Cut, Foley Indicates." *Washington Post*, 25 August.

Browning, Edgar K. 1989. "Elasticities, Tax Rates, and Tax Revenue." *National Tax Journal* 42, no. 1 (March): 45–48.

Buchanan, James M. and Richard E. Wagner. (1978). "Dialogues Concerning Fiscal Religion." *Journal of Monetary Economics* 4, no. 3 (August): 627–636.

Byatt, Ian. 1989. "The Record of Tax Reform in Great Britain and its Contribution to the Supply Side." In *A Supply-Side Agenda for Germany*, edited by George M. von Furstenberg, 355–376. Berlin, Heidelberg, New York: Springer.

Carlson, Keith M. 1989. "Federal Budget Trends and the 1981 Reagan Economic Plan." Federal Reserve Bank of St. Louis. *Review* 71, no. 1 (January/February): 18–31.

Cukierman, Alex and Allan H. Meltzer. 1989. "A Political Theory of Government Debt and Deficits in a Neo-Ricardian Framework." *American Economic Review* 79, no. 4 (September): 713–732.

Daniel, Betty C. 1989. "One-Sided Uncertainty About Future Fiscal Policy." *Journal of Money, Credit and Banking* 21, no. 2 (May): 176–189.

Dewald, William G. 1988. "The Budgetary Importance of Either Eliminating Inflation or Accounting for It." *Business Economics* 23, no. 1 (January): 34–38.

DRI/McGraw-Hill. 1989. "U.S. Forecast Summary." (September).

Eisner, Robert. 1986. *How Real Is the Federal Deficit?* New York: The Free Press.

Friedman, Benjamin. 1988. *Day of Reckoning: The Consequences of American Economic Policy Under Reagan and After.* New York: Random House.

Gandhi, Ved P., ed. 1987. *Supply-Side Tax Policy: Its Relevance to Developing Countries.* Washington, D.C.: International Monetary Fund.

Gillis, Malcolm, ed. 1989. *Tax Reform in Developing Countries.* Durham: Duke University Press.

Herd, R. 1989. "The Impact of Increased Government Saving on the Economy." OECD Department of Economics and Statistics *Working Papers*, no. 68 (June).

Hoffman, David. 1989. "President Strikes Out at Democrats." *Washington Post*, 23 September.

Holtz-Eakin, Douglas, Whitney Newey, and Harvey Rosen. 1986. "The Revenues-Expenditures Nexus: Evidence from Local Government Data." Unpublished paper. Columbia and Princeton Universities (March).

Keating, Michael and Geoff Dixon. 1989. *Making Economic Policy in Australia, 1983–1988.* Melbourne: Longman Cheshire.

Kimmel, Lewis H. 1959. *Federal Budget and Fiscal Policy 1789–1958.* Washington, D.C.: Brookings Institution.

Larkey, Patrick D., Chandler Stolp, and Mark Winer. 1984. "Why Does Government Grow?" In *Public Sector Performance: A Conceptual Turning Point*, edited by Trudi C. Miller, 65–101. Baltimore: Johns Hopkins University Press.

Lee, Dwight R. and Richard B. McKenzie. 1989. "The International Political Economy of Declining Tax Rates." *National Tax Journal* 42, no. 1 (March): 79–83.

Leiderman, Leonardo and Mario I. Blejer. 1988. "Modeling and Testing Ricardian Equivalence: A Survey." International Monetary Fund *Staff Papers* 35, no. 1 (March): 1–35.

Manage, Neela and Michael L. Marlow. 1986. "The Causal Relation Between Federal Expenditures and Receipts." *Southern Economic Journal* 52, no. 3 (January): 617–629.

Maynard, Geoffrey. 1988. *The Economy under Mrs Thatcher.* Oxford: Basil Blackwell.

Miller, Preston J. 1989. "Gramm-Rudman-Hollings' Hold on Budget Policy:

Losing Its Grip?" Federal Reserve Bank of Minneapolis. *Quarterly Review* 13, no. 1 (Winter): 11–21.

Montiel, Peter J. 1989. "Empirical Analysis of High-Inflation Episodes in Argentina, Brazil, and Israel." *International Monetary Fund Staff Papers* 36, no. 3 (September): 527–549.

Niskanen, William A. 1978. "Deficits, Government Spending, and Inflation: What is the Evidence?" *Journal of Monetary Economics* 4, no. 3 (August): 591–602.

Noyes, Alexander D. 1926. *The War Period of American Finance 1908–1925.* New York: Knickerbocker Press.

Peacock, Alan. 1985. "Macro-economic Controls of Spending as a Device for Improving Efficiency in Government." In *Public Expenditure and Government Growth*, edited by Francesco Forte and Alan Peacock, 143–156. Oxford: Basil Blackwell.

Pechman, Joseph A., ed. 1988. *World Tax Reform: A Progress Report.* Washington, D.C.: Brookings Institution.

Peele, Gillian. 1989. "Contemporary Conservatism and the Borders of the State." In *The Economic Borders of the State*, edited by Dieter Helm, 153–179. Oxford: Oxford University Press.

Pierce, Lawrence, C. 1971. *The Politics of Fiscal Policy Formation.* Pacific Palisades, CA: Goodyear Publishing.

Plesko, George A. 1988. "The Accuracy of Government Forecasts and Budget Projections." *National Tax Journal* 41, no. 4 (December): 483–501.

Roubini, Nouriel and Jeffrey Sachs. 1989. "Government Spending and Budget Deficits in Industrial Countries." *Economic Policy* (U.K.), 8 April: 100–127.

Stein, Herbert. 1989a. *Governing the $5 Trillion Economy.* New York and Oxford: Oxford University Press.

————. 1989b. "Confessions of a Tax Addict." *Wall Street Journal*, 2 October.

————. 1988. "The New Parkinson's Law." *Wall Street Journal*, 13 July, op. ed.

————. 1984. *Presidential Economics: The Making of Economic Policy from Roosevelt to Reagan and Beyond.* New York: Simon and Schuster.

Stockman, David A. 1986. *The Triumph of Politics.* New York: Harper & Row.

Tanzi, Vito. 1989. "The Impact of Macroeconomic Policies on the Level of Taxation and the Fiscal Balance in Developing Countries." *IMF Staff Papers* 36, no. 3 (September): 633–656.

————. 1977. "Inflation, Lags in Collection, and the Real Value of Tax Revenue." *IMF Staff Papers* 24, no. 1 (March): 154–167.

Tanzi, Vito, Mario I. Blejer, and Mario O. Teijeiro. 1987. "Inflation and the Measurement of Fiscal Deficits." *IMF Staff Papers* 34, no. 4 (December): 711–738.

U.S. Congressional Budget Office. 1989. *Reducing the Deficit: Spending and Revenue Options, A Report to the Senate and House Committees on the Budget-Part II*, Washington, D.C.: U.S. Government Printing Office (February).

U.S. Office of Management and Budget. 1989. *Historical Tables: Budget of the United States Government, Fiscal Year 1990*. Washington, D.C.: U.S. Government Printing Office.

von Furstenberg, George M. 1983. "Fiscal Deficits: From Business as Usual to a Breach of the Policy Rules?" *National Tax Journal* 36, no. 4 (December): 443–457.

von Furstenberg, George M., R. Jeffery Green, and Jin-Ho Jeong. 1986. "Tax and Spend, or Spend and Tax?" *Review of Economics and Statistics* 68, no. 2 (May): 179–188.

————. 1985. "Have Taxes Led Government Expenditures? The United States as a Test Case." *Journal of Public Policy* 5, no. 3: 321–348.

Wakefield, Joseph C. 1989. "Federal Fiscal Programs." *Survey of Current Business* 69, no. 1 (January): 29–35.

————. 1988. "Federal Fiscal Programs." *Survey of Current Business* 68, no. 2 (February): 19–24.

Walters, Alan. 1989. "Supply-Side Policies: The Lessons from the U.K." In *A Supply-Side Agenda for Germany*, edited by George M. von Furstenberg, 185–214. Berlin, Heidelberg, New York: Springer.

Walters, Alan. 1986. *Britain's Economic Renaissance*. New York and Oxford: Oxford University Press.

Weidenbaum, Murray L. 1983. *Confessions of A One-Armed Economist*. St. Louis: Center for the Study of American Business, Publication no. 56.

West, Darrell M. 1988. "Gramm-Rudman-Hollings and the Politics of Deficit Reduction." *The Annals of The American Academy of Political and Social Science* 499 (September): 90–100.

Wilcox, David W. 1989. "The Sustainability of Government Deficits: Implications of the Present-Value Borrowing Constraint." *Journal of Money, Credit and Banking* 21, no. 3 (August): 291–306.

COMMENTS ON "TAXES: A LICENSE TO SPEND OR A LATE CHARGE?"

William A. Niskanen

I would first like to acknowledge how much I admire George von Furstenberg's writing skills and mordant perspective. His "typical middle-age American male" is all too descriptive of the one person whom I know best.

Most of this paper bears on the long-term relation between spending and taxes. The arithmetic is correct, and I have no problems with the inferences that George draws from it. This is a valuable tutorial for any policymaker who can be induced to follow this argument.

The dilemma is that there does not appear to be any clear relation between spending and taxes in the short run, either over time or across governments. Several empirical studies of this relation, by George and other scholars, have produced only weak results and no agreement on the direction of the relation.

The reason for these weak results, I suggest, is that the relation between spending and taxes depends on the fiscal rule of the specific government at a specific time, and that these rules have changed over time and differ across governments. The primary difference among these rules is whether the *ex ante* deficit is exogenous, whatever its magnitude.

In the absence of a rule about the *ex ante* or target deficit, the relation between spending and taxes will be very different than under a deficit rule. One hypothesis about this relation, by Buchanan and Wagner, is that an increase in taxes would *reduce* spending, by increasing the tax price of government services to the current generation of voters. In this case, a tax increase would reduce the deficit by more than the increase in revenues. My own crude test of this relation produced results consistent with the Buchanan and Wagner hypothesis, although I must acknowledge that the later tests of this relation produced mixed results. Alas, as I approach early senescence, I recognize that some of the views that I hold most strongly are not clearly supported by the evidence. With this caveat, my judgment is that the Buchanan and Wagner hypothesis described the

U.S. federal fiscal experience from about 1953 through 1985 and, during this period, tax increases contributed to spending restraint. This relation also seems to have described the British fiscal experience, at least in the 1980s.

For this and other reasons, I supported the 1982 tax increase, to the consternation of my supply-side colleagues. And in retrospect, I believe that the Reagan administration was wrong to reject the 1981 proposal by then-House Budget Committee chairman Jim Jones to make the third step of the individual tax rate reductions conditional on implementing spending cuts equal to the amount identified by Stockman's "magic asterisk." On this issue, Milton Friedman's advice to Reagan was wrong on economic grounds, but probably not on political grounds. In effect, Friedman argued that we were then operating under a fiscal rule by which approved spending was equal to estimated revenues plus the maximum tolerable deficit. In one sense, of course, this argument is a truism. As a group, our major mistake is that we enormously underestimated the maximum tolerable deficit in the early 1980s. During this period, the *ex ante* deficit was clearly a residual of spending and tax decisions, not a binding exogenous restraint.

I suggest that beginning in 1986, all of this changed. The Gramm-Rudman-Hollings process, for all its warts, should be recognized as a major revision of fiscal rules. Approved spending is now equal to estimated revenues plus the target deficit plus $10 billion. As long as the target deficit is not changed, the derivative of approved spending on estimated revenues is plus one; tax increases have *no* effect on the expected deficit. This has not proved to be a rigid rule, of course; Congress has already increased the deficit targets once and, I expect, will do so again in the summer of 1990. And the relation between actual spending and tax revenues is complicated by both the shameless manipulation of the GRH process and the variance around the spending and revenue forecasts. The GRH process, however, should be improved, not repealed. At the margin of the target deficit, the GRH rule requires that all incremental spending be financed by additional taxes, and this has had a powerful effect on disciplining spending growth.

A personal note: One curse apparently overlooked by Kismet's poet is the curse on every policy analyst: "May your favorite-proposal be implemented." In 1973, the American Enterprise Institute published my monograph on *Structural Reform of the Federal Budget Process*. In that monograph, I proposed a new congressional budget process centered on a joint budget resolution, the creation of a congressional budget office, and what I then described as a "marginal balanced budget" rule. As it turned out, Congress implemented most of what I proposed in the Congressional Budget Act of 1974 and the marginal balanced budget rule in the 1985 GRII legislation. You may regard this process as an ungainly monster, and I will acknowledge that it is ungainly. This process has proved to be a great burden to Congress, it is subject to considerable abuse, and its outcomes are far from satisfactory. For the first time in 15 years, however, I am prepared to acknowledge at least partial paternity for this awkward teenager.

A final note. What are the implications of my perspective for near-term fiscal policy? Specifically, am I concerned about the deficit? The answer is yes; in the eighth year of economic recovery the unified budget should have a surplus, possibly as high as the current net revenues from Social Security. More importantly, do I favor a tax increase? My current answer to this question is no, because under the current GRH rule a tax increase would increase spending by an equal amount and would not reduce the deficit. On the other hand, I would favor a tax increase to reduce the deficit. To achieve that outcome, however, the GRH rule would have to be changed to reduce the target deficit by the expected increase in revenues from the change in taxes. After approval of this new rule, I would eagerly join the crowd calling for a tax increase but, under this rule, most of the tax increase crowd would probably have disappeared. Watching my high school band, my mother used to ask "Why is everyone out of step but my Billy?" I have yet to sort out the answer to that question.

COMMENTS ON "TAXES: A LICENSE TO SPEND OR A LATE CHARGE?"

Edward M. Gramlich

Since I largely agree with George's message, and since nobody can tell better stories, my own comments will be rather bland, just refining around the edges.

George's main message is the rejection of what he calls the marginal Parkinson's Law (MPL) of fiscal policy: higher taxes simply raise spending and do not permit the budget deficit to be reduced. George criticizes MPL in the strongest terms, as would I, and he says that in their mistaken belief in MPL, the two most recent presidents have conducted a disastrous fiscal policy. With such criticism from Republicans like George, who needs Democrats?

Along with this main message, George brings some harsh criticism of those who favor tax cuts now. Such tax cuts entail higher tax rates in the future for two and a half reasons (a half because I am not sure George believes the third):

☐ As long as the present value of future program spending is fixed, the present value of future tax revenues is also fixed. In this mechanical sense, tax revenue cuts now entail tax revenue increases later.

☐ Tax cuts now followed by increases later on generate inefficient intertemporal shifts in labor supply, causing intertemporal deadweight losses in output and higher future tax rates to fix the present value of tax revenues.

☐ Tax cuts now may fool the populace into thinking the cost of public goods is lower than it really is, and may cause larger public spending; if this spending cannot be reversed, tax cuts now may cause a higher present value of future spending and future taxes.

He also adds a point relevant to the debate about Ricardian equivalence, the theory that tax cuts do not affect the present generation's living standard because farsighted households just save to cover future tax increases. This theory then implies that tax cuts do not make households any better off. How can that be true, George asks, when both citizens and their political representatives fight so hard for lower taxes? Good question.

While I am thus in substantial agreement with George, I do have some minor criticisms:

□ George feels that any discussion of fiscal policy cannot be value neutral. In regard to the value of farsightedness, this is quite true. It is hard to condemn deficits unless one thinks that national saving rates should be higher. But regarding the usual question of whether public spending should be higher or lower, it is not obvious. Why can't those who favor higher public spending also favor a tax increase and cuts in the budget deficit? Or those who favor higher public spending also favor no change in taxes and increases in the budget deficit? In a word, the big government spending question is independent of the national saving question.

□ George feels the limit to sustained deficit spending is found in the condition that the public debt-GNP ratio be stable. But this confuses stability with desirability. While it is better to have a stable debt-GNP ratio than an exploding ratio, simple stability in the debt-GNP ratio says nothing about whether this path of fiscal policy is desirable from a national saving standpoint. To make this assessment one needs to get into difficult intergenerational equity considerations.

□ The whole MPL discussion is oversimplified because it presumes the type of budget bargaining to take place. If there is an absolute constraint on the federal deficit, then tax increases may indeed stimulate equal changes in public spending. But if budget bargainers can horse trade to reduce the deficit, those reluctant to accept tax increases might well gain spending cuts, not increases, as their reward for going along with the tax increases.

□ As one of the leading present day econometric researchers, George makes maddeningly little use of numbers. What is the econometric evidence against MPL? In this day and age I would have liked to see at least reference to some kind of formal testing of hypotheses, flawed though these tests may be. I would also have liked George's description of why some evidence was more credible than other evidence.

ABOUT THE AUTHORS

James R. Barth is Lowder Eminent Scholar in Finance at Auburn University. He was formerly Chief Economist for the Office of Thrift Supervision, U.S. Treasury Department, and has been a Visiting Scholar at the Congressional Budget Office and at the Federal Reserve Bank of Atlanta. He holds a doctorate in economics from Ohio State University.

John F. Helliwell is Professor and Head of the Department of Economics at the University of British Columbia. He has done extensive research on the quantitative assessment, for many countries, of the domestic and external effects of fiscal and monetary policies. In 1991–92 he will be Mackenzie King Professor of Canadian Studies at Harvard University. He holds a doctorate in economics from Oxford University.

George Iden is a Principal Analyst at the Congressional Budget Office, where he specializes in analysis of fiscal issues. Before joining the CBO, he held academic posts at American University and the University of North Carolina. He holds a doctorate in economics from Harvard University.

Rudolph G. Penner is a Senior Fellow at The Urban Institute. He was director of the Congressional Budget Office before joining the Institute in 1987. Earlier posts in government included Deputy Assistant Secretary for Economic Affairs at the Department of Housing and Urban Development, and Senior Staff Economist at the Council of Economic Advisers. He has published numerous books and articles, particularly in the areas of tax and spending policies. He recently coauthored *Broken Purse Strings: Congressional Budgeting, 1974–88* (Urban Institute Press, 1988) with Alan J. Abramson. He holds a doctorate in economics from Johns Hopkins University.

Frank S. Russek is a Principal Analyst at the Congressional Budget Office, where he specializes in measures of fiscal impact and other fiscal issues. Before joining the CBO, Mr. Russek was on the staff of the Federal Reserve Board. He holds a doctorate in economics from the University of Maryland.

George M. von Furstenberg is Rudy Professor of Economics at Indiana University in Bloomington. Several years of work at the International Monetary Fund (1978–83) and at various U.S. government agencies, such as the President's Council of Economic Advisers (1973–76) and, most recently, the Department of State, have punctuated and enriched his academic pursuits. The latest book of which he is contributing editor is *Acting Under Uncertainty: Multidisciplinary Conceptions* (Kluwer, 1990). He holds a doctorate in economics from Princeton University.

Mark Wohar is Associate Professor of Economics at the University of Nebraska-Omaha, and was a Visiting Scholar at the Office of Thrift Supervision, U.S. Treasury Department, when much of the work on this paper was performed. Mr. Wohar holds a doctorate in economics from the University of Illinois.

ABOUT THE DISCUSSANTS

Frank de Leeuw is Chief Statistician of the Bureau of Economic Analysis, U.S. Department of Commerce. He has worked on measuring and interpreting Federal fiscal actions at the Bureau and in his previous position, Assistant Director of the Congressional Budget Office. His other research has been in the fields of macroeconomics, economic statistics, and housing.

Jacob A. Frenkel is Economic Counsellor and Director of Research at the International Monetary Fund. Prior to assuming his current position in 1987, he was the David Rockefeller Professor of International Economics at the University of Chicago. He is the author and editor of numerous books and articles on international macroeconomics, inflation, and financial markets.

Edward M. Gramlich is Professor of Economics and Public Policy at the University of Michigan and Director of its Institute for Public Policy Studies. He has served as a staff member at the Federal Reserve Board, as Director of the Policy Research Division at the Office of Economic Opportunity, as a Senior Fellow at the Brookings Institution, and as both Deputy and Acting Director of the Congressional Budget Office. He has written both books and articles on budget policy, macroeconomics, fiscal federalism, and income redistribution.

John H. Makin is a Resident Scholar and Director of Fiscal Policy Studies at the American Enterprise Institute in Washington, D.C. Earlier, he was a Professor of Economics and Director of the Institute for Economic Research at the University of Washington. He is the author of more than sixty scientific articles and has authored or edited more than a dozen books on a wide range of economic subjects.

William A. Niskanen is Chairman of the Cato Institute and editor of *Regulation* magazine. From 1981 to 1985, he was a member of the Council of Economic Advisers, serving as acting chairman during the last nine months of this period. His latest book is *Reaganomics: An Insider's Account of the Policies and the People*. Mr. Niskanen also served in a number of other federal positions, and he is a specialist in public policy and public choice.

John Williamson is Senior Fellow at the Institute for International Economics. He was formerly Advisor to the International Monetary Fund and Economic Consultant to Her Majesty's Treasury. He has published numerous studies on international monetary issues, including *IMF Conditionality, Political Economy and International Money*, and most recently *Latin American Adjustment—How Much Has Happened?*